Getting A Stand

By Miles Gilbert

Illustrated by Bill Leftwich

LIBRARY OF
FEF
FRANK E FETTER

Getting A Stand

by Miles Gilbert 1986

Illustrated by Bill Leftwich

An anthology of the writings of buffalo hunters who were engaged in the hide business between 1870 and 1882.

The method used in shooting buffalo was queer. The hunters could usually slip up within three or four hundred yards, and then they would shoot the buffalo that seemed to be the leader. They never shot to hit it behind the shoulder in the heart. An animal so hit would pitch, buck around, and break the stand. They always shot far back in the body behind the ribs. Such a shot would make the buffalo sick. It would hump up, walk around, and lie down. If another animal started to lead out, it would be shot next; each new leader in turn was shot, until the animals began milling around. Then the hunters had a stand on them, and they could kill all they wanted.

Paraphrased from the journal of
Mrs. Ella Bird, wife of a Texas hunter.
Lee (1964)

Reprint – Softcover – 1993
Published by: Pioneer Press
P.O. Box 684 – Union City, TN 38261

Library of Congress Catalog Card No. 86-091351

ISBN 1-877704-14-8

Illustrated by Bill Leftwich
Cover Design by Clair Millett

Dedication

This book is dedicated to my mother, Josephine Oliver Gilbert, who encouraged my boyish interest in old guns, and to Floyd Foltz and Carlyle Smith, who knowledgeably helped to develop that interest.

Autobiography of Author and Artist

Miles Gilbert was born 21 November 1942 at Pampa, Texas. His sixty some published works range from articles in popular magazines like *Muzzle Blasts* to professional journals including the *American Journal of Physical Anthropology*. He has written and published two popular books on bone identification. His interest in firearms and the American West was rekindled in college by Carl Smith and Floyd Foltz. After 15 years in academia, he repented of secular humanism and now preaches for the Church of Christ in Sedona, Arizona where he resides with his wife, Randi and their children, Ty and Polly.

Bill Leftwich was born 21 June 1923 at Duncan, Oklahoma, and was reared in Texas. A sergeant in the 92nd Cav. Recon. 12th Armored Division, E.T.O, he recieved the silver star, three battle stars, and the Colmar Coat of Arms, French 1st Army Veteran's Medal. His published works include over seventy illustrated articles and eight books. He has done eleven murals and twenty-six bronzes, including a statue of Audie Murphy for the Texas National Guard at Austin.

Past President of the Texas Cowboy Artists' Assoc., Bill lives in Ft. Davis with his wife Mary Alice.

Table of Contents

List of Illustrations and Photographs

Introduction

The history and significance of the extermination of bison during the Indian Wars period has been told often and well. Among the classic works are *The Extermination of the American Bison* by W.T. Hornaday, *The Great Buffalo Hunt* by Wayne Gard, and *The Buffalo Hunters* by Mari Sandoz. The story is dealt with in smaller scope by other authors whose main focus was the natural history of bison, among which *The North American Buffalo* by F.G. Roe, *The Time of the Buffalo* by Tom McHugh, and *The Buffalo Book* by David Dary are outstanding references.

Two autobiographies of men who were directly engaged in hunting buffalo for their meat and hides are John R. Cook's *The Border and the Buffalo* (which served as the basis for Zane Grey's *The Thundering Herd*) and Billy Dixon's *Life and Adventures of Billy Dixon of Adobe Walls*. Frank Mayer's autobiographical account of buffalo hunting (*The Buffalo Harvest*, by Mayer and Roth) is informative, but many details he recorded have been challenged as inaccurate or at least as very atypical.

The aim of this anthology is to make available in one volume some of the original sources cited by Gard, Sandoz, and others, and to present some previously unpublished manuscripts by buffalo hunters. I feel that the serious student of the buffalo harvest will appreciate and enjoy these firsthand accounts by men who made their livings on the prairie and who profited from getting a stand.

Henry Raymond's contribution to this anthology is rich in the details of a buffalo hunter's daily activity. He arrived in Dodge City at the peak of the buffalo hide business there, and he left after a year and nine days. During that time, he spent 129 days himself hunting or in skinning for others. He personally killed at least 186 buffalo between November 24, 1872 and September 2, 1873. Of these, 63 were bulls, 41 cows, 3 spikes, 2 calves, and 77 were not recorded as to age or sex. His largest stand was 10; his largest daily kill was 17. Some days he would hunt hard and long without seeing a buffalo; another time he killed five buffalo without even leaving his camp. Although Raymond was a good shot, by W.S. Glenn's standard, Raymond was only a common hide-skinner.

Henry Raymond wrote only a few lines in his diary each day, but these provide us with a vivid picture of his life as a buffalo hunter. The weather figures prominently in his diary, as it might be expected to with anyone whose best shelter was a canvas tent. Sometimes the weather ran him into town. Once the wind was so high that it blew the spring seat off his wagon onto his head. Another time the wind blew down his bunk and scattered dried buffalo hides for half a mile.

His diary shows the neighborliness of fellow hunters. Besides news, they exchanged coffee, yeast, flour, gun powder, a bullet swage, and even a rifle. Raymond mentions some of the big names in the history of the hide business. He hunted with Tom Nixon, Bat Masterson, and Jim White; he worked in Rath's store and hide yard; he repaired J. Wright Mooar's rifle and wagon.

Henry Raymond became quite adept in the skills of the hide business. He lightened his rifle mainspring to improve the trigger pull; he made cross-sticks of hackberry for himself and Bat Masterson. He skinned off hides, pegged out hides, poisoned hides, folded hides, stacked hides, baled hides. He learned the value of a dollar earned. He paid 75 cents for a restaurant meal, equivalent to wages for skinning three buffalo. He once sold 895 pounds of buffalo meat for a penny a pound.

In contrast to Raymond's diary, the recollections of W. Skelton Glenn were written almost 40 years after the time of the events he reported. Almost exactly one half of these recollections deal with the minutiae of hide hunting. Glenn describes the various methods of hunting which preceded the stand method. He tells at what time of year animals were shot specifically for their robes. He tells of following fascial planes between muscle bundles in order to butcher out muscles as is commonly practised in many European countries today. He tells of the many uses made of buffalo tallow: to lubricate guns, cartridges, wagon hubs; to eat; to fuel fires and lamps.

Glenn tells of the time when Bill Hillman skinned 70 buffalo cows in eight hours and ten minutes, and then pegged them all out before complete dark. He speaks of well-known Texas hunters Pat Garrett, Hi Bickerdyke, and Billy Dixon. He tells of Jim White's revenge on the Mexican lancers who broke his stand.

The balance of Glenn's narrative describes the Hunter's War and the Battle of Yellow House Canyon. It is included here for several reasons: it documents the hunters' long-range shooting ability; it describes the Indian menace to hunters; and it offers an interesting comparison to John R. Cook's account of these events in his oft-quoted *The Border and the Buffalo.*

By far the most widely experienced individual whose own written record appears herein was Oliver Perry Hanna. Explorer, farmer, guide, hunter, Indian fighter, mail carrier, miner, postmaster, scout, settler, teamaster, trapper, Hanna was all of these. His autobiography is the stuff of which good western novels and movies are made. His grit was the right stuff for pioneering western America.

Unlike the minutely detailed account of Raymond and Glenn, O.P. Hanna's story is broadly sweeping in its generality, but no interesting or authentic. While the former were concerned with hide counts and weather, Hanna was concerned with where; his acute sense of geography and topography are reminiscent of Osborn Russell's *Journal of a Trapper.*

The brief introductory remarks of Josiah Wright Mooar, known as Wright to his companions, are even more general than those of Hanna, but they serve to set the stage and to floodlight the driving market force behind the action. Thousands of unemployed men, many of them Civil War veterans, saw opportunity literally on the hoof.

One of these men was P.C. Bicknell, whose letter is the shortest document in the anthology. By his own admission he was a newcomer to the hide business, as Henry Raymond had been at first. His naiveté is interesting in showing what in particular struck him as newsworthy to his correspondent. Its details correspond with those of Raymond and Glenn.

We can but wish that George W. Reighard's story, which first appeared in the *Kansas City Star* for November 30, 1930, was much longer. What there is agrees with the other accounts as regards the methods used in getting a stand. Earle Forrest interviewed Reighard in Dodge City in 1926. From that account we have a brief biography of Reighard, and a photograph.

The final chapter in this anthology is by Robert Loren Chambers, excerpted from his autobiography by an unknown member of the Laramie (Wyoming) Corral of Westerners and placed in the University of Wyoming Library in 1970. It documents the end of the game on the northern range the winter of 1881-1882. Chambers noted that in that winter of '81-'82, there were 82,000 buffalo hides shipped out of Miles City. The next winter, there were only 8,000. Men turned from hunting hides to gathering bones.

Acknowledgements

I am grateful to the men whose texts provided the hides from which this garment was sewn together. I am culpable for the poor stitching and gaps where they exist; even so, I trust that the reader will find it a serviceable covering for the subject.

Many people have given their time, lent their guns or gear, and in some tangible way encouraged the completion of this little book. Those whose contributions come readily to mind, and to whom I sincerely express appreciation are hereby listed:

Stan Anderson, Pablo Ballentine, Bob Edgar, Dave and Debbie Floyd, Gerry Garneau of the Sedona Public Library, Jerry Mayberry, John Schoffstall, and Tony Silveus of Silver Images Photography. The generosity of Charles Hanna Carter deserves special recognition, as does the encouragement and sacrifice of my wife, Randi, and our children, Ty and Polly.

I am grateful for the institutional support of Northern Arizona University, the Museum of Northern Arizona, the Kansas Historical Society, the Panhandle-Plains Historical Museum, the University of Wyoming Library, the Historical Society of Western Pennsylvania, and the West Texas Historical Association.

Finally, Bill Leftwich deserves the greatest acknowledgement of indebtedness on my part. Bill's contribution goes beyond the obvious work he put into his excellent illustrations; he has given of his time and talent and especially of himself. Gracias, amigo.

Miles Gilbert
Sedona, Arizona
July 1986

Chapter 1

It seems appropriate to begin these accounts by buffalo hunters with a brief history of the hide business told by one of them who was more successful than many. In 1870, Josiah Wright Mooar sent some raw buffalo hides to his brother, John, in New York, who sold them to a tannery in Pennsylvania. The tanners were satisfied with the results of their tanning process and they ordered 2,000 more hides at $3 each. This market interest was created by the decimation of the Argentine cattle hide supply, which had provided leather for many of the markets until 1870.

The hide harvest began in earnest as eastern U.S. and foreign markets for buffalo leather and tanned robes sky-rocketed. Virtually every middle and upper class American family had buffalo robe bedspreads, couch covers, buggy and sleigh lap robes. Also, for the next 20 years, all British Army leathergoods were from the American bison.

Mooar's remarks are here presented as they first appeared in the *West Texas Historical Association Yearbook*, Vol. 6, 1930, with two footnotes I have added for clarity.

The First Buffalo Hunting in the Panhandle

J. Wright Mooar

Commercial buffalo hunting was commenced at Fort Hays, Kansas in 1870 by Charles Rath and A.C. Myers, who shipped the meat (without removing the hides) to Kansas City and St. Louis. Rath hunted on Walnut Creek and Myers on Pawnee Creek.

I commenced in the fall of 1870 on Smoky Hill River. Shipped from Hays. In 1871 we hunted on Arkansas River above Fort Dodge. Five men in our party. Several other parties took to the business. We used the Springfield Army rifle, a center fire cartridge, 70 grs. of powder, a swadge ring ball 50 caliber. In 1872 the hide market was established and the Sharps Rifle Mfg. Co. developed the big 50 rifle, 90 grs. of powder, a slug ball 11 to 16 oz of lead with paper patch,[1] the weight of the gun was from 12 to 16 pounds. This was a success and is the one that exterminated the buffalo herd. In 1872 the ATSF RR came to Fort Dodge and Dodge City was established and became the principal shipping and supply depot for buffalo hunters. A.C. Myers engaged in merchandise, bought hides and meat and shipped to W.C. Lobenstein at Leavenworth, Kansas. Business was rushing and (there were) many new hunters. Early in the spring of 1873 many hunters went south to the Cimarron River, then supposed to be the south line of Kansas and the north line of the Indian Territory, the strip known as the neutral strip between Kansas and Texas, 34 miles wide. Hunters were all under the impression (that) if we crossed the Cimarron the US Army at Fort Dodge would seize and confiscate our teams. The river was patrolled once a month by a company of soldiers.

Buffalos now were very scarce in Kansas.[2] In July of 1873, John Webb and I made a trip on horseback south. Each carried 200 rounds of ammunition, big 50 guns, and a pocket full of salt. We crossed Beaver Creek 12 or 15 miles below where Beaver City now is in the strip. Went south across Wolf Creek, up the divide between Canadian River and Palo Duro Creek, went west until we could see the breaks of Blue River. Buffalo, a solid herd as far as we could see, all day they opened up before us and came together again behind us. We now turned north across Palo Duro, San Franciso Creek, Coldwater, and Beaver Creek back to the Cimarron River over 100 miles west of our camp, then down the river to home camp. We now went to Dodge City and told many hunters and Myers and Rath about the trip to Texas and the many buffalo we had seen there. All contended it was not safe to cross the strip as it was Indian territory. A young hunter named Steel Frazier proposed we go to Fort Dodge and ask the commanding officer, General (Major) Dodge, what would be the penalty should we cross the strip to Texas or perhaps kill some buffalo in the strip. So we slicked up some, (put on) new clothes, to be presentable, went to the fort six miles from town, and asked for an interview with the commanding officer. The officer of the day said the general was very busy, but he sent an orderly to tell the general two

[1]A slug weighing an ounce (437.5 gr) or 11/16 ounce (300 gr) is not typical. According to Sellers (1978) the .50 paper patched slug weighed 473 gr.

[2]The *Wichita Eagle* Nov. 7, 1872 reported that there were from one to two thousand hide hunters locally. By February 1873, the ATSF had shipped 43,029 hides, representing about 50,000 killed.

buffalo hunters desired an audience. The general said bring them right in at once and dismissed his other engagements and received us very cordially. We introduced ourselves, were seated, and asked the general what his policy to us would be if we crossed the neutral strip to hunt buffalo in Texas. General Dodge was very much interested and surprised as we told him about the trip. He asked many questions about buffalo, their habits, migratory and otherwise, methods of hunting, and profits derived and seemed to enjoy our visit. Finally we got ready to go. I said, "General, you have not answered my question." He said, "What was it?" I repeated the question. General Dodge said, "Boys, if I were a buffalo hunter, I would hunt buffalo where buffalo are." He then shook our hands, bid us goodbye, and wished us success.

Late in September 1873 I crossed the neutral strip into Texas with our hunting outfit. Ten men went south to the Canadian River, killed some buffalo, moved back to Palo Duro Creek in November and wintered. We made a good hunt. Lane and Wheeler with ten men camped six miles above us. They made a good hunt, until late in February they were attacked by Indians and Wheeler was shot, badly wounded, from which he died. Later during the winter several hunters from Dodge came to our camp prospecting, some went as far as the Canadian River but did not make permanent camp.

In March, Myers moved a branch store from Dodge City. He located on Canadian River and gave the new trading post the name of Adobe Walls. Myers brought hunters and built a large stockade, corral, and store house. Rath, his competitor, also came with a stock of supplies and hunters and teamsters, and built a sod house. Nearby James Harrahan (Hanrahan) built a sod house for a saloon. Tom O'Keafe built a blacksmith shop and picket house. All got to doing a good business. About May 1st more hunters came from Dodge and the stores did a big business and bought many hides. The Indians were very troublesome, and killed out some small outfits. The small parties now began to merge together for strength against the Indians. Buffalo were plentiful and this plan worked well until June 28th when a large party of Indians attacked the stores, made a desperate fight, and were repulsed with a great loss to the Indians. In August the stores were abandoned. Indians destroyed all improvements (at Adobe Walls). The hunters went to Dodge City, but returned to Texas in October and continued killing buffalo for hides until about 1879 when buffalo

Mooar and Webb crossed the Cimarron, July 1873

were exterminated (in Texas), which resulted in the subjugation of the Indians and the civilized occupation of the Pampas of the Texas Panhandle.

Letter of J. Wright Mooar to J. Evetts Haley, November 25, 1927

Courtesy Panhandle-Plains Museum, Canyon, Texas*

I was born in Vermont in Bennington County in 1851. I began hunting (buffalo) for meat out of Fort Hays, Kansas when I was 19 years old in 1870. A.C. Myers had an outfit and Charley Rath had one. Both had big outfits. Then my brother and I began hunting. We did not know that the hides were worth anything, but we shipped the meat by carloads to Quincy and Kansas City.

We would kill a buffalo, cut it half in two in the middle, leave the hide and hair on, and ship the hind quarters in that way. We got three cents a pound for it, and we could make a hundred dollars a day at the work. The buffalo saddles weighed from 160 to 300 pounds each.

My correspondence with Sharp (the Sharps Rifle Co. in Hartford, Conn.) led to his making the Big 50 buffalo gun. We were using the Springfield Trapdoor infantry gun. It was the best thing we had before the Sharps. They were too light, though, and I wrote Sharp that we wanted a heavier bore. He said a larger one would not be true, but he made the heavier gun.

In loading our Sharps we wrapped paper around the bullets instead of greasing them, and this kept the guns from 'leading.' The bullets were made with a concave butt. When the barrels of our guns got so hot that they began swelling, the bullets with this concave butt would be expanded when shot by the charge of powder, thus filling the barrel and making it true.

John Webb and I scouted south from Dodge across the Cimarron, the Beaver, and down toward the eastern panhandle to the Canadian in 1873. There was no one else in that country. All we carried to eat

*These reminisences were originally recorded as Mooar's stream of consciousness flowed. Thus, many events were not related chronologically, and details differ from his previous account. He was 76 at the time this letter was written. The text has therefore been rearranged chronologically for ease of reading.

was a pocket of salt. We crossed the breaks of the Wolf Creek and went on to the Canadian, then we turned west and rode until we could see Tucumcari Peak and the water of the Blue, though it was unnamed, then. We turned north, crossed the Beaver and San Francisco Creek and struck the Cimmaron again 100 miles west of where we had crossed it when we started out. We were out ten days, looking over the buffalo range to see where the most were. We carried about 300 rounds of ammunition apiece. We carried no packs, but slept on our saddle-blankets. We saw buffalo by the million. When we got back to Dodge, Webb decided that he would not go south again, because it was too risky; I had only a small outfit.

There was another big outfit there in Dodge by Cox and Frazier. Cox was rather backward like my brother, but Frazier was adventurous. We decided to go into that country to hunt buffalo.

When Webb and I were down there, we knew we were in Texas. We knew we struck Texas after crossing the 34 mile strip. We decided that we had better go to see General (Major) Dodge, the commanding officer at the fort, before we left. We went down to the post and told them that we were a couple of buffalo hunters and wanted to see the commanding officer. The officers we talked to reported to General Dodge and he gave us an interview immediately. He gave us comfortable seats. I told him of our trip south and asked him what the officers would do if we went down and hunted buffalo. He laughed and laughed and then began asking questions: How they migrated, what their habits are, how they acted in a stampede, and so on. We answered them. While we were answering he was jotting something down on a piece of paper. I did not know it then, but he was taking down in shorthand what we told him. At Abilene a year or two ago his report on the habits of buffalo was read and I recognized it as almost verbatim what we had told him.

He got through questioning us and started to dismiss us. I asked him to answer our question. He said, "If I were hunting buffalo, I would go where the buffalo are." That was all he said, and we knew that we were going!

We had made our scout in September of '73. In October we set out, striking the Canadian about 18 miles above the Old Adobe Walls (remains of the Bent's post). There we ran into some Mexican outfits that were running a contraband trade with the Indians. They were afraid that we would break into this. There were twelve or thirteen of us in our party and we had trouble with them. We had two or three fights with them and we killed several. Twenty-five of them came into our camp one day to kill us, but they got it pretty bad. On that account we turned back to the headwaters of the North Palo Duro and camped about where Jimmy Cator settled later on. We camped there all winter.

Hunting for hides did not begin until the year after the railroad reached Dodge in 1873. I made the first wagon track to the Panhandle of any citizen, when I brought my outfit down from Dodge in October. The Old Adobe Walls were three or four miles above where the Indian fight took place (at new Adobe Walls).

A.C. Meyers and Charley Rath were competitors in business in Dodge and in the buffalo hunting business. Myers started the first store at Adobe Walls, bringing down about $50,000 worth of goods. Rath said he would have to put in a place too, to compete for the trade. I suppose that he did not bring over $20,000 worth of goods. Fred Leonard was clerk for Myers. Hanrahan ran the saloon and store for Rath for half the profits.

Another outfit that belonged to Lane and Wheeler came down and camped about seven miles west of us. Each of us would take a wagon, a keg of water, a roll of bedding, and a little grub, and with a four-mule team we would drive out on the divide that separates the north Palo Duro from the Canadian. There we intercepted the buffalo herds that were crossing east to west from the headwaters of Wolf Creek, to the Blue and Coldwater. We stayed there on the divide until we loaded our wagon with hides and meat. We could haul 10,000 pounds with four mules when the ground was frozen. We would load, come back to camp, unload, and go out again.

We kept track of Wheeler's outfit, and he of ours, by the sound of the guns. If either of us got into trouble the other would know it because the sound of the buffalo guns would be interspersed with the report of lighter guns used by the Indians.

Wheeler was killed that winter. Not finding enough buffalo, he went on to the Canadian, which I had never done again. He was camped near a bluff and one morning at breakfast eight or ten Indians rode into camp. They dismounted and one of them picked up something in the camp. Wheeler, who had a mean temper, hit the Indian with a blacksnake whip. The Indians grunted, got on their horses, and rode down the river. They circled back above the bluffs and the one whom Wheeler had hit with the whip crawled up on the bluff and shot him just below the collar bone.

Wheeler's brother came over to my camp, and I told him to bring Wheeler. They could feel the bullet under the flesh in his back, and it had not gone on through. I told him that I would take a sharp knife and cut the bullet out. Wheeler was a big, husky fellow and might pull through, but I told his brother that if they tried to take him to Dodge in a wagon, he might not.

His brother wouldn't hear of it. He carried him to Dodge and then sent him on to Wichita by train. Wheeler was feverish by the time they got to the railroad, couldn't eat anything on the way, and he died in Wichita.

Among the larger outfits that were in the Panhandle in 1874 were those owned by Lane and Wheeler, Cox and Frazier, Galloway and Sisk, and my brother, John, and I. There were a lot of others who ran smaller outfits. When the Indians got bad we went out together and camped together hunting out in different directions from the common camp. These outfits belonged to one class of men. On the buffalo range there were two classes of people, just like there are two classes in any other pursuit of life.

Red Lummis, Brick Bond, and Fred Singer had outfits and belonged to the other class from us. Billy Dixon was with this other class, but he was rather a better man than the outfit he ran with, though he was of that stripe. Some horse thieves dropped into the country then, and they never stopped with us but hung around the other class of outfits. Red Lummis tried to stir up a row with our outfit at Adobe Walls, but he go his hand called real sudden.

Tobe Robertson, who was later sheriff of Tascosa, and John Webb were with us in 1874. I was the first man to take Tobe out on the Plains. Tobe was a regular wag (joker). He was the man who said that when he first came to the western country, the antelope were about the size of jackrabbits. He was a good mixer, and he was in partnership with Webb. He said that Webb spoiled their gun by shooting too straight up a hill at a buffalo. The only time I ever saw him mad was when he came in one night after his team ran away with him and tore up his wagon. He said, "The man that can't make a living during the day is a damned fool and ought to starve to death anyway!"

Lane and Wheeler, Cox and Frazier and us came down the fall of '73, and others came in March and April of 1874. I guess there were fifty outfits at Adobe Walls (different times) before the fight. Dave Dudley and Tommy Wallace were killing buffalo down at the mouth of Red Deer. They were killed there by the Indians who caught them asleep in camp during the day. They staked Dudley to the ground through his abdomen and mutilated him horribly. Antelope Jack and Blue Billy were killed over the head breaks of the North Fork of Red River, east of where Amarillo is. They were in Anderson Moore's camp. This was just before the Adobe Walls fight. Moore got away but lost his teams. He made it to Adobe Walls. I think he was still there when the fight came off.

[1](John Mooar told me of the impending Indian invasion.) He brought news also that the buffalo had got as far north as the Canadian River, so we lost no time loading up and starting to Adobe Walls. All were anxious to kill buffalo near the stores.

It began raining the second day of the journey. Noon camp was made near the headwaters of Red Deer between two lakes. The horses and mules were grazing, about half the number in each lake. Suddenly a large band of Indians appeared a mile back, following our trail. A rush was made to get the horses and mules to the wagons. I ran toward the stock on the left. The Indians came on like soldiers, one in the right column blowing a bugle.

Phillip Sisk and Lem Wilson were just ahead of me. They had left their rifles uncleaned since killing the last buffalo and so were unarmed. It became evident that something had to be done to halt the oncoming attack, or we should be cut off from our teams.

As he ran, Wilson looked back at me and yelled, "Is your gun ready Mooar?" "Yes," I replied, "and I have forty rounds of ammunition."

"Well, for God's sake, hold'em back, and we'll get the teams."

The situation was desperate and seemed all but hopeless. I dropped down on one knee and taking aim, I sent a big .50 ball screaming across the front of the charging column. Instantly the horses were jerked to their haunches, and the Indians stopped in a confused huddle. They didn't like my music. Seeing my advantage, I sent bullet after bullet whistling and skittering along, each one a little closer to the Indians than the last. They became more disconcerted and fell back. Precious time was gained. A glance showed me my companions still running for the horses and mules. Would they have time to make it? I took careful aim and brought down a horse, his redskin rider

[1]The following is from Mooar's account in *Holland's* March 1933, as told to James Winford Hunt.

I got down on one knee and took aim

going over his head and flinging himself flat on the prairie. The bugler tried to rally his followers. They swung back and started forward again. Again the old .50 spoke in deadly language, and the group broke up and fell back. A wild yell arose, and some began shooting, but their shots fell short.

Again glancing around, I saw that the boys had reached our teams and were rounding them up. In a few moments they came thundering by me and reached the wagon. I continued the bombardment until the boys got the teams hitched, and we drove on furiously to Red Deer Creek, a mile away, and crossed it near its head at upper Cottonwood Tree. Sisk and Wilson never allowed their rifle barrels to stay dirty again on that trip.

Camp was made across the Canadian River (the following day). Supper was in preparation when a whooping band of redskins dashed through the camp, shooting right and left. They got a warm reception, the roar of our big rifles mingling with the popping of the Indian's lighter arms and the savage yells of both reds and whites. No hunters were hurt, and the invaders carried off their dead and wounded. Next morning, the entire outfit arrived at Adobe Walls post.

Meyers began loading his wagons with hides to be hauled to Dodge City. John and I loaded our wagons to go along also, and lent our extra rifles to Myer's outfit so they would all be armed. I asked Myers and Rath if they were going to stay, and they said they were. I did not believe them, because I knew they had kept warning of the Indian attack on Adobe Walls post from the hunters, and that only Myers, Rath, Hanrahan, John and I, and possibily one or two others knew of the report the scout Amos (Chapman) had brought, or what his mission was: This was done to keep the hunters and helpers around the post for protection.

The last trek from Adobe Walls to Dodge was begun the next morning. Eight miles out the freighters met Dirty Face Jones, alone with six mules loaded with powder, lead, and guns. He had driven 90 miles without sleeping himself or unharnessing his mules. He drove on to the post, discharged his load, slept five hours, put on a half load of hides, and overtook the big caravan at Palo Duro Creek. I was driving the rear team of the long train. Jones said, "Now I can drive as slow as need be."

The next day we met Ike Shadler with four six-yoke teams at Rifle Pits on the Palo Duro. John Webb said, "Ike, you hurry back or the Indians will get your scalp."

On the Beaver the next morning, Myers and Rath came into camp on good horses. They stayed with the train one day, and made a night ride into Dodge. Myers left Fred Leonard in charge of his store (at Adobe Walls) and Rath left James Langdon in charge of his.

At Sharp's Creek the wagon train met a hunter named Burr, with four men. Billy Tyler, one of the four, told of a fight they had had with Indians on the Cimarron the day before. Burr remarked, "Yes Billy, and you are going to fall early in this war."

The prophecies of Webb and Burr were soon fulfilled. Shadler and Tyler were killed at Adobe Walls June 28th, and this is the date that Amos had predicted for the attack.

Billy Dixon had a bullet hole through the calf of his leg. In his book it is claimed that he got this at Buffalo Wallow, but I dressed that wound for him. We were camped at a big tree off from Adobe Walls in 1874 and I was there by myself. I looked up and saw him coming into camp. I picked up my gun and slipped a cartridge into it. He unloaded his gun, walked over and set it against the wagon. He wanted to know if I was the only one there, and if I would do a favor for him. He pulled up his trouser and showed me a bullet hole through his calf.

We always kept a sort of first-aid outfit, so I washed the wound with some Castille soap, put on some Carbolic salve, bandaged it up with linen, and sewed the bandage on. He got up, shouldered his gun and said, "I don't care for anyone to know how I got that." He walked off without limping or flinching. I never knew how he was shot and I never told this until he was dead. He was not the man who killed the Indian on the hill (the 1538 yard shot from Adobe Walls). The ridgepole did not crack that night like he claimed in his book, and some time I am going to tell about that.

There was a military road from Fort Hays to Ford Dodge. Eleven miles from Hays, Billy Dixon had a road ranch in a picket house on the Smokey. A man named Finn kept it for him. Whiskey and tobacco were their two main stocks in trade, but they had a few groceries. Dixon freighted on the road between Hays and Dodge with a four-mule team, then he took a two-mule team and began hunting buffalo in the latter part of 1872.

In 1875 General Buell told me not to go over twenty miles out from the fort (Griffin), because the Indians would give me trouble. He said if I did he would have to come out and arrest me. I had sixteen wagons in my outfit and I hired nine outlaws. I worked outlaws a good deal. You never saw a lazy one. When one is down and out and tells you he wants to work, he will work, attend to his business, and make a good hand as long as he is with you. I got some of them in Griffin and some out in the brush, and then I pulled out 140 miles from the fort.

My brother John was behind and when he caught up he asked what Buell had said. I told him, but that he would never come after us. We all had those Sharps Big 50's and could have made quite a stand.

[2]On the morning of October 7, 1876 we pitched camp on Deep Creek where the Mooar Ranch now stands. Camp was pitched about ten in the morning, and I spent the rest of the day riding my horses in a wide circuit west and southwest, surveying the country. As I was returning near sunset, from the top of a ridge a mile and a half west of the camp, I saw a herd of buffalos not far from the wagons, and the sun flashed on a white object in the midst of the herd, which I quickly saw was a white buffalo. Only seven white buffalo were ever seen or killed by white hunters, so far as the records show. I had killed one of these in Kansas.

Galloping into camp, I inquired how long the herd had been there, and the men answered that the buffalo had been grazing along and approaching for some time, but they had not noticed the white animal. Turning to Dan Dowd, I said, "Get your knives, we'll get some meat."

We slipped down the creek on foot, keeping under the high bank for six or seven hundred yards, and then crept out on the prairie through the grass near the white buffalo. It was a four year old cow, her white coat a freak of nature. Whispering to Dan, I said, "Take a look. There is the gamiest animal on earth, a white buffalo."

I then took aim and pulled the trigger. At the crack of the big rifle, the cow fell, and as the herd rushed together, we narrowly escaped being trampled; in fact, I shot three bulls down to prevent being run over.

George Causey had some other men in with him. He had a pretty big outfit and hunted the longest of anybody I know. I quit in 1879,

[2]This account of the white buffalo is from Mooar's recollection in *Hollands*, May 1933, as told to James Winford Hunt. It was the only white buffalo killed by hunters in Texas.

but he hunted around until about 1882. He was a grader on the railroad when it was built into Dodge. He quit that in 1873 and went to hunting.

In February of 1877 Jim Ennis was camped on what is now called Sweetwater Creek, a tributary of the Double Mountain Fork of the Brazos in what is now the northern part of Scurry County. The buffalo were rather scarce around him. One morning he got up in a heavy ground fog. He set off hunting afoot and finally killed two or three bulls. He did not take his skinner with him, but when he killed a bull, he skinned it himself, rolled up the hide, and left it by the carcass and continued hunting.

In the afternoon he wounded another buffalo bull and it started walking off. Jim hurried after it to get another shot. When wounded, a buffalo will when followed, stop every little while and turn broadside to see you. Then you shoot him again. It is no use to shoot at one going directly toward or away from you. Jim hurried to get another shot, and in the fog he got closer than he realized. The buffalo whirled around and came straight for Jim. He dropped his gun and ran for a mesquite tree.

He beat the buffalo to the tree and jumped up in it. But, the bull didn't stop, he ran right into the tree full force. It was a dead tree and snapped off; Jim fell out onto the buffalo. He rolled off on the ground, but the tree fork stayed across the bull's back, scaring him, and he ran off.

Jim was a little rattled then, but got up and began looking for his gun. He found it, but still being rattled, he didn't know which way to go through the fog to find his camp. He wandered around awhile and finally came upon one of the carcasses he had skinned. It was about dusk so he built a little fire, cooked some of the meat by throwing it on the coals, and ate. Then he took the buffalo hide and spread it out with the hair side up, laid down on one edge and rolled himself up in it.

In a little while a blue norther blew up and soon froze the hide, casing Jim in. There were a great many lobo wolves in the country then. Buffalo carcasses were all over the country so the wolves could get plenty to eat. The carcass and the meat Jim had roasted attracted some wolves. They began eating on the flesh left on the hide. Jim began yelling, but that did not bother the lobos. They just continued stripping the meat off the hide. When one would bite the hide, Jim would feel it tearing his clothes. The wolves stayed until they had stripped the hide and most of the carcass. When morning came they sneaked off to hiding places. The sun came up and by ten o'clock the hide thawed so that Jim could unroll.

His skinners in camp were having a lot of fun joking about the boss being lost, because he had raw-hided them about it some time or other. They knew he had matches and could build a fire, so they weren't worried. About noon they looked up and saw an old man coming into camp. He was bent, white-haired, and his face was all creased. One of the boys recognized Jim's gun and asked the old man where he got it. Another recognized Jim's clothes and jumped right in asking where he got them. Jim Ennis went out a black headed man and came in looking old and gray. His own men didn't recognize him!

Lobenstein bought hides, pelts and furs of all kinds in Fort Worth. Some people wondered why he located there. It was because that was a centrally located point for business. In 1878 he offered me $100,000 and a letter of credit for me to go to Buenos Aires to open a hide house. I refused. It might have been better had I accepted. After I refused he let the matter drop. His offer came about in this way.

In the summer of 1877 all the buffalo hide hunters were in Fort Worth. Bates of New York had a hide man there and there were always a bunch sitting around the hotel watching Lobenstein's movements. All of us would go to Lobenstein's hide house where a man named J.T. Hickey was in charge. Lobenstein was a Jew, but he always hired Irishmen to handle his money. He had about 40 Irishmen scattered over the western country.

We would go down to the hide house and Hickey would pass around little slips of paper in a hat. Each man would draw one. Then he would have a Nigger bring a hide and throw it on the floor. We would all just look at it. We were not allowed to touch it. After we had looked at it, it was turned over and we guessed at its weight and class, and wrote our guesses on the paper slip. The slips were taken up in the hat, and then Hickey turned the hide over and announced its class. Then the Nigger threw it on the scales and weighed it and Hickey announced the winner from the slips. We made sport out of it, making the losers set us up to cigars and the like.

We kept that up to pass the time for about three weeks, day after day. There were always about ten or twelve in there and sometimes as many as twenty. We did not know it at the time, but Hickey had a bookkeeper behind a screen keeping account of each guess. I was a young man of 26 then, and after this was over, Hickey communicated the results of our sport to Lobenstein. I had gotten the highest score and he wanted to hire me to go to Buenos Aires.

When we first came to hunt out of Griffin after the fight at Adobe Walls, we shipped our hides to Lobenstein from Denison, freighting them to Denison ourselves. That first load was 4500. We sent the next hides to Fort Worth and Dallas. Sometimes we made one trip a year, and sometimes two, bringing hides and hauling back enough supplies to do us.

The most buffalo I ever killed at one stand was 96. That was about eight or nine miles north of where I live here (Snyder, Tex) I killed about 6500 with my 14 lb. gun, and about 14000 with my 11 lb. gun.

One day at Snyder I was talking with some fellows and among them was a high-collared gent from Dallas. He said he was a jeweler. I told them that I was the first citizen of Scurry County to make a wagon track in it. He asked, "How big was Snyder then?" I did not say a word, just turned around and walked off.

Chapter 2

George W. Brown was born in Newton County, Missouri on March 20, 1847. He enlisted in Capt. James K. McLean's company, third regiment, volunteer cavalry, Union Army, on December 22, 1863. He was mustered out in October 1865 and returned to farming for three years near Greenville, Bond County, Missouri. By 1870 he had migrated to south of Denver where he worked as tie hack for the Kansas Pacific RR. Narrowly escaping being caught and hung for his unwitting part in rustling, he headed east to Fort Wallace, Kansas and began hunting buffalo. His account as here presented is excerpted from *Kansas Historical Collections* vol. 17. Editorial changes and insertions are indicated by parentheses.

The Adventures of George W. Brown, Buffalo Hunter, 1870-1874

George W. Brown

(The first night out we camped at an old stage station called Russell Springs about 25 miles east of Fort Wallace.) The evening we got there we saw a few buffalo. The next day we spent hunting buffalo and we succeeded in killing eight. We butchered these buffalo and the next day I took the meat to Fort Wallace. The meat sold fairly well as there hadn't been any there for a good while. So the next day I pulled out for camp with my wagon loaded up with grain, ammunition, and provisions, and the men felt so elated over our success we concluded to remain hunting for awhile.

Every day we were there the buffalo seemed more plentiful; they were working their way up the Smokey Hill river. I made one more trip up to Fort Wallace with meat and it sold pretty well. I told the men there was no use to hunt here any longer as there was buffalo within eight miles of Fort Wallace. So we moved our camp back west to another old station, Henshaw Stage station. We camped in the old building which had been used by the stock tender in the earlier days.

This house was dug into the bank on the east side of the (Turkey) creek, and walled up with rock, but it had no cover on it. We covered it with canvas and lived there all winter.

There was a little valley a mile wide right in front of the door on the west side. Every morning when we'd wake up and look out of the door we could see this little valley full of buffalo. We could go out the other way from the top of the house and see the country black with them. We hunted out of this camp all winter until the middle of March.

We sent Bob Robb to Denver to sell meat for us. We could send him a load of meat every day for quite awhile. We shipped meat enough to amount to about a thousand dollars, but that work was all thrown away as Bob Robb never sent us a cent of money, but one time he did send us about $85 worth of provisions and ammunition. We kept his team, worth about $150, and he never showed up. We made enough that winter to pay our expenses and feed our team.

John Burdett and I bought out the other partners (John Stover and Jacob Tigg). Then he and I went to hunting on our own account, and this is where I made my first start as a buffalo hunter. Along about the middle of March the buffalo started to go south. The country was all new to us; we didn't know where the next creek was. We knew nothing. The buffalo hunting all had to be learned.

In butchering the buffalo we cut them in two at the first rib and left the first rib on the hind quarters, and that's all we wanted. The tongues and front quarters were left on the prairies for the wolves to eat. The hide was left on the meat. We would sell a saddle of this meat for five dollars. We never sold it by the pound.

(About the first of May 1871, we met some more hunters in Fort Wallace.) We told them the weather was getting so warm it was almost impossible to get the meat to market before it spoiled. (They asked why we didn't just take the hides and leave the meat. I asked what the devil I would do with the hides. They said to send them to Lobenstein in Leavenworth and he would send us a check.) So John Burdett and I went out the next trip and went to skinning. We both worked on the same buffalo. It took us about an hour to skin one. we were then starting on a new occupation we knew nothing about. We finally got about 40 hides and we shipped them to W.C. Lobenstein. It was but four or five days until we got our check for our hides. We received for our cow hides $1.25 and for our bull hides we got $1.75. Mr. Lobenstein paid the freight.

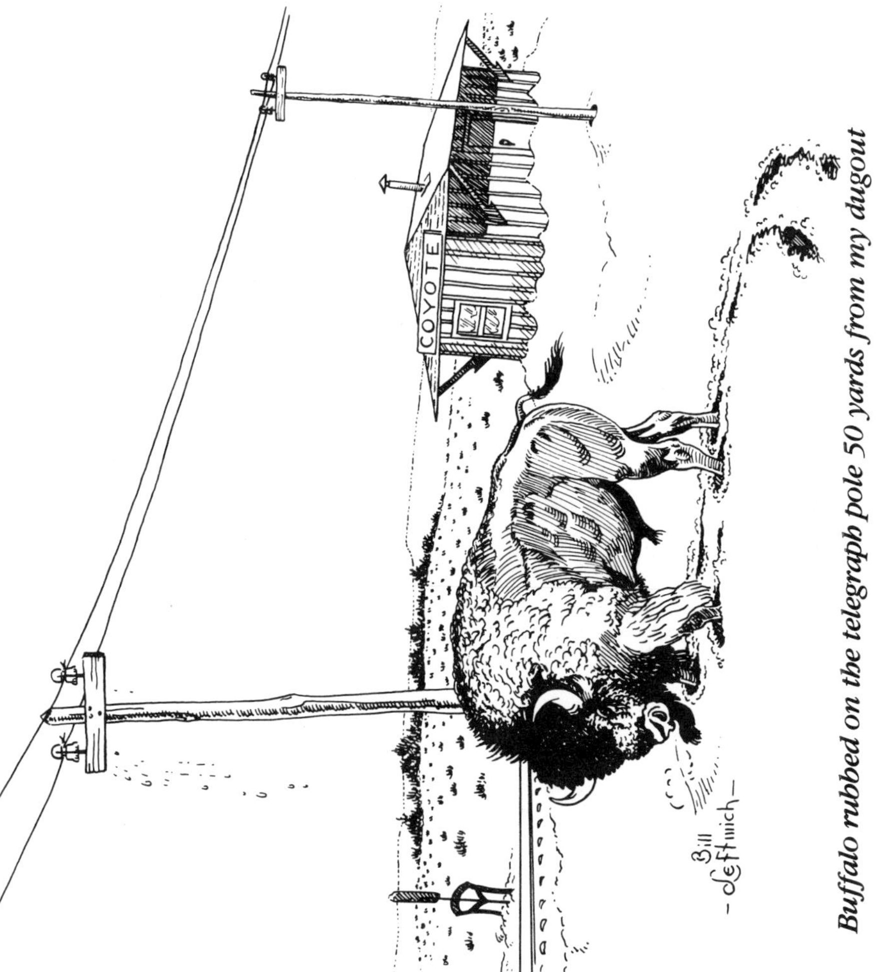

Buffalo rubbed on the telegraph pole 50 yards from my dugout

Coyote Station on the old KP RR was the second station west of Ellis, Kansas and this is where I had a good camp almost all winter (1871-1872). I camped right at the railroad station and had me a good dugout and burned coal. I hired one of the section hands, a young German named Louie, and he made a good, faithful hand all winter. An old man named Richardson and his wife boarded the section hands. (Often when I'd come in late with a load of green hides he would invite me over for supper.) It was music to my ears. And he would often have a good hot fire going in my dugout when I'd get there. To show my appreciation for what Mr. Richardson had done for me I would bring him his meat. He did not have to buy any meat that winter. Often when I would look out of a morning I would see buffalo rubbing themselves on telegraph poles not more than 50 yards away.

On the 15th of November, 1871 Louie and I skinned 20 buffalo. It was rather warm that day and drizzling rain. We rolled our hides out of the wagon calculating to stretch them out the next morning. But next morning came and we never unrolled our hides for the next six weeks as a big norther came up about midnight. I staked my horses out about 200 yards from the dugout that night. The next morning when we looked out we couldn't see 20 steps. The wind was blowing about 60 miles an hour and there was a blinding snow. Louie wanted to go up and get the horses. (I wouldn't let him go. Nothing more was said for about half an hour, when again Louie said he'd better go get the horses. I made him promise not to leave the creekbed, but to follow around its bends. Even so, I was afraid I'd never see him again. After a short time I saw him coming leading one horse. The other had frozen to death.) Then we dug the door down a little and put part of the horse in and covered the other part.

In about four days we made our way to the station. Mr. Richardson told me that the thermometer registered 20 below zero and you may know it was cold with the wind blowing 60 miles an hour. There was a man named Happy Jack (camped at Five Mile Hollow, five miles out of Fort Hays.) Every man in the outfit froze to death that night; and there was also a big Newfoundland dog froze to death lying on the bed.

(The year 1872 was always spoken of as the year of the big hunt. There were more buffalo killed that year than any other. I was hunting in the vicinity of Fort Wallace and became acquainted with many of the people there and at the little station. There were Wheeler &

Clark, post traders; Jack Williams, Prairie Dog Dave Morrow, Lin Guilford, and Billy Tyler, who was killed at the Adobe Walls fight in 1874.)

Lin Guilford and I went out on a hunt together (about 35 miles southwest of Fort Wallace, on Beaver Creek.) We got hides enough to load one wagon. Lin had a team of his own, two horses, and I had two horses and a mule. This mule was about 40 years old; she was very slow and hard to get along. (I started for Fort Wallace with the hides and reached there the same day.) Lin told me the next morning after I left that there was six or eight Indians came over the hill shaking their buffalo robes, hollerin' their war whoop and shouting, which stampeded his two horses and also the mule. He told me afterwards that he couldn't help but laugh when he saw that old mule stick her tail straight up and she actually outran his horses. He said if he lived to be a hundred years old that he never would forget this happening on the Great Plains.

One day Tom Nixon told me that the Indians came and ran off all his horses and mules but one, so he had to go to Dodge City and get teams to haul his hides in. After he got his hides in, he bought five two-horse teams and hired fifteen men. He went about 35 miles southeast of Dodge to Rattlesnake Creek. In this camp he killed 3200 buffalo in 35 days. He told me that one day he killed 120 in forty minutes. There was a large herd came past his camp. He used two guns. When one got too hot, he threw the breechblock open, ran a wet rag through it and took the other gun till it got too hot. We nearly always carried a bottle of water for that purpose.

I have told this story several times to people that didn't know anything about buffalo hunting, and they always showed that they didn't believe it. One man who was working for Tom at that time later worked for me. He said that Tom Nixon did that very thing. Tom Nixon is a very truthful man, and no none who ever knew him in those days ever doubted him in the least.

(My men and I hung around Dodge City for several days, and while we were there, some hunters from the north brought news of the massacre of the Jordans and the capture of Dick Jordan's wife.) There was a little band of Northern Cheyennes that had been down visiting the Southern Cheyennes. Bob and Jim Cator met these Indians between the Pawnee and the Arkansas before they murdered the Jordan family. When they saw the Indians coming, Bob Cator got up on his wagon and motioned the Indians not to come, but they kept coming as fast as their horses would bring them. Then the men fired a volley into them and killed one Indian. The Jordan family were the next whites the Indians met up with.

It wasn't long until we went back again to Fort Wallace, as the buffalo were scarce on the Arkansas river. Then I made a trip to the Arickaree river about 65 miles northwest of Fort Wallace. I think this trip was made in February, 1873. We arrived at this creek about two o'clock in the afternoon. This was one of the best camps I ever had while hunting buffalo. The buffalo would pass within a hundred yards of our camp fire.

I had four men working for me (Andy O'Harrow, Abraham Wilks, Squaw Bill Wilson, and Peake). I had two two-horse teams, two men to each team. I told the boys to hitch up both teams and they could tell by my shooting where I was. I commenced shooting before I left camp. The buffalo beat back into the sand hills to the north. The boys commenced to skin while I was shooting all the time. Finally the sun went down and I had killed 65 buffalo that afternoon. When I got to camp I busied myself with cooking our supper. Pretty soon the wagons commenced coming in with the hides that had been skinned that afternoon. They had skinned 51 buffalo. They also brought with them about 500 pounds of tallow that we used to make a fire at nights. When they would skin a nice, fat buffalo they would cut it open and take the tallow off its entrails. We made our fire of buffalo chips as there was no wood there. When our supper was eaten we renewed our fire and went to making cartridges for our guns.

I used a big fifty caliber Sharps rifle. It shot a hundred and twenty grains of powder, and the bullets were an inch and a quarter long. When one of these big (slugs) would hit a buffalo, whether it hit the right place or not, it would make him sick. It wouldn't be long until I put another into him. I have often shot a buffalo ten or fifteen times before I got him down.

These buffalo hadn't been fired into for a long time and were very gentle and easy to get a shot at. The first evening I hunted there I killed 35 at one stand. What we called a stand is when we killed a buffalo the first shot, the others would smell the blood and begin to hook the dead one and paw the earth. Then we would shoot the outside ones, and the more blood there was scattered around the better they would stand. I have often shot two belts of cartridges away at one stand. Each one of these belts would hold 42 cartridges. My gun weighed 14 pounds; the gun and these two belts of cartridges made quite a load to carry around over those prairies.

The second day I hunted there I killed 86 buffalo. The third day I killed 45. Then I was getting ahead of the skinners, so I took my skinning knife and went back and helped skin. By this time I got quite handy with my knife. I could skin a buffalo in fifteen or twenty minutes by myself. Some of my skinners could beat that.

We hunted from this camp until we had 500 hides. It took ten days to do this work. I got on my saddle horse and rode into Kit Carson City, Colorado and I hired Pat Shanley to come out with his mule train and haul these hides for me. I gave him 50 cents a hide for this hauling. I sold the bull hides for three dollars and the cow hides for two dollars to Chick & Brown.

I paid my men off and we spent our money lavishly in Kit Carson City. While we were there a man came in with a carload of shave-tail mules from Missouri. (He sold all but three. I asked him how much he wanted. He said $500. I had $250 left. I told Jack Williams, whom I knew from Fort Wallace, about them, and he agreed to go partners on them and in a hunt). So we bought the mules, and we went over to Chick & Brown and bought two new wagons, and two sets of new harness and we had thirteen head of mules and horses. We owed Chick & Brown over $1000. The buffalo hunter's word was a good as gold anywhere on the range.

Most of what I've been telling was in '73. This trip to Dodge City was in 1874, sometime in September, I expect. Myself and a man named Gus Johnson made a trip together. He was a young Swede and a pretty good hunter. (Before we got to the buffalo, he proposed a contest to see who could shoot the most in one day. In about two days we came to Tipi Creek about 100 miles southwest of Dodge, and buffalo were everywhere. When we came in at night I had killed 12, and he had killed 65.) You must recollect that there is a good deal of luck about killing buffalo, which all old buffalo hunters will tell you is the way of it. The skinners were keeping pretty close to our heels, as buffalo were getting rather scarce by that time. In a few days we loaded our wagons and went back to Dodge City, sold our hides and lay around town a few days. We only made about enough to pay our expenses on this trip.

POSTSCRIPT

George Brown continued to hunt buffalo and poison wolves in Kansas and the Texas panhandle until the herds thinned out by 1876. In May of that year he married Sally Lemon, and they lived in Dodge City until 1878.

George R.T. Gill joined his brother, Will, in Dodge City in 1869. They hunted buffalo commercially for several years. George brought this compass and canteen from service with the Union Army. He needed 5 shots from his Spencer carbine to finish off a wounded bull which charged him. Collection of George W. Gill. Photo by Univ. Wyoming Photo Service.

Chapter 3

George W. Reighard was 85 and the oldest settler in western Kansas when he died in the early 1930s. A native of Pennsylvania, he fought through four years of the Civil War with the 22nd Pennsylvania Volunteer Cavalry. Like many other young veterans, both Union and Confederate, he found that the life he'd known before the war was just too tame, so he headed west.

His first stop was at Ft. Hays, where he got a job as a teamster with Custer's 7th Cavalry. In 1871 he was a teamster in Col. Grierson's 10th Cavalry of black "buffalo" soldiers, trailing Kiowas who had escaped from Ft. Sill. He began hunting buffalo in the fall of 1871, and continued until the spring of 1873. During that time he killed over 5,000; his first big stand was 68.

His recollections, as written here, are from his article in the *Kansas City Star* and an interview with him by Earle Forrest in Dodge City in 1926, published by Forrest in the Los Angeles Corral of Westerners Brand Book XIII.

Recollections of the Buffalo Hunt

George W. Reighard

I came west in 1867, and for several years I drove a government team in the reserve train for General Custer and the 7th Cavalry. Our route was from Ft. Hays to Ft. Dodge on the Arkansas River, and then on south to Ft. Supply in Texas, then back again. This was through the heart of the buffalo country.

I have read many writers who described the herds as "blackening" the plains. They never herded that closely together. A grazing herd undisturbed would be divided into small groups, each group close together, but distinct, with 25 to 30 buffalos to the acre. They drifted along about as closely clustered as cattle do when grazing loosely on the range. But, looking at a buffalo herd from a knoll or hill, it did seem

George W. Reighard in Dodge City, 1926
Photo by Earl Forrest, courtesy of the Historical Society of Western Pennsylvania.

to be almost a solid mass, with the green sod showing only here and there between groups.

In 1872 when I went down into the Texas panhandle with a buffalo hunting outfit, it was estimated that the southern herd numbered three million head. By that time, buffalo hunting had been developed into an exact science. I organized my own outfit and went south from Ft. Dodge to shoot buffalos for their hides. I furnished the team and wagon and did the killing. Jim Whalen, Tom Rooney and Zeke Ford furnished the supplies and did the skinning, stretching, and cooking. They got half the hides, and I got the other half.

I had two big .50 Sharps rifles with telescope sights, using a shell three and a half inches long, (that is, the entire cartridge was three and a half inches, the cartridge case itself was 2.5 inches) with 110 grains of powder. Those guns would kill a buffalo as far away as you could see it, if the bullet hit the right spot.

We had flour, coffee, sugar, salt, blankets, four ten gallon kegs for water, a dutch oven, two frying pans, a big tin coffee pot, a camp kettle, bread pan, tin cups and plates, but no table knives, forks or spoons. We used our skinning and ripping knives for carving. We had four butcher steels and a grindstone for sharpening knives, and that just about completed our outfit. Our diet was mostly buffalo meat, fried, stewed or raw, any way, and since there was plenty of that we saved the expense and worry of toting a lot of provisions around.

We kept moving the camp as the herd moved, often staying a week in a camp. Each morning I would ride out or walk, depending on how far away the heard was. Usually I went to the top of some rise to spy out the herd, and I could creep and crawl, taking advantage of gullies and ridges, to sneak up to within good ranges. Between 250 and 300 yards was all right, the closer the better. I would choose my spot, behind some natural screen, a soapweed, cactus, sagebrush, or the like. I would lie flat on my stomach, get my guns ready, spread a lot of cartridges out on the ground, adjust the gunsights, and be ready to shoot. Usually I carried a gun rest made from a tree crotch, which I would stick in the ground to rest the gun barrel upon.

Each group (of buffalo) always had a leader. The general belief is that the leader was an old bull, but that is not so. The leader was the oldest cow in the group, so the first move of the still hunter would be to drop her. If aimed true, the bullet would pierce her lungs. She would make a startled movement, a sort of little leap forward, looking around, the blood gushing from her nostrils. Hearing the report of the gun, the animals near her would look to her with an idea of running if she would lead the way. Without the initiative to start a stampede themselves, they would see her standing still, and so they would resume their grazing. The wounded cow would wobble weakly, stagger forward, and fall.

Meanwhile, I would have jammed another shell in the breech, and watching the herd carefully, I would note any movement on the part of any buffalo that might take fright and start to move off. That one would be the next victim. It would begin bleeding, lurching unsteadily, and then would fall. Several would walk up and sniff the two on the ground. Then they would throw up their heads and bawl. One or two might start off, and I had to stop them. Sometimes the whole herd would start, and I had to shoot quickly to stop the leaders, and thereby turn the others back. The whole idea was to keep the herd milling, round and round in one restricted spot, shooting those on the outskirts that tried to move away.

While this was going on, the only strange thing that the buffalos could see was a little white puff of smoke now and then from a distant bush or rock. This was usually not alarming, and they would stay milling and bawling, bewildered, until most of them had been shot.

The time I made my biggest kill, I lay on a slight ridge behind a tuft of weeds 100 yards from a bunch of a thousand buffalo that had come a long distance to a creek. They had drunk their fill and strolled out on the prairie to rest. I followed the tactics I have described. After I had killed about 25, my gun barrel became too hot and it began to expand. A bullet from an overheated gun does not go straight, so I put that gun aside and took the other one. By the time that one became hot, the other had cooled, but the powder smoke in front of me was so thick that I could not see through it. There was not a breath of wind to carry it away, so I had to crawl backward, dragging my two guns in order to work around to another position on the ridge. From there I killed 54 more. In one and a half hours I had fired 91 shots, as a count of the empty shells showed afterwards, and I had killed 79 buffalos. We figured that they all lay within an area of about two acres of ground.

My right hand and arm were so sore from working the gun that I was not sorry to see the remaining buffalos start off on a brisk run that soon put them beyond range. On that trip I killed a few more than 3,000 buffalos in one month, which was an average of about 100 a day.

You who have never seen a herd of wild buffalos cannot realise that once all these plains were covered with them like cattle in a field. There were millions in those days, and we never dreamed that the hunting would ever come to an end. In the spring when they traveled north you were never out of sight of a herd, no matter where you went. I have seen buffalos all the way from Ft. Dodge to Camp Supply, a distance of two hundred miles. In 1870 when I was freighting for the army I saw them so thick on the very ground where Dodge City now stands that I had to stop a thirty-six mule team to let them pass. Now you can't find even a bone in this whole region.

The big year for the hunters was 1872. You could hear guns booming all over these plains; so many that it sounded like a battle. By the spring of 1874 the herds in this vicinity had either been killed or driven south. Then the hunters moved their headquarters to Adobe Walls, where the big battle was fought.

I got from a dollar to three dollars and forty cents each for hides, depending upon the condition of the hair. One of the best known of the old-time hide firms in the southwest was Lee and Reynolds. They ran an Indian trading post at Camp Supply and they made a specialty of trading for tanned and painted robes. They bought many thousands of them from the Indians. In those days I purchased good painted robes for six dollars each. If you had one today (1926), you could get anywhere from a hundred to two hundred dollars.

About September 1, 1872, I went to "Soldier's Grave" where Ashland (Kansas) now stands, about 50 miles south of here. The hunting was good, and I killed about 2,000. A band of Indians camped eight miles south of us, and they ordered us to leave the country. One big buck came to camp and threatened to shoot us if we did not get out in "one sleep." We refused to move, and they didn't bother us. Buffalo hunters were all good shots, and the Indians had little stomach for a fight with more than one at a time.[1] They fired the grass, and we had to move camp about six miles, where we had good hunting until Christmas.

[1]According to Brick Bond, "No, the Indians seldom bothered us. They were not looking for a tough proposition like a buffalo hunter's outfit. The hunters were the best shots on the frontier. We had to be, and any man who followed in any capacity had to have plenty of guts. The Indians had a wholesome respect for good shooting when combined with courage."

Bond died in Dodge City in May, 1927, aged 77. He held the records for the most buffalo killed in a single day, and the most killed in a week. He claimed to have been out for three years without seeing a town, and to have averaged 150 buffalo a day, keeping as many as 15 men busy as skinners.

A few weeks later I was hunting with George Pratt on Sand Creek, and I killed five cows for the meat. A big Indian came to our camp one morning, and said that he belonged to Romeo's band of scouts at Ft. Dodge. We were suspicious when he refused to eat with us, and after we had loaded up and driven up on the divide we saw a large war party. About 30 bucks came up to the wagon. I ordered them back at the point of my .50 caliber Sharps buffalo gun. The big Indian tried to talk us into going back after more buffalos, but they only wanted to separate us and I knew it. They would have killed us before we got many of them, but Indians never liked to take a chance with buffalo hunters. That was all that saved us. Pratt drove the wagon. I sat up on top of the load and held those Indians off until they finally gave up. I quit buffalo hunting in the spring of 1873 and went to freighting from Ft. Dodge to Ft. Elliott.

Thomas C. Nixon, Henry Raymond's friend and sometime boss.
Photo courtesy Kansas Historical Society.

Chapter 4

It was very cold in Dodge City when Henry Hubert Raymond, 24, stepped off the recently completed AT & SF at 6:55 a.m. on November 16, 1872. "It was just showing signs of the arrival of a new day, and, seeing a light across the street - there was but one street open on one side (the now famous Front Street, along the railroad tracks) - I wended my way to this light. In entering, there appeared a card table with men around it; and on the table were stacks of pokerchips and piles of money, indicating that the game had perhaps been going on all night. The man with his back to me as I entered wore a blouse, and protruding below it were the barrels of two large revolvers. I learned later that he was Bill Brooks."

Raymond also learned later that Bill Brooks was an ex-marshal of Newton, and a former policeman of Ellsworth. Within four months of this first sighting of Brooks, Raymond recorded in his diary of the attempted murder of Brooks in Dodge City.

Henry Raymond had taken the train from his home in Carlinville, Illinois on November 11. He bought a violin at his stop in St. Louis that same day, and an E string for it in Kansas City the next day. The violin proved to offer him and his hunting partners many hours of pleasure for the next 12 months, as his diary records.

Henry's older brother, Theodore, whom he refers to throughout with the abbreviation "The," had settled near Sedgwick, Kansas and had worked on a railroad leveling contract with Ed and Bat Masterson. When Henry arrived at the Masterson home near Sedgwick, however, he was directed to the home of Thomas C. Nixon in Dodge City. There, Mrs., Nixon, ". . . on learning my identity, kindly suggested that, since I was just from 'The States' the town would be a rather rough place for me; and if I wished, might remain there until my brother came in, as he was camped with her husband, hunting buffalo."

This same Tom Nixon set a record for one stand, and had witnesses to prove it. The *Hutchinson Herald* for Feb. 26, 1928 gave the following details. One September day (probably preceding Henry Raymond's arrival in Nov, 1872) Nixon boasted to his friends in Dodge City that he would set "a record for buffalo killing which would last for all time." Nixon's friends agreed to observe the event. All set off southward, across the headwaters of Bluff Creek, in Meade Co. They found a herd large enough, and properly situated so that Nixon could get a stand. In 40 minutes he killed 120 buffalo. Later, he broke his own record by getting a stand on 204.

Henry Raymond's diary entries are more brief than we'd like, but they are laconic nonetheless. We find mention of using bullet swages; grinding knife blades; making hide pegs; trading for flour and gunpowder; daily records of the killing and skinning of buffalo. His diary was first sent to the offices of the *Kansas Historical Quarterly* in July, 1931, and finally published first in the Winter 1965 issue (Vol. 31, No. 4). The present publication preserves virtually all of the footnotes made by the first editor, Joseph W. Snell, and it adds a few more of interest to the specialized audience of this anthology. Footnotes attributed to H.H.R. are from later articles he wrote for newspapers.

Raymond's record of his first year on the frontier shows his development from a greenhorn who paid $5 for a "soldier's overcoat" his first night in Dodge City, to an experienced hunter and blacksmith. Within six months he'd worked as a ranch hand, post-cutter, skinner, hide-stacker, wolfer, buffalo hunter; he learned the value of a dollar earned. With this experience, he bought a "military dress coat" for $1.50. We'll follow his diary from its first entry, omitting only his narrative for four months while he was in town.

Diary of a Dodge City Buffalo Hunter 1872-1873

Henry H. Raymond

Nov. Monday 11. 1872
Started to Kansas bought violin, in St. Louis. left there at 11 oclock at night for Kansas City.

Nov. Tuesday 12. 1872.
At Kansas City. bought violin string, E. left there at 5 oclock and 15 min. pm for Topeka.

Nov. Thursday 14. 1872.
Went to Mastisons. Staid all night.[1]

Nov. Friday 15. 1872.
Came back to Sedgwick. started to Newton at 8 1/2 oclock, pm. from there to Dodge City. got pair boots $6.50. Stoped at Newton for express train. got shaved. got cakes & box prize candy.

Nov. Saturday 16. 1872.
got to Dodge City at 6:55 A.M. stoped at Nixons.[2] Wrote to Seth.[3] Bought soldier overcoat this evening, paid five dollars.

Nov. Sunday 17. 1872.
down at town; got box of boot grease, 50 cts. crackers and cheese. left shirt to get washed at dug out. terrible cold and windy. bought pistol scabbard for 50 cts.

Nov. Monday 18. 1872.
Went to Fort Dodge with teamster, to get load wood for Mrs. Nixon; found The[4] when come back; him and I got dinner at restaurant. The and I went to the dance house at night; one of the fair Dolcinas[5] sat by me, and invited me to dance.

[1]The Masterson family consisted of seven children, five boys and two girls. Probably all but Edward and William, the two oldest, were still home. Their 80-acre farm was in Grant township, Sedgwick county, the E. 1/2 of the S.W. 1/4 of Sec. 24, T. 25 S., R. 1 E.

[2]Thomas C. Nixon, whose ranch lay about one-fourth mile west of Dodge City. Twice assistant marshal of the town, he was shot and killed while in office by his predecessor, "Mysterious" Dave Mather, July 21, 1884.

[3]Henry's older brother, Seth L. Raymond, who was probably still at home near Carlinville, Illinois.

[4]Henry's nickname for his older brother, Theodore D. Raymond.

[5]Raymond probably meant Dulcinea and was referring to a "dance hall girl."

Nov. Tuesday 19. 1872.
cold and windy. went to town, went out into river with The, helped him to get wagon out,[6] put bottom in wagon box for him, Nixon came home, all went to town, at night; started to write to L.

Nov. Wednesday 20. 1872.
In town. went to Fort Dodge with The and got corn and oats. crossed river. stayed at Myers'[7] corral, all night.

Nov. Thursday 21. 1872.
started for Chiwa camp.[8] camped out on prairie. saw antelopes and kyotes. shot at kiotes with pistol in morning. very cold at night.

Nov. Friday 22. 1872.
mistake. started for Chiwa on Friday. at Nixons camp. saw Bat[9] kill 4 buffalos.

Nov. Saturday 23. 1872.
went out, helped skin 17 buffalos. very warm and pleasant. The killed 5 of them. Abe Mayhue[10] came in, saw badger and prairie dogs.

[6]Theodore's wagon had broken through the ice and bogged down in the Arkansas River on his return to Dodge City. Having heard that Henry was at Nixon's, Theodore abandoned the wagon and hurried to greet this brother whom he had not seen for three years. Later the two retrieved the vehicle.

[7]Possibly Alexander C. Myers of the firm Leonard & Myers, Dodge City.

[8]Probably a camp on Kiowa Creek which crosses the northeast corner of Clark county.

[9]William B. "Bat" Masterson, whom Raymond variously refers to as Bat or Bart, both of which are accepted diminutive forms of Bartholomew. In 1962 Raymond's daughter, Mrs. Blake, told W.E. Koop that "Bat's folks always called him Bat at home, and that his middle name was actually Bartholomew. . ." Confirmation of this appears in a biography of Thomas Masterson where reference is made to a son, Bartholomew, who was then marshal of Trinidad, Colo. This was, of course, Bat. At least one newspaper article, in the *Kansas City* (Mo.) *Star*, December 10, 1897, named him Bartholomew.

Certainly Bat did not earn his nickname, as legend has stated, from his habit of batting opponents over the head with his cane, since the incident which caused him to use a supporting staff occured three and one-half years after Raymond's use of "Bat" in his diary.

If Bat's middle name was Bartholomew, originally he changed it some time before August 3, 1907, when he signed his will as William Barclay Masterson. This is the only known use of his full name in his own handwriting.

[10]A.B. Mahew (or Mayhew) was a Sedgwick county neighbor of the Raymonds and Mastersons. — "Kansas State Census," 1875, Sedgwick county, Grant township, p. 34.

Nov. Sunday 24. 1872.
killed two buffaloes myself. helped skin 4. Very windy.

Nov. Monday 25. 1872.
Abe and Bat started for Dodge City this morning. Ed[11] killed 19 buffaloes. Skinned 15 of them. I killed one at night. Saw jack rabbit. Saw pack of wolves. Sent for pants and over alls, and cup and camphor gum, by Bat. made ring of hoof.

Nov. Tuesday 26. 1872.
killed and skinned 20 buffalos. I killed 3 of them. beautiful day untill night, turned very cold and windy.

Nov. Wednesday 27. 1872.
Cold day. The and me skinned 14 buffalo. Steve and Jim fixed shanty.[12] Ed killed wild turky. saw village of prairie dogs.

Nov. Thursday 28. 1872.
Killed and skinned 13 buffalo. I killed one. The sick. Abe and Steve went to town, or rather started.

Nov. Saturday 30 1872.
Ed and Bat and me killed and butchered 17 buffalos. Jim pegged.[13]

Dec. Sunday 1. 1872.
Ed and me butchered 10 bulls. Jim pegged. Indians at camp.

Dec. Monday 2. 1872.
hunted with Nixons outfit. Butchered 23 today. Jim and me 13.

Dec. Tuesday 3. 1872.
Butchered 17 buffalo, The, Ed and me. Abe got back, bot ein gallon Schnaps mit gebraucht (brought a gallon of whiskey along). Nixons teams came back.

Dec. Wednesday 4. 1872.
Butchered 20 buffalos, The, Ed and me. three Indians in camp today.

Dec. Thursday 5. 1872.
butchered 19 buffalos, Ed, The, Bat, and me. I shot some wounded ones. Spring day. Some little rain at evening, turned cold and clear. went to Yahoo's camp at night. The, Nixon, Hunt, and me.

Dec. Saturday 7. 1872.
Skinned 26 buffalo. Nixon moved camp today.

[11]Edward John Masterson, oldest of the Masterson children. As marshal of Dodge City, he was killed in the line of duty, April 9, 1878.

[12]Steve Mahew, son of Abe Mahew, and James P. Masterson, third in age of the brothers.

[13]Buffalo hides were nailed to the ground with wooden pegs for drying.

Dec. Sunday 8. 1872.
Shaved with pocket knife. Ed Jim and me went to Indian village. Saw the squaws tanning robes. Arapaho tribe.

Dec. Monday 9. 1872.
Skinned 30 buffalo. Very cold a(ll) d(ay). Cloudy and windy at night. I killed 3 of buffalo.

Dec. Tuesday 10. 1872.
first snow, last night. warm today. wounded buffalo this morning. Big John here. Jim and I went aft turkys. Abe came at night brought (word illegible) letter from Liza Lane

Dec. Wednesday 11. 1872.
Bat, Abe, Ed, Jim, Rigny[14] and me went to Indian camp to trade. The went to Dodge with Nixen. Killed my first grouse today. Saw Indians eating lice.[15]

Dec. Thursday 12. 1872.
Sat up nearly all night last night. So cold did not work. hauled load wood. went to Yahoos camp at eve.

Dec. Friday 13. 1872.
butchered 4 buffalos. Snow on ground. quail hunting. Abe tried to kill some. I shot a kyote on run, grazed his back.

Dec. Saturday 14. 1872.
terrible windy and cold. did not work, only pegged a few hides. The came in at night.

Dec. Sunday 15. 1872.
did not work, went to Big Johns camp to take saddle and ammunition. bought Navy pistol of Big John for five dollars. two strange Indians in camp to day. Jim Barber here. went to Yahoo camp at night. Abe and Ed started to Dodge.

Dec. Monday 16. 1872.
The, Bat, and me butchered 6 buffalos, Cold in fore(noon). three Indians in camp today.

[14]Probably James Rignyer.

[15]"Sitting on the ground was a 'Brave,' his back against a log on which sat another while at his back still another was standing; the two latter carefully searching their companions' heads for what we sometimes hear called 'Jerusalem Creepers' and judging from the frequency of the hand to the mouth, they must have found a rich harvest. I don't know whether they eat them for the nourishment they furnish or whether it is simply to rid themselves of the pests." H.H.R.

Dec. Tuesday 17. 1872.
Jim and I went to East Chiwa to kill turkeys, had Dutch Freds gun. got ball fast[16]. killed grouse, didn't work.

Dec. Wednesday 18. 1872.
Staid in camp. Yahoos hunted with our boys today. I thawed and pegged hides. Rigny here in morn. boys killed 12 buff (their part). wrote to Seth.

Dec. Thursday 19. 1872.
terrible wind and snow storm last night and this morning. bull train came last night. borrowed flour of Yahoos. cold day.

Dec. Friday 20. 1872.
very cold day. Shook snow off hides. The and Bat went to Big Johns. Started to town. 4 bull whackers here to spend eve. Sang songs and played violin. Snowed.

Dec. Saturday 21. 1872.
Jim and I at camp alone. Shot a grouse. came near shooting Moore. Jim Barber here after shovel. boys did not come.

Dec. Sunday 22. 1872.
went to other creek to hunt turkeys. all gone. beautiful day. boys didnt come. Borrowed flour of Yahoos.

Dec. Monday 23. 1872.
terrible cold and windy all night and to day. Wright Moore[17] called on his way to Nixens. boys did not come.

Dec. Tuesday 24. 1872.
cold day. two of Yahoos here. Moore here aft(er) yeast pwd (powder). Abe and Ed came at night. Ed bought pair gloves $3.00. got letter from Seth.

Dec. Wednesday 25. 1872.
Christmas day. Shot at mark to see whos treat. Ed and me best. fine day in morning. Wind rose about noon. went to Nixens camp. played fiddle for stag dance in dug out.[18] terrible windy and cold. Stayed all night. I slept with boss Jim White.

[16]Probably stuck a ball in a muzzle-loader.

[17]Josiah Wright Mooar, a well-known frontiersman and very successful buffalo hunter, who settled Snyder, Texas, formerly called Hide Town.

[18]"We were invited to Nixon's camp. They were to have a pie and cake like they do 'back in the states' and a dance at night. Of course, there were no girls there, so half of the men had to take the role of the gentler sex in the quadrille." H.H.R.

I fiddled while Tom Nixon and Boss Jim White had a Christmas dance

Dec. Thursday 26. 1872.
Came home from Nixens camp. nearly froze to death. staid in camp a(ll) d(ay). Texan Jim came here crazy with tooth ache. Jim and me went to Yahoos to hear boys sing. Bat didn't come.

Dec. Friday 27. 1872.
In camp a(ll) d(ay). Snowed all day, not very cold, I killed grouse with needle gun. Jim went to Yahoos to play cards. Bat did not come.

Dec. Saturday 28. 1872.
Ed, Abe and me went to Yahoos, got Abes gun, went to main Kiwa to hunt turkey. Saw fellow with cap made of hide off antelope head, with horns and ears on.[20] Saw 4 antelope and lots of turkeys but killed none. Bat did not come. thawing today.

Dec. Sunday 29. 1872.
beautiful warm day. Ed and me shot at mark two hundred yds. I made 2 best shots. piled hides, made dug out. I killed buffalo cow on run. Ed and me skinned her. Nixens teams came.

Dec. Monday 30. 1872.
In camp a(ll) d(ay), damp drizzly day, fixed up old wagon and greased it. Ed, and Abe, went to Nixens camp. Dutch Fred here. fixed box to put things in.

Dec. Tuesday 31. 1872.
got balls and pwd from Yahoos to load revolver. fixed over shoes. In dug out. warm day. loaded 30 hams and the tongues on The's wagon. Nixens teams and the Yahoos loaded up and went to Big Johns. Jim Barber and Wright Moore (Mooar) skinned 3 grey wolves here this eve.

March Saturday 1. 1873.
At ranch most all day. went to town got no mail. Saw wolf chase and saw them catch jack rabbit. played ball. Bat and me and George M. and Pat Baker shot at marks. I made best shot. wrote some for Carlinville Dem(ocrat). played accordian, beautiful day.

March. Sunday 2. 1873.
beautiful day. went to town twice. shot at mark down there. made best shot (at) 300 yds. Nixon and Jim hunted jack rabbits, got one. Tom's came in. made fiddle bow; didnt go to town at night.

[20]An unidentified man who - "was dressed almost, if not entirely, with the furs of wild animals: a coat of antelope skin and on his head was the skin of a buck antelope with the antlers on, the nose coming down over his forehead making an apt portraiture of the 'Evil One.'" H.H.R.

March. Monday 3. 1873.
beautiful spring day. went to town, no mail train on Monday. came back to ranch, took a walk out north; to look at country. had thought of going out to camp but changed notion. went down town at night. Rigney, Barber and (Dave) Dudly[21] left today. in town at night.

March. Tuesday 4. 1873.
beautiful day. down in town Bill Brooks got shot at with needle gun the ball passing through two barrels of water lodging in outside iron hoop. Jerdon shot at him.[22] I was down town most all day. Pat and Bat went to hunt the horses. Soldier got beat over the head with boot and $5 taken from him in town.

March. Wednesday 5. 1873.
Nice day. in town most a(ll) day. Saw Brooks and Jerden compromise today.[23] Pat Baker and me made fiddle bow. I made silk E string. in town at night. come home played vio.

March. Thursday 6. 1873.
Started with Nixon outfit for the Cimarron. got to Crooked Creek and camped. eat some hmp(?) that we found in bushes. saw lot of poisoned wolves. saw antelope. very windy. Nixon turned off Haily. Jim White got back.

[21]Dudley was killed by Indians near the Canadian River in June 1874. "A fine fellow" was Raymond's estimation of him.

[22]Billy Brooks was an ex-marshal of Newton and former policeman of Ellsworth. He appeared in Dodge City sometime late in 1872. According to a later statement by Raymond, Jake (?) Jordan was intent on killing Brooks for the latter's murder of a friend. Jordan, lying in wait, raised his rifle "holding it against the door-facing and was about to pull the trigger when someone stepped out of a building between him and Brooks. He then raised the gun as he did not want to shoot another party; but Brooks, ever on the lookout, caught the motion of that gun barrel. He suddenly threw himself to a sitting posture on the ground behind two bbls. of water, trying at the same time to draw one of his guns. Somehow the gun hung and he failed to pull it from the scabbard. Jordan fired at the barrels and the bullet lodged against the last iron hoop next to Brooks. Brooks sprang to his feet before Jordan could reload and someone helped to hide him." H.H.R.

[23]Jordan had left town following the previous day's shooting but someone arranged a compromise between the two. "It happened . . . that Jordan came riding in unarmed. Rode up to the hitching rack just a few feet from where I was standing," Raymond recalled. "I heard him say 'Boys, you've got me into it!' Just then from a nearby building came Bill Brooks in white starched shirt, and with no gun on him. I never saw him thus before. He approached Jordan with a broad smile offering a friendly handshake. Jordan gave his hand, but there was no friendly smile on his face. Jordan says, 'What we've got to say we don't need to say to this crowd. Let's go inside!'"

Brooks was hanged as a horse thief in Sumner county, July 29, 1874. H.H.R.

March. Friday 7. 1873.
go to Simiroan. saw antelopes. Tom killed buffalo cow, skinned her and took horns.

March. Saturday 8. 1873.
drove up the Simmaroan about 15 miles to the springs. Pat killed bull. Jim White killed two antelope and two bulls. beautiful day. saw lots of antelope and some deer.

March. Sunday 9. 1873.
Started to go back to Dodge. nice day. Saw good many buffalos. Saw 5 wild horses. saw some deers. Jim killed buffalo cow. Saw nice chase aft a swift (fox) did not get it. come to puddle of water about middle aftnoon and camped. Tom killed a bull. Chisler and me stretched tent.

March. Monday 10 1873.
killed and butchered 5 buffalos. started for Crooked creek. not certain about country. turned and drove for the Arkansaw. crossed sand hills and crossed river. I got stalled in river in the quick sand. Chisler helped me out. pitched tent on other side.

March. Tuesday 11. 1873.
Started. Saw lots of buff. killed and butchered 11. got to ranch about 3 oclock. I went down town at night. got two letters one from The, and one from Simonson. Pat brought home quart of schnaps.

March. Wednesday 12. 1873.
last night the vigilance committee shot Mcgill, a buffalo hunter for firing pistol in dance hall. I went down town saw him. went down town. pegged the hides. cut up and salted the meat, did not go to town at night. boys all went. mailed letter to Seth and one to Chicago.

March. Thursday 13. 1873.
Tom Sherman shot (Charles?) Burns last night.[24] Nice day. teams all

[24]Raymond had heard Sherman's shots. "I hastily rose and ran downtown," he later wrote. "Just as I neared the edge of the little town I could see some fellows gathering and, as I drew closer, could discern a man down and moving his legs & arms. Possibly he may have had consciousness enough to feel that he was fleeing from his pursuer with whom I almost collided. This was Tom Sherman, a big lubberly fellow, who ran with a limp. He had a large calibre revolver in his hand which he was emptying into the boy that was down . . . Tom, panting for breath, said to those gathering, 'I'd better shoot him again, hadn't I boys?" He stepped at once to where he lay struggling; stood over him holding a big revolver in both hands, aimed at his forehead and fired. The bullet went a little high and scattered his brains in his hair . . . All I could learn was that Sherman had killed a friend of Burns and thought it would be safer to have him out of the way." H.H.R.

went out but mine. Tom sold little mules and bought team of horses. I got letter from E. Lawton. I took pitcher of milk to Lill Thompson at night. heard nice music at Kelly's. Italians played harp and vio. wrote to Simonson. Decker came in.

March. Friday 14. 1873.

Terrible windy and warm. I went down town got letter from The. mailed letter to him and one to Simonson. got 25 cents to Levy to get stamps. helped Weber to unload car load of coal. got drink of schnaps. brought home the new team. Decker started out.

March. Saturday 15. 1873.

went down town. cold and windy in morning but turned very pleasant. got no leter. Ed gave me glass of beer. Shot army rifle at mark 350 yds. Made good shot. me and Nixon at ranch alone at night. made scabbord for knife today.

March. Sunday 16. 1873.

me and Weber stared to go to rattlesnake,[25] got on wrong track went most to East Kiowa. turned to come back to Dodge. stoped at O'brians ranch. concluded to try it again. Slept in wagon. terribly windy and Cold night. didn't sleep much.

March. Monday 17. 1873.

went back to old Supply road[26] and took another start but not being rightly directed did not go far enough so turned and came back to Dodge. nice day. went down town at night. saw one of the fairs with Zouave suit on.

March. Tuesday 18. 1873.

Salted meat and tongues for Rath,[27] in car, in forenoon, got dinner at restaurant. Weber paid my dinner, got veil weins (much wine) at Raths at noon, got schnaps at night. Load hydes for la comp in aft. noon. at dance house at night. at both dance halls, nice day.

March. Wednesday 19. 1873.

helped bail and load hides for Rath all day recd. $2.00. got dinner and supper at restaurant. paid C.W. Weber $1.00 dollar that had borrowed. Hat veil wein getrunk (drank much wine). Nixons outfit came in and Ed Jones and Tom Decker. Mrs. Nixon came home. got letter from The; very windy.

[25]Rattlesnake Creek which flows in a northeasterly direction through parts of Ford, Kiowa, Edwards, Stafford, and Rice counties.

[26]The military road from Fort Dodge to Camp Supply in present Oklahoma.

[27]Charles Rath, an early merchant of Dodge City, did business in partnership with Robert M. Wright under the name of Charles Rath & Co.

March. Thursday 20. 1873.
bailed & loaded hides. piled some. loaded some bones. worked all day for Rath. hauled two loads corn from car. hat veil wein getrunk. nice day. Recd. $5.00 of Rath. in dance house at night. splendid music. got sup at restaurant. nice day.

March. Friday 21. 1873.
Salted meat for Rath until noon then went with Nixons outfit to the Sawlog.[28] played on Ed Jones vio. nice day. $2.50 still coming to me. Charley owes me 25 cts. hat ein glass wein (had a glass of wine). Ed Jones gave me powd to load revolver.

March. Saturday 22. 1873.
got up early in morning. crossed Buckner and Dry creeks, got to Pawnee.[29] drove up it. saw but little game. passed one small outfit on Pawnee. camped about middle aft noon. beautiful day. Warped Eds vio bow and played on his vio at night.

March. Sunday 23. 1873.
Turned terrible windy and cold awhile aft went to bed. stock all got loose. Spring seat blew off wagon onto my head. blew off Whites hat found it one half mile away this morning. drove up Pawnee. turned to go back to D(odge). C(ity). found piece of izinglass. Decker didn't turn. cold all day. pitched tent and camped at Beards & Moores camp.

March. Monday 24. 1873.
pulled up and drove to head of Buckner and took out. fed team & got dinner and came to Dodge. nice day until about middle aft when it turned fearful windy and cold and began snowing. White killed antelope. killed 4 buffalo. went down town. got hair cut 75 cts. wretched cold.

March. Tuesday 25. 1873.
Cold day though moderated some. in town, got letter from The with one enclosed from Seth. got $12.00 from White and put $3.00 more with it. Sent to Seth fifteen dollars paid expressage one dollar. wrote to The, Ed showed me letter from Nellie.

[28]Saw Log Creek flows from Ford country, north of Dodge City, into the Pawnee River near the Hodgeman-Pawnee county line.

[29]Pawnee River, an east flowing stream, empties into the Arkansas River at Larned.

March. Wednesday 26. 1873.
Loaded up and came to the horse shoe bend (of) "Crooked creek."[30] Cold windy day. most of the boys getrunken war (were drunk). arrived at Crooked creek about two hours by sun. Ed gave me the magazine today.

March. Thursday 27. 1873.
cold windy day, drove down the creek about 10 miles then turned and went across to head of Bear creek.[31] killed two buffalo cows and one calf and bull. lost Blucher & Runner. turned back to Crooked creek. struck it below the Manerby. camped, very windy.

March. Friday 28. 1873.
drove back to Horse Shoe bend or Walker timber and cut some poles and camped. pleasant day though windy. Tom and Jim went across to look for pups but didn't find them.

March. Saturday 29 1873.
finished cutting and loading poles and came back to Nixon ranch. went down town. no letters. in town at night. beauty day all day. very warm. Levy hat der ochs schussen dieser abend (shot the ox this evening).

March. Sunday 30. 1873.
Worked for Rath. folded hides and unloaded car loads of oats. Engaged weeks board at hotel, beginning at noon. pleasant day. Billy, Louis, Nelson and me worked.

March. Monday 31. 1873.
folded hides for Rath all day. folded and piled. very windy, warm at night and windy. Came to ranch at night and wrote letter to Seth. George Mitchel also writing.

April. Tuesday 1. 1873.
me and the Sweed (Andrew Johnson) unloaded and weighed car load of corn and potatoes. worked all day at unloading car and putting corn away in back room. Windy day. got letter from Seth. states Mothers started to Kan.

April. Wednesday 2. 1873.
worked for Rath. Haly and me bailed hides. George Mitchel and Bat and the Sweed hauled and put in car in afternoon. I got pair of boots of Rath this morning $7.50 got pr sock with them. hat ein hemd georgen

[30]Crooked Creek is a tributary of the Cimarron and flows southward from Gray, across the southwest corner of Ford county and through Meade county.

[31]In Clark county, flowing south through Ashland.

von (borrowed a shirt from) George. Kelly and Rhine had row tonight. Columbus (Crouse or Kruse) left today.

April. Thursday 3. 1873.

Kelly got head put on him last night and Jim Redman today. Haly, Andrew and me bailed hides today. George and Bat hauled. Haly and I got quart of sherry $1.00. gave Johne's w(ife) and apfel, heutenacht (apple this evening). warm day. left shirt at dug out to get washed. at dance hall at n(ight).

April Friday 4. 1873.

very warm spring day, though in aft noon terrible windy. Haly and me bailed hides. other boys hauled. at dance hall (at night).

April. Saturday 5. 1873.

nice day. bailed and shifted hides all day. Haly, Andrew and me. the boys hauling. not many hides taken in today. got shirt of Hank at night. price $2.25 cts. called at D(ance). H(all). Ed got letter from Nellie.

April. Sunday 6. 1873.

Windy and cold. rained some during the night. rained some in morning and snowed. covered up hides and helped haul 4 loads of bails to cars until Bat and George came, when all worked, cold and windy all day.

April. Monday 7. 1873.

Very cold and windy all day. George and I worked till noon for Rath. at noon George began working at restaurant. snowing some today. Rath went east and also Nixon.

April. Tuesday 8. 1873.

got breakfast at hotel. in town most all day. got in with fellow with ox team to go hunting. Bob Wright [32] settled Rath account with me. paid $10.50 cash. got military dress coat, $1.50. paid board bill. $7.25 got valice today 75 cts exp(ress).

April. Wednesday 9 1873.

pleasant day got gun of Jim White to go hunting with (J.A. or Samuel?) Carr and James. got of Hank Cable 200 rnds ammunition $9.00 and one steel $1.75 got bill of same $10.75. drove out to Saw Log and camped with Barber and Rigny, Dudly and Butterfield.

April. Thursday 10. 1873.

drove toward the head of Saw Log. then turned toward the river. Struck river about 4 miles below first station. drove up river about two miles above the station and camped at dug out in river bank. killed one cow.

[32]Robert M. Wright, partner of Charles Rath, was later mayor of Dodge City.

April. Friday 11. 1873.
drove up river, most to Huntington, went out to the lake. Saw no game, turned for Dodge. Stoped and eat snack where we camped. Cleaned out gun and pistol. beautiful day. killed duck but could not get it. drove within 4 mi of Point of Rock[33] and camped, with fellow from Huntington.

April. Saturday 12. 1873.
drove in to town got dinner at Nixons. got letter from The stating mothers arrived at Sedgwick. wrote to The. nice day though windy. Jim White came in from Crooked creek this eve. got sup at ranch.

April. Sunday 13. 1873.
got breakfast at ranch and went down town. got dinner at hotel and went to work for Rath in aft noon. about 5 oclock there came a terrible wind storm continued until late in night. had to quit work, got nichol of Ed. mailed letter to The. Bat worked. borrowed Andrews coat.

April. Monday 14. 1873.
Wind still blowing and very cold today. bailed hides for Rath after finishing car load of hides began yesterday. very windy all day and cold. Emigrant train camped in town to night bound for Colerido Bart[34] didnt work.

April. Tuesday 15. 1873.
got breakfast at ranch. went down town. aweful cold and windy. got letter from Seth, Bat took (Raymond) Ritter prisoner.[35] I went on train got his valice. did not work. got two meals at hotel. wrote to Seth at night.

April. Wednesday 16. 1873.
Snowing this morning and cold all day. wind died about night. mailed letter to Seth. Staid at ranch most a(ll) d(ay). Rath came today. played vio at ranch today and tonight. Levy and Chisler came in from plowing today. got 25 cts fm Ed to get stamps.

[33]There were at least three "Point of Rocks" landmarks on the Santa Fe trail; two were in Kansas. The most prominent in the state was on the Cimarron River in Morton county but here Raymond was referring to the Point of Rocks on the Arkansas River west of Dodge City.

[34]Bat Masterson.

[35]Ritter was a Santa Fe railroad contractor from whom Bat and Ed Masterson had subcontracted some grading between Dodge and Fort Dodge. Legend has it that Ritter refused to pay up and that Bat eventually collected their money at the point of a gun. Raymond's diary confirms this story.

April. Thursday 17. 1873.
Cold in morning and clear. went down town. did not work. went out with Ed, Bart, Scoty, Charles, Hunt, Ed House and Kelly to kill some buffalo. got 5. Kelly fell off his horse got badly hurt. Sent for doctor.[36] Sold hides, Ed owes me two dolars. got book and pencil 75 cts. at hall at night.

April. Friday 18. 1873.
Beautiful still day. at ranch most all day. took shot gun went up the river to kill some ducks. killed sea gull, but no ducks. went to town at night. gave Bat $1.00. Kelly very bad tonight. made will.

April. Saturday 19. 1873.
beautiful day. Jim White, Bart, and me went out to kill meat for restaurant. got 11 buff. Didnt go to town at night. Mrs. [N.B. (Sally)] George fixed salve and ties my finger up. rising pained me very much. mrs. N(ixon). hat mir candy gegeben (gave me candy).

April. Sunday 20. 1873.
nice day. went down town. got no mail. at ranch most all day. went up river bottom to Col. (Isaac) Young claim to tell the man to bring plow down. went aft cows at night. Ed here tonight to stay all night.

April. Monday 21. 1873.
found old six blade knife this eve. Went up the river above Point of Rock. got two loads poles. very warm day. Saw old Indian camp and lodges. lost my revolver. Charley Trask went to look for it. boys found it in load. Sick at night.

April. Tuesday 22. 1873.
turned real cold awhile before morning. very windy this morning. saw company of infantry soldiers go by & 6 six mule teams and an ambulance. I did not go to town today. Snowed some. traded my ripping knives to C. Trask for dirk knife. made handle and put on dirk.

[36]Later Raymond explained that Kelly had been drinking quite heavily on the hunt. While in a drunken state, he mounted his horse, Calamity, and rode off with his dogs after buffalo. "It was not long until we saw someone on horseback on the ridge about a mile away who seemed to be motioning." Raymond later wrote, "We all looked awhile and saw him take off his hat and wave. Bat took Dutch Albert's pony and rode over to see what was wrong. He came back saying that Kelly's horse had stepped in a prairie dog hole and Jim was badly hurt. We took the wagon and loaded him in. Bat went ahead on horseback and got a spring-wagon & came to meet us. He was badly hurt and thought the end was near. Made his will — he owned considerable property." H.H.R.

April. Wednesday 23. 1873.
At ranch all day. cold and snowing a(ll). d(ay). Emigrant train of 13 wagons passed going to Colerado. copyd Gary Owen and Sailors Hornpipe. played vio at night. Jim Lochren here.
April. Thursday 24. 1873.
Still cold, though moderated some. Chisler and Sam (Wilson?) quit this morning. Jim put in my care.[37] Boys all down town. two fellows came up here for fear of being shot. all the boys went to town tonight except N.B. George. made out bill of goods for Lochren this eve.
April. Friday 25. 1873.
fixed place in stable for curry comb and brush. rode Michigan Jim first time this morning. took grey horse down town. got Kellys pony and drove up the stock. nice day. Nixon started at 11 o clock for Lawrence, Kan.
April. Saturday 26. 1873.
Helped to get the boys ready and started on their trip to Camp Supply. helped load teams with corn. came back to ranch. Cleaned horse and rode him out for exercise. cleaned up Winchester rifle and shot at carcas. went up the slew tried to kill duck. Ed here most all day.
April. Sunday 27. 1873.
at ranch all day. Ed here most ad (all day). Sam Willson here. played vio. rode Jim out. nice day. wrote to Barbara, enclosed picture. Mrs. Nixon went to Sunday school. Seen one of the fairs come out on the hill[38] and set down, read letter.
April. Monday 28. 1873.
helped Levy to plant potatoes. nice warm day. Ed came up at night, did not go home. showed me letter which he got from his father. Emigrant train passed 14 teams. Mrs. Bridges[39] came here today. her man gone with soldiers to take horse thieves.
April. Tuesday 29. 1873.
got kicked last night while looking out for theives. windy all day. planted 5 rows of potatoes Levy and me. In aft had light thunder storm.

[37]Michigan Jim, a race horse owned by Tom Nixon and Dog Kelley. Later Raymond said he was paid $40 a month to care for the animal. H.H.R.

[38]Probably Boot Hill which was near Nixon's ranch.

[39]Mrs. Ada Bridges. Her husband, Jack, was deputy United States marshal for the area.

June. Sunday 1. 1873.
Little Ring died. warm and cloudly all day. Teams came in. I went down town to meet them. got sack of oats. got glass schnaps at p.o. tended horse. made bed in garden. Levy R. here.

June. Monday 2. 1873.
got shot gun tonight. drizzling rain all day. I took 49 sacks down to Collars.[40] got 10 cts apiece in trade. got Jim 1 pr. drawers $1.50. the balance for myself. Nixons outfit started out with 6 teams 14 hands besides themselves. got for self 1 shirt $2.00, comb 40 cts, bottle ink 50 cts. paper and envelopes cts.

June. Tuesday 3. 1873.
got molasses. 3 pound berry at Irvense nice day. carried some milk down to town for Fred. got little axe at Zimmermans[41] for $1.75. got shovel plow at shop and made stock for it at ranch. helped old woman to make some garden. Joe caught young antelope.

June. Wednesday 4. 1873.
finished shovel plow. got pr clevis at Zimmermanns for 50 cts, and Joe and me plowed the potatoes. this morning the town surrounded by soldiers trying to arrest the murderer of Taylor who was killed last night.[42] Ed Jones here.

June. Thursday 5. 1873.
beautiful day. hitched up the mules went down town to get feed. Soldiers again surrounded the town, put five men in jail. viz. (Tom) Sherman, (A.D.?) Gilkerson, Cook and the two Micks's. Jones here at

[40]Morris Collar's dry goods store on Front Street between George M. Hoover's wholesale liquor store and F.C. Zimmermann's hardware.

[41]F.C. Zimmermann's, dealer in hardware and firearms.

[42]William Taylor, a Negro, was killed by John Scott and William Hicks. Since the newly organized county had no effective police as yet, Maj. Richard I. Dodge requested and received permission from the governor to arrest the killers. Raymond later wrote: "A bunch of drunken toughs hired the driver of this man's (Taylor's) team to take them and some of the girls of the town to drive them to Fort Dodge to a dance. He had made two or three trips, and they wanted him to go again. He objected and when they insisted he went to the owner, a restaurant keeper, who came on the scene and said they should not go again. It was then 2 a.m. He said the team should not make another trip whereupon one of the toughs put a gun to one of the mule's head and shot it. The owner made such a remonstrance at this that they turned their guns on him and riddled him with bullets while he begged for his life saying that he was a law-abiding citizen. This man had been a private cook for the colonel (Maj. Dodge) at Ft. Ddoge. This is why Uncle Sam took a hand." H.H.R.

eve. got sack of oats and had it charged to Moore. 135 lbs. got ret letter for The.

June. Friday 6. 1873.

nice day. warm and cloudy. George James here, die fraue kammen in morgen (the women came this morning) awhile. went down town to see Col. Young about claim. Joe and me plowed corn patch and in eve I commenced digging new well, found water.

June. Saturday 7. 1873.

finished digging well. put in two barrels and one half bbl (as a liner for the well). made lid. die alte zuriike kammen zu blieben (the old woman came to stay). got letter from The and answered it. went to town to mail it. Chisler came in eve.

June. Sunday 8. 1873.

very warm and cloudy; rode Jim up to Co. Y's claim. came back went with Bowen up to Anthonys got two of his planes. made vio fiddle box. Surveying outfit came today. camped here. Harris and Lochren came in this eve. old woman gone to Anthonys to stay. got hinges to fix vio box.

June. Monday 9. 1873.

beautiful day. Jim came near getting away from me. der Sallie[43] hat heir kommen huete (Sally came here today). fixed lining n vio box. hoed beans. carpenter at work on house today. de alte zu Anthonys bleiben (the old woman is staying at Anthony's). (Emanuel) Dubbs here today. Tom and one of hands came.

June Tuesday 10. 1873.

nice day. went across river to see the mare, found her at ranch with a little colt. went over in eve got her. Jones hitched up, brought the colt over in wagon for me. I traded my two pistols to Joe for his Smith and Wesson No. 2, and $4.00 to boot. Ben came in with hides.

June. Wednesday 11. 1873.

nice day. at ranch all day. hoed some in garden. Shot little revolver at telegraph pole 30 yds. C. Trask here at night.

June. Thursday 12. 1873.

rode Jim up to Col. Youngs and down to shop. Saw Courie and Dutchy up the bottom. had talk with them. Ben and me plowed potatoes.

[43]Sally (Mrs. N.B.) George.

June. Friday 13. 1873.
plowed corn. finished went down town. got poison and soda to poison hides. Trask proposed to me to go hunting. shot pistol at mark.
June. Saturday 14. 1873.
nice day. turned over the hides and poisoned other side, and piled them up. took old woman buggy riding to Col. Y's. die alte (the old woman) and Tom gone to Anthonys at night.
June. Sunday 15. 1873.
nice day untill eve when there came a hard wind storm. went to town twice to see Charley (Trask) but failed to see him. in eve piled the hides. rode Jim in morning, and grazed him. rained at night.
June. Monday 16 1873.
tended horse. Charley gone to help Haney find horse. Frenchy came to get me to go and hunt for him. offered me half.
June. Tuesday 17. 1873.
Started out. N(ixon)s bull train pulled us across the river. drove to head of Mulberry and camped. I rode ahead and found camping place.
June. Wednesday 18. 1873.
Started early for the Simaron. took dinner below Walker timbr. kill buff cow. drove to Bascoms crossing of crooked creek. camped.
June. Thursday 19. 1873.
drove to sand hills of Simaron. made camp in canyon. killed old bull.
June. Friday 20. 1873.
hunted. killed only four bulls. nice day. saw plenty of buff but were wild. came mid aft.
June. Saturday 21. 1873.
hunted out west in the flat. killed 10 buff. Charley killed two of them. very nice day. C. and me hat gin getrunk (C(harley) and I drank gin) at night.
June. Sunday 22. 1873.
moved camp to the lake on old Basquin (Fort Dodge-Fort Bascom) trail. killed 10 buff six cows and four bulls. Saw another camp below us at the lake nice day. reloaded some cartridges at eve.
June. Monday 23. 1873.
very warm & clear day. did not hunt. went back to other camp to get the hides that were left, and to get peg timber. killed but 4 bulls. a large Mexican outfit passed our camp this eve. at night Charley and I went to Harris's and Cochren's camp. came near looseing the way.

[44]Bullet swage for truing bullets.

June. Tuesday 24. 1873.
hunted north east. got 17 buffalo, 10 in one stand and 7 in another. killed another bull and some one else skinned him. cloudy and thundering but not much rain.

June. Wednesday 25. 1873.
went to Harris's camp and ground knives. took the swedge[44] to them. killed 7 old bulls today. nice day though windy. looked like rain at night.

June. Thursday 26. 1873.
killed 7 buffalos 4 bulls and 3 cows. killed one of them aft dark. nice day. went to Harris's camp in morning to get swedge. found it broke. came home and reloaded some.

June. Friday 27. 1873.
hunted in the sand hills today. killed 9 buffalo two in one place and 7 in another. went to the springs near the Cimaron and got good cool drink. pleasant day. Charley went to Harris's this eve.

June. Saturday 28. 1873.
Saw scarcely any buff, did not hunt. killed one spike. killed large black and white snipe. cooked and eat it. at night went to Harris camp, he had 4 letters for me 2 from The one from Seth and one from George Mitchel. got lost and slept on the sand hills as came back.

June. Sunday 29. 1873.
Started for town. drove to hollow within 6 miles of Crooked creek and camped at puddle of water. during the day I rode part of the time with Golaway. looks very much like rain in morning but blowed over.

June. Monday 30. 1873.
drove on to Crooked creek. stoped and got our breakfast. water soaked up during the night where we were camped at night. drove to within 5 miles of Mulberry (creek), camped.

July. Tuesday 1. 1873.
got nearly drowned aft. came thunderstorm. drove to Charleys crossing. rode Jim over the river. Nixons outfit crossed to night.

July. Wednesday 2. 1873.
Staid all night at the stable tended Jim. Charly came over. I got pr shoes. wrote to George Mitchel and to Seth and The. Haney came over with the teams.

July. Thursday 3. 1873.
nice day. tended Jim. Haney passed here going aft his pony. Charly and I went down town in dance house at night. got quart of whiskey at Raths. Tom discharged Fred.

July. Friday 4. 1873.
mailed letter to The with $5.00 in it. nice day. in town most all day. Haney and Charley had a fight. Settled with Mrs. G. got pr of pants and overalls. Went down town at night. at dance house. got little looking glass 50 cts.

July. Saturday 5. 1873.
nice day. went in to Col. Youngs. wrote letter to The. took gun down town got it recited (resighted). paid $3.00.

July. Sunday 6. 1873.
worked for Myers in forenoon, 1.25. settled in bill of goods for hunting. gun got out of fix took it down to shop and fixed it myself. Nigger broke needle (firing pin) of my gun; got one dol of Dudley to pay for fixing it.

July. Monday 7. 1873.
crossed rivr. camped at Jones. stuck nail in my knee last night. pained me so did not sleep at all. got pen of Jones this noon. drove to big hollow between Mulberry (creek) and Kiowa (creek) and camped. stopped at (Emanuel) Dubbs got some salve of Sallie (George). Saw remains of Jester.[45]

July. Tuesday 8. 1873.
rained in night. got wet. went and slept with Jim (White). leg pained me very much. drove to N(ixon')s old camp on Kiowa (creek). stoped and got dinner and dried blankets. in aft drove to (Mike) Obrians camp near mouth of Bluff creek.

July. Wednesday 9. 1873.
drove below mouth of main Kiowa, on Bluff creek and camped. Dudly hunted in aft killed 3 buffalo. rained in the night.

July. Thursday 10. 1873.
Dudly hunted. killed 5 buffalo 2 bulls and 3 cows. N(ixon')s teams passed. 6 buffalo 3 bulls and 3 cows. rained in night.

[45]Alexander Jester, a Sedgwick county resident, had killed a young man, and was caught and convicted but escaped. He next was reported in southwest Kansas where he attempted to murder a sick man for his team. The intended victim escaped and found help at the ranch of Mike O'Brien. An informal posse set out which claimed to have found and killed Jester, though years later he turned up in Wichita.

July. Friday 11. 1873.
drove about 10 miles east killed but 1 cow. my leg pained me so very bad had to come in to camp. rained in the night.

July. Saturday 12. 1873.
beautiful day. leg pained me so very bad had to stay in camp. I slept none last night. Dudly killed two old bulls before breakfast I pegged their hides. killed 6 buffalo today. Jim got some drug to put on my leg.

July. Sunday 13. 1873.
I staid in camp. my leg pained me all night and all day. boys killed 4 buffalos. came in early. very warm and windy. Jim went down to Obrians to get some lineament for me at eve.

July. Monday 14. 1873.
Jim got some sugar of lead (lead acetate) at Obrians. leg some better today. made me a bunk of hollow cottonwood snags. boys killed 6 six buffalo bulls today. nice day though windy.

July. Tuesday 15. 1873.
staid in camp. nice day. shot mocking bird with my pistol. leg some better. boys killed 5 buffalo bulls; I and Jim pegged them out.

July. Wednesday 16. 1873.
I went out and helped skin buffalo today. got 9 bulls. leg great deal better. fixed swedge at eve and helped Jim peg and pile the hides.

July. Thursday 17. 1873.
very warm and cloudy. killed but 3 old bulls. Obrian called and got some flour.

July. Friday 18. 1873.
hunted over in the flat. lost my knife. killed 12 buffalo. 10 bulls 1 cow, and one calf. nice day very warm.

July. Saturday 19. 1873.
hunted north east. got 12 bulls

July. Sunday 20. 1873.
hunted. got 8 buffalo 4 bulls and 4 cows. nice day. Obrians men here to supper and Jar Johnson.

July. Monday 21. 1873.
Tom Nixon and Obrian here in morning. I wrote letter to The before breakfast. Nixons bull train came along. we sent 54 hides to town by him. Seen Bat sent letter by him. I killed 8 buff and Dudly 3.

July. Tuesday 22. 1873.
killed 10 buffalo 6 cows and 4 bulls. I killed 3 Dudly one. nice day. came in mid afternoon. no buff in sight. I killed two more at dusk

July. Wednesday 23. 1873.
Dudly hunted. killed 3 buffalo two cows 1 bull. headed off Jim Whites train. got some flour. moved Jim and Ed Masterson and their outfit from the train down to our camp.

July. Thursday 24. 1873.
I killed one old bull before breakfast. Dudly hunted. killed 11 buffalo. Ed and Jim helped us skin them. N.B. George stayed all night with us on acct of Jim White. Labeau and one of his men here at eve.

July. Friday 25. 1873.
killed 9 buffalo. Dudley hunted. all bulls but one. Ed and Jim out with us.

July. Saturday 26. 1873.
I killed two old bulls before breakfast. Dudley killed one cow and one bull aft breakfast. came in. did not hunt. dug a well found heap good water.

July. Sunday 27 1873.
nice day untill about night. there came a most terrible wind and rain storm. blew our hides a half mile away and blew my bunk down. Loaded Dudly up with 44 or 50 hides. he started to Dodge. some of freighting outfit here.

July. Monday 28. 1873.
gathered up hides that were scattered. fixed up my bunk again. nice day though cloudy. Jim B(arber). and Ed went to other camp in aft.

July. Tuesday 29. 1873.
cloudy all day. no buff in sight. Ed and Jim Barber went in aft noon and killed young spike. two boys from other camp came and got some flour.

July. Wednesday 30. 1873.
nice day. very warm Jim M(asterson). and me went over the hill to try to get some buffalo for meat. did not get any. came back by other camp. Ed and Jim came thru got some flour and turnips.

July. Thursday 31 1873.
in camp. teams did not come untill night. Lochren and Harris passed here. Webbs outfit camped with us over night. got some grub of him. Bat and Dudley came in at night. Bat brought me postal cards from Seth.

August. Friday 1. 1873.
Dudley and I went out on a scout to find buff. went to Nuskatunga.[46] found Johnsons camp. went down creek and across to the Cimaron. Dudley shot two grey wolves at once (with one shot). Jim White and Obrian went off in opposite course.

August. Saturday 2. 1873.
rained some in the night. camp at a dismal looking place. saw quite a number of buffalo. Came back to camp. arrived at 2 oclock. the other parties came in soon after.

August. Sunday 3. 1873.
Jim White killed a buffalo bull near our camp. gave it to us. him and Obrian pulled out. we, Jim Barber and me, skinned him. I sent to town for mail by Jim Lane.

August. Monday 4. 1873.
Mastersons and us moved camp to the springs on Cimaron below mouth of Bluff creek. I killed two chickens, dressed them had them for supper.

August. Tuesday 5. 1873.
went out south 5 miles did not see any buffalo. came in to camp. Bat shot and hit kiote on run. I got some ripe grapes around spring. got hackberry stick split it and made gun stick. made one for Bat.

August. Wednesday 6. 1873.
made mistake. moved camp on Sunday. Tuesday went beyond salt plains and most of Buffalo creek. got but one buff. fixed gun spring weaker and easy on trigger. I killed (Wed) 9 buffalo 8 cows and one bull. Dudly, Bat and I all went to same herd. I killed 2 others none.

August. Thursday 7. 1873.
went way over into the Nation[47] Saw but few buffalo. did not hunt. returned to camp went over the river turned the hides over. M(asterson) boys got 8 hides 5 cows 3 bulls, looked very much like rain at eve but did not rain.

August. Friday 8. 1873.
did not go out to hunt. I killed 5 bulls and 1 spike that came in sight of camp. killed rattlesnake. nice day.

[46]Nescatunga Creek, a Comanche county tributary of the Salt Fork of the Arkansas.
[47]Present Oklahoma.

August. Saturday 9. 1873.
killed 7 buffalo today. I killed 6 of them. 6 bulls and one cow. Jim Lane came back from town. brought me two letters, one from Seth and one from The.

August. Sunday 10. 1873.
Went over to other camp. took letter and sent to town by Wm. Harris to The. I went out in eve and killed 8 buffalo. Shot the head off a jack rabbit. had it for sup. gethered some grapes and stewed in syrup. heap good sup.

August. Monday 11. 1873.
did not hunt, went over and piled up the hides. concluded to move camp. I sewed and made new back to my vest. wrote letter to Wm. Barnett. nice day. Jim Lochren here.

August. Tuesday 12. 1873.
loaded up 55 hides. Started for Dodge, drove to slew opposite Bluff creek. halted and got dinner then drove across mouth of main Kiowa to a little spring creek and camped.

August. Wednesday 13. 1873.
drove to crossing of west branch (of) Kiowa (creek). stoped. spread out hides to dry, got dinner, a beautiful spring here, drove to big hollow and camped. I killed old buffalo bull took out tenderloin.

August. Thursday 14. 1873.
drove to Mike Obrians ranch. found Jim White and outfit there. got dinner there. Jim pulled us across river. came to Dodge. unloaded hides. got 75 cts and 1.50 in trade[48]. got sup at Kelleys.

August. Friday 15. 1873.
got breakfast at Kelleys restaurant. got new hat at Myers $4.00 came out to Ns ranch to get mare shod. Jim B. got him hat $4.05 and shoes $2.50. loaded up buckboard drove to Obrians. crossed river at Fort. met Bat going to town bet(ween) Fort and town.

August. Saturday 16. 1873.
Obrian, Jim White and us started for Ninnesquaw.[49] drove to big hollow. got dinner then drove to hollow about 6 miles beyond big hollow and camped on old East Kiowa trail.

[48]Probably 75¢ for a cow hide; $1.50 for a bull.

[49]Ninnescah River, south central Kansas.

August. Sunday 17. 1873.
Saw good many buffalo above head of East Kiowa. drove across to head of Mule creek. passed Labeau in afternoon went out to hunt. went to head of Medicine.[50] saw but a few buff did not hunt. shot at antelope.

August. Monday 18. 1873.
Jim and I staid in camp and made pegs. Dudly went out horse back to find white buff (word illegible). rained at night. I killed buff bull on Thompson creek.

August. Tuesday 19. 1873.
started again for Ninneskaw. drove across main and north Medicine and crossed Thompson creek and camped at springs east of Thompson. killed some buff for meat. saw man from Sun City, said buff were plenty.

August. Wednesday 20. 1873.
started for Sun City. crossed Spring creek and Soldier and Turkey (creeks). arrived at Sun City a little aft noon turned back and started up Turkey. found first settlement at mouth of Spring creek.

August. Thursday 21. 1873.
left camp on Turkey creek. drove past head of Turkey across country started for Rattlesnake. camped at noon at lake south of sand hills. I fixed my belt to hold 45 cartridges with some buck skin Billy Tyler[51] gave me. found Deckers camp at lake. Decker came in after night from town.

August. Friday 22. 1873.
White and Obrian started back for big hollow. we pulled up foot of sand hills about 3 miles above Deckers and camped. killed 8 buffalo. me 4 and Dudley 4. nice day.

August. Saturday 23. 1873.
went away over east beyond breaks of Turkey and killed two cows. (Dudley) came back to camp. Scarcely any buff in country. saw outfit of Ks team going east to Chikaska[52] to camp. nice day.

August. Sunday 24. 1873.
Staid in camp. Jim went down to lake. I killed big rattlesnake very near our camp fire. Made me a straw tick and filled it. loaded up at noon

[50]Medicine Lodge River, Barber county.

[51]Billy Tyler was killed in the battle of Adobe Walls, June 27, 1874.

[52]Chikaskia River in Harper and Sumner counties.

and started for Kiowa (creek). drove to Thompson creek, where a Navahoe Indian is camped and camped for night.

August. Monday 25. 1873.

drove to Medicine, and stoped for dinner then drove across to where we camped on Mule Creek.[53] got two hides that Jim White left, then across to our old winter camp on Kiowa (creek). found Masterson boys camped here. Dudly killed 2 buff.

August. Tuesday 26. 1873.

went out to hunt. buffalo so scarce and wild came back to camp. I washed some shirts. dug out springs, and killed two old bulls that were passing. Charley Wright and Levy came in and camped for the night.

August. Wednesday 27. 1873.

went most down to Mike Obrians old camp hunting. I killed 6 buff and Dudly 2. nice day.

August. Thursday 28. 1873.

loaded up all the plunder and moved to Obrians old camp at mouth of main Kiowa (creek). I killed 5 buffalo on the way.

August. Friday 29. 1873.

Started over east to hunt. went up on high hill. crossed over Bluff creek at our old camp. I killed 9 buff and 4 cows. went on high peak west of Bluff creek. got in very late.

August. Saturday 30. 1873.

went way over west to hunt. I killed one spike, saw no more buffalo. came back to camp. moulded 200 balls and reloaded 110 cartridges.

August. Sunday 31. 1873.

hunted about 12 miles east. killed 15 buffalo I killed 12 of them Dudley 3.

Sept. Monday 1. 1873.

rained last night. went over east to get some buff that I killed yesterday. wolves had torn some of them. Dud killed two spikes and I one bull.

Sept. Tuesday 2. 1873.

Did not hunt. an outfit of 5 teams stopped here for dinner. we went aft dinner to a pond up main Kiowa (creek) to ketch fish. made some hooks. caught 28 fish. Jim and I went in swimming. very deep. I killed cow for tallow. got in late.

[53]A tributary of the Salt Fork which flows south from Kiowa county through Comanche and Barber counties.

Sept. Wednesday 3. 1873.
Staid in camp. I washed and sowed up my overalls. reloaded some cartridges. loaded up hides and plunder and crossed creek.

Sept. Thursday 4. 1873.
started to Dodge, drove to west (or) main branch Kiowa (creek). got there at noon. stopped for the night. found Jim White and Obrian here building a ranch. Levy and C. Wright here. Jim B(arber). and me went fishing. got mess and gave to J. White.

Sept. Friday 5. 1873.
cold and rainy. Drove to Mike Obrians ranch. camped opposite, on the Mulberry. got in with another outfit.

Sept. Saturay 6. 1873.
rained most all night. got up. got breakfast. drove to post and crossed river. drove to Dodge. sold hides for .80 and 1.50 to Myers. got burnsides shaved off. had some mellon to eat at Myers.

Sept. Sunday 7. 1873.
in town most all day. went to the race. race to be run over again. got pr boots $6.00. socks 40 cts. box cartridges 75 cts.

Sept. Monday 8. 1873.
went up and run horse race. Straffort won by 6 feet. I hired to Nixon to work in (blacksmith) shop at $30.00 per month and board. in town at night. wrote to The. at dance hall at night.

Sept. Tuesday 9. 1873.
Settled with Dudly and Jim. got $30.00 in cash. got pr pants & vest and shirt $13.50. paid Rath $10.00. went to work for Nixon in shop. began at noon made 1 inch pins and nails.

Sept. Wednesday 10. 1873.
Heinrich (Henry Kramer) shod one span horses all around and set 3 shoes for Decker. I made two hooks to put in back hand, and made gate hinge. Jim White Bat and Ed and Levy here. got new razor $2.25. pd Levy 24 cts.

Sept. Thursdy 11 1873.
nice day though windy. Heinrich shod horses. I mad(e) hook and put on log chain. fixed up tools.

Sept. Friday 12. 1873.
very windy. fit up some tools. I made wagon rod and wedged bollers in wagon wheels for some Texans. fixed some hinges for Walk. Ed James here. got 3 letters last night. Wm. B. str. 21s. at dance h.

Sept. Saturday 13. 1873.
worked some on Moores wagon, and some wagons for Texas outfit. worked some on Warrens wagon. Ed James helped me carry bunk down & played some on his fiddle last night.

Sept. Sunday 14. 1873.
fixed gun hammer for Wright Moore (Mooar). went up to ranch got valice. paid Mrs. N(ixon) 50 cts for Sunday school library. came down town got shave left razor to get put in order pd 50 cts. got brush and bol 70 cts. windy.

Sept. Monday 15. 1873.
Heinrich and me mad(e) steel bridle bit for race horse. made some new tools. I made two new heading tools. I welded tongue rod and put tap on for a hunter. Henry shod one mule. hat tovat milons (had two wattermelons). very warm.

Sept. Tuesday 16. 1873.
I made clevis and lap ring, and clip for Ed Jones partner. made picket pin for Texan. Tom at shop. old Charley got bucket of beer and brought to shop. bull train came got postal card from Seth and answered it.

Sept. Wednesday 17. 1873.
I mended brace on spring seat and mended a spring for another man. out $1.00. Henry shod some horses. took in $10.00. went to dance house at night. warm day.

Sept. Thursday 18. 1873.
made some locks for coupling rods to bull train. made some staples for walls.

Sept. Friday 19. 1873.
Bat and the boys came in. Chisler also. I made some corner straps to go on coal box for wells. welded tongue rod and made spring key. Henry shod old Jim.

Sept. Saturday 20. 1873.
worked on bull train in fore noon. In aft went to see big horse race. Tom won the race. set wagon tires at eve. went to dance house at night. big time there.

Sept. Sunday 21. 1873.
worked a little on bull train. Cloudy and looked like rain. Charley Trask and the Texiean ran a race. I was one of the outcome judges. I

lost the drinks on betting length of a stick of timbir on cars. throwed race.

Sept. Monday 22. 1873.

I worked on bull train most all day. fixed neckyoke and singletree for Walts. settled board bill at Kelleys and began to board at Peters. sup first meal.

Sept. Tuesday 23. 1873.

worked some on bull train. made 3 clevis's. made some hooks. gave Joe 50 cts to go and get us a melon. bull train started. took bed to Peters. got wort (malt sugars for brewing beer) at Raths $1.25.

Sept. Wednesday 24. 1873.

made cleviss. rapaired log chains. put lock chain on Larrys wagon.

Sept. Thursday 25. 1873.

fixed log chains. made 11 bolts and cut them. made 80 staple keys and fit up lot of ox shoes. Henry done some shoeing.

Sept. Friday 26. 1873.

large Mexican train came in camped near shop. done some work for them. black smith from Colerado here. I talked of buying his tools. Jim White came in with outfit. I loaned him $1.00.

Sept. Saturday 27. 1873.

worked on Mexican outfit most all day. I fixed wagon for a Colerado man. had several drinks of him. ziemlich trunk war (was rather drunk). took in over $26.00 this week. shod two horses for Jim

Sept. Sunday 28. 1873.

miserable cold & rainy day. in shop made ring and broke it Spielen (played) on der harmonica at Peters. done a little work on sicle drives for A(ndrew) Johnson.

Sept. Monday 29. 1873.

made some linch pins for the Mexicans and a bolt. made two bolts for sickle driver for Frenchy. made 4 new cleviss. Mexican train left. took lounge down to Peter Yashettes [Peter Tashetta].

Sept. Tuesday 30. 1873.

done work on hack for Italian Frank. I made bar to go across store door at Raths. made clevis and two corks. Frank brought us a big melon. J. White and Decker started for Texas today. Obrian out bed.

POSTSCRIPT

Henry Raymond eventually settled in Sedgwick county where he married Sarah Armstrong in 1874. The marriage produced eight children three of whom were still living at the time this diary was first edited in 1965. After several years farming in the Sunny Dale community, the Raymonds moved to Oklahoma where Mr. Raymond died, at Homestead, October 16, 1936. He is buried in Maple Grove cemetery, Sunny Dale, Kan.

Henry H. Raymond in 1869, three years before he arrived in Dodge City. Photo courtesy Kansas Historical Society.

The west end of Trail street, formerly the Santa Fe trail, south of the railroad tracks, September, 1872. The wagons, loaded with dried buffalo hides, are stopped in front of the Smith, Edwards & Co. grocery store. Jones' dance hall occupies the building at the left. Photo courtesy Kansas Historical Society.

Chapter 5

Joe S. McCombs was born in Randolph Co., Alabama May 12, 1854. His family moved to Texas in 1868 when Joe was 14. They traveled by boat from New Orleans to Galveston, and thence by the H&TC RR to Calvert, Texas. The next year they moved on to near Hillsboro, and in 1870 they moved further west to near Desdemona. At that time the nearest town was Stephenville in Erath Co. It boasted two stores.

When Joe was 17, he got a job hunting cows, at $15 per month. This took him up the Old Chisolm Trail with a herd of about 1,000 steers owned by Stewart, Strawn and Bartholomew. (The town of Strawn was later named for Belliol Strawn. N.L. Bartholemew became judge at Albany, Texas and was cashier at the First National Bank.) Joe and his bunkies gathered the wild, old steers out of the sand hills of Eastland Co. and headed them for Colorado, via Coldwell, Kansas where they wintered, and eventually sold the herd right there.

Joe returned to the vicinity of Ft. Griffin, assembled the first outfit to hunt buffalo strictly for hides, and eventually married his childhood sweetheart, Betty Hale, June 29, 1879, after the buffalo were hunted out. They settled in Albany in 1881. The following account is here published for the first time, so far as is known, from a manuscript copy in the Panhandle-Plains Museum of Canyon, Texas.

First Buffalo Hunt Out of Ft. Griffin

Joe S. McCombs

About Christmas, 1874, John Jacobs, John Poe and I rigged the first buffalo outfit ever to leave Ft. Griffin on a buffalo hunt for hide purposes. Ft. Griffin afterwards became the greatest hide market in Texas. We left out on Christmas Day, going out the Mackenzie Trail and up Paint Creek in Haskell County and established our camp six or seven miles northeast from Haskell near Mocking Bird Springs. There was no house or settlement west from the Stone Ranch at the time but we did not strike buffalo until we got on Paint Creek. They always kept west of the white man. They occupied the prairies of Shackelford and Throckmorton counties by the hundreds of thousands.

Around our camp at Mocking Bird Springs the hunt was good. I did all the killing, and Poe and Jacobs did the skinning. From the low ground I would creep along hunting afoot and getting into scattered bunches of from ten to a hundred head. I would always shoot the leader, usually a bull, and if I could get him, the herd or bunch would start milling around until another bull assumed leadership and headed out and then I would try to get him. The idea was to always shoot a leader so the group would keep milling around. Most of the herds had moved south at this time of year, but I killed 700 and we were out only two months. Nothing of consequence happened on the hunt. We saw neither white man nor Indian, and we didn't hear any other hunters.

After returning to Griffin, Poe and I decided to leave Jacobs with the wagon to haul in the hides and to go further west on another hunt. So we rigged up a pony team and headed out up the Clear Fork of the Brazos by way of Fort Phantom Hill, finally locating our camp about where Rotan[1] is now. We stayed until May first and got 1,300 hides. After hauling in the hides of the first hunt, Jacobs followed our trail and located our camp,[2] and we were sure glad to see him because we had been out of bread for ten days. It was on this hunt that one of our ponies slipped a shoulder so we had no way to haul our hides into camp. We would just skin and peg the hide down on the ground and when Jacobs arrived, we hauled them in. In pegging down we simply stretched the hide and drove pegs at intervals in the ground using about 14 to the hide.

I remember a close call that Poe had with a buffalo. I had downed several bulls right together. Poe was only a short distance away and as we approached the kill together, he was slightly in the lead. When he was about fifteen feet from the bull, it got up and charged straight at him. I shot past him and dropped the bull at his feet. Poe just had time to shoot his pistol as the bull fell.

[1]About 50 miles NW of Abilene, in Fisher Co., south of the Double Mtn. fork of the Brazos River.

[2]John Jacobs' account of this reunion follows in this chapter.

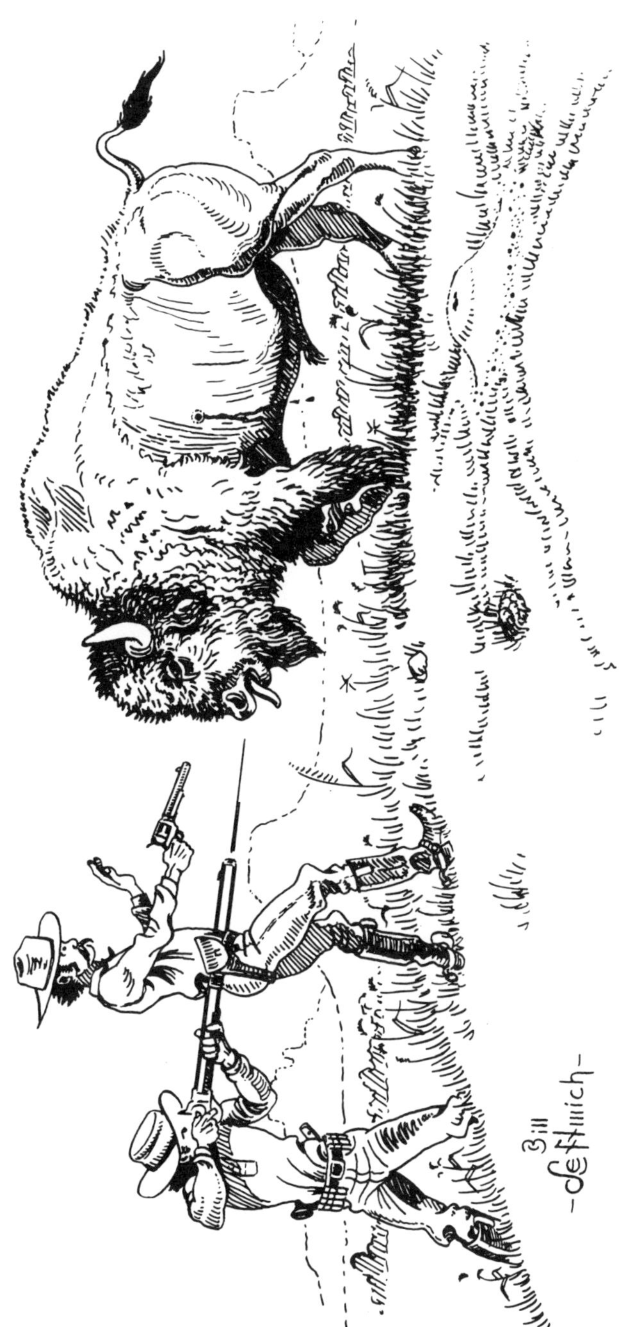

I shot past him and dropped the bull at his feet

Our kill for the two-hunt season was 2000. We sold them at Griffin for $2 each robe hide, and $1.50 for the rest. They were the first hides of any consequence marketed at Griffin. There had been some hides sold there from buffalo killed for meat, but our sale was the beginning of the hide industry at Griffin. It ended abruptly at the close of 1878 with the extermination of the herds which were killed completely for their hides.

Conrad and Rath, to whom we sold were the big buyers there. Their hide yard in the big years of the kill 1876-77 looked much like a cotton bale yard of today.

In the fall of 1875 I organized an outfit of my own with three skinners. One was Bob Pitcock, now an oil man of Ranger, Texas, one was Westley Tarter who died in the seventies, and the third was Sol Pace, who died in Ft. Worth several years ago. I had a span of mules and a wagon on this trip and took along 800 pounds of lead, five kegs of powder, a 16 pound Sharps Sporting Rifle, and my reloading outfit.

We struck out by Phantom Hill, going to where Sweetwater now stands. I killed several hundred while we were camped there. Next we moved to Champion Creek just this side of Colorado City, Texas. There we made permanent camp and stayed until April 1, 1876. My total kill was just a little more than 2000 hides. During this entire trip of over six months we did not see anyone outside of our own outfit. In fact, there were no settlers in that country so far as I knew and the hunting had not gotten much underway. Upon my return to Griffin I hired five or six ox-wagons to go after the hides. Each buffalo wagon had a trailer and six yokes of oxen were used to the wagon. They made two trips for these hides.

By the time of my next hunt in the fall of 1876, buffalo hunters were coming pretty thick. The northern hunters were following the herds on their migration south. I had about the same outfit and struck out on the same trail as the year before but did not stop until we reached Morgan Creek which is over the divide west of Colorado City. There we made permanent camp and our winter kill was 2300 hides. All the time now the herds were being drifted west by the hunters who were after them from morning til night. We could hear the guns of the other buffalo hunters at times but most of them were to the east of us (the prevailing wind was from the west and south). I always tried to keep on the outer edge of the herd.

On the way home to Griffin we met several meat hunting outfits from the settlements to the east. It was this year, too, that hide buyers started following the hunters and buying the hides at the camps. I disposed of most of my hides in camp at $1 each hide straight through. The hides we hauled in brought $1.50.

In September 1877, I took the same number of skinners and a Mexican to stake down the hides, 1000 pounds of lead and five kegs of powder. We struck the same old trail that we had blazed two years before. This time our permanent camp was at the big springs where Big Spring City is now located. Later, however, we moved to Mossy Rock Springs, which we named. They are near Signal Mountain, ten miles south of Big Spring. On this hunt, from September to May, I made my biggest kill. I personally killed 4900. Poe and Jacobs had an outfit north of us that killed 6200. There were several camps around us and the hunters were getting too thick. Two outfits stacked hides at our camp and we had 9700 there altogether.

I account for our big kill that year by being favorably located at these springs where the animals would come for water. I killed 1000 bulls at Big Spring. The bulls always led the herds on the migration and they were usually 30 days in advance of the cows. At Mossy Rock springs I killed 2200 buffalo (over several months' time) so close together that I could see all of them from one place. We decided to poison our hides to carry them over until the low market improved. After doing this I struck out in advance of the wagon for Ft. Griffin. I met W.H. Webb, a hide buyer, at Phantom Hill. He offered me $1 per hide camp delivery for the whole 9700 hides, and I sold. I had authority to sell for the others, as well as my own outfit.

Webb and I returned to camp where he received the hides and our outfits returned to Ft. Griffin. That was the last year of the big kill, and the biggest year for the buffalo hunters in Texas. The hunters followed the herds north that summer and back again in the fall. The buffalo were being hunted all the time.

In the fall of 1878 I went out on my last hunt. This time I located camp on Mustang Pond, where Midland is now. This year, although I stayed out from September until the middle of March, my entire kill was only 800 hides. Buffalo were scarce and wild and they started north early on what was the very last migration. They never came back. They never even got to their summer range. Hunters finished them this spring of 1879. All that remained from the once vast herds of a few years back were a few straggling bunches, mostly calves. I do not recollect seeing a buffalo on the range after my return from my last hunt. There was no buffalo hunting in Texas after that.

Although I killed altogether about 12000 buffalo while on these hunts, I never saw a white one. I saw some that looked white in the herds, but the several I killed always turned out to be grizzly color.

Letter of John Jacobs to Joe S. McCombs, July 13, 1924

Courtesy Shackelford County Archives, Albany, Texas

My Dear Joe:

About next Saturday a man will drive up to your feedstore in a car. It will be John Jacobs. You are to get in with me and drive down on the creek where we will camp and break bread together after all these years. No one but you and I must know of this. I am at last beautifully fixed in life, but Joe I would give it all up for my old Sharps .45 and my old team back again that I might follow you and good old John Poe up on the buffalo range with supplies. I well remember it has been fifty years ago when we broke up camp on Paint Creek. You and John took the horse team and struck out for a new range leaving me behind with the ox team to haul hides to Griffin. No road, nothing but dim trails. I told you and John that anywhere the trail forked you were to take thirty steps from the fork and dig a little square hole with a spade beside the trail you were to take so that I could follow and at every fork the welcome hole was there. I gave you and John a little board about two feet long and four inches wide. Where you and John left the trail and struck off for our camp you were to bury this stake in the ground with a note by it in a primer box, the note telling me the distance to your camp and the direction. Now, Lord, how good that stake did look when I came to it. It was getting dark and I could not see to keep my course so I concluded to camp there for the night. I was out of matches so in order to cook a little food I picked ravelings out of a flour sack, drew the bullet out of a .45 shell, poured most of the powder out, stuck the ravelings in, and fired into a handfull of dried grass and caught the fire. After putting wood on I let down my ox bells, hobbled my steers, and was cooking my bacon and hoe cake when you and John walked up to the firelight and you had heard the bells and the report of my gun at your camp two miles away and it was indeed a happy meeting. Poor old John has crossed the divide. You and I are about the only ones of the buffalo hunters left. If you cross over the range first and join John don't forget the spade and the stake and just thirty paces from every fork of the trail dig a little square hole that I may find and be with you again on that dear shore. And when the shades gather and I am about due listen for my ox bells and if you hear them jingling in the dim distance come again to my rescue as of yore and we will pitch our camp beside some gurgling stream. Our occupation will be whatever the Great Spirit wills and so may it be.

Your Lifelong Friend,
John C. Jacobs

According to Dr. R.L. Moore, Jr. (1985), "Jacobs did make the trip out to Albany as referred to in this letter. They went out on the creek and had some target practice with their old Sharps rifles. McCombs won the match and Jacobs sent him a fine rifle as a prize on his return to San Antonio."

McCombs was presented an engraved Remington No. 1, Smoot's Patent New Model revolver inscribed on the front grip strap, "To J. McCombs from John Poe, Ft. Griffin, Texas 1874." A photograph of this revolver appears on page 305 of *Firearms of the American West 1866-1894*, Garavaglia and Worman, (1985).

The Last of the Buffalo[1]

John Cloud Jacobs

When I was a young man in 1872 the great body of the Kansas and northwestern buffalo herd crossed the Red River and the famous Texas hunt began. Fort Griffin in Shackelford County, 175 miles from Dallas, was the principal trading-point for all the hunters. From Fort Griffin west, there was not a settlement nearer than old Fort Sumner, 200 miles away, on the Pecos River in New Mexico. And this was practically the width of the buffalo herd. And it stretched in length from near the north line of Texas southward 400 miles to the head of Devil's River Canyon. In parts of the range one might travel a hundred miles, as I have done, and never be out of sight of vast herds.

In those days my partner, John W. Poe, and I expected to be buffalo hunters all our lives. He is now president of the Citizens' National Bank of Roswell, New Mexico, but he was not anything that looked like a banker when I first met him on the frontier of Texas in 1872.

When we started to the range for the winter hunt, we bought one ton of ammunition; 1600 pounds of lead, 400 pounds of powder, besides shells, patchpaper, caps. etc.

We took with us four skinners and two other men to stretch and carry hides, eight in all. We had two wagons and two teams of mules and an ox team of four yoke to make frequent trips to the trading post for supplies.

My partner and I did the hunting, each with a wagon and two skinners. It must be remembered that a successful hunter must make his own ammunition, as old ammunition is most unreliable. The shells seemed to sweat after a time, and often the whole charge of powder would be found in one solid lump. Hunters would have nothing but the best single-F powder, and if there were any cartridges left over from the last winter's hunt, the shells were emptied and recharged. A man who has hunted as a business knows the importance of good, fresh, ammunition. It frequently happened that a man's life depended on a cartridge that neither snapped nor flickered.

We used to put 50-80 pounds of lead in a large iron skillet and get a good blue heat on it. Then we would dip out the lead with a spoon

[1]This first appeared in "The World's Work" magazine for January, 1909, Doubleday, Page & Co., New York and Chicago. Walter Page, ed.

and mold our bullets. Any ball with the least bit of flaw we put back. Nothing but smooth, true balls were used.

It was easy enough to find the buffalo. We would go a mile or so from the camp to begin the day's hunt. When we saw a bunch in about the right kind of a place and about the right size (the hunter can handle a bunch of from 20-70 better than a larger herd), we would stop the wagon and get out with gun, wiping-rod, and ammunition.

As a first precaution we always picked a few blades of dry grass, held them up, and let them sift through our fingers. This gives you the true course of the wind, for if Mr. Buffalo ever gets the wind on you his hide is lost for good.

We used to leave the wagon and start for the herd when at a distance of from a half to three-quarters of a mile. This distance is governed by the way the herd is acting. We would start for the herd in a straight line. At a distance of 400-600 yards we would see the sentinels on the look-out. Then, in a stooping posture we went straight as an arrow for the herd. So long as our course was straight, up to about 400 yards, they could not make out what we were, but if we ever took just one step to the side the herd was lost.

Right here is where the skill of the hunter is matched against instinct. When we encountered obstacles in our direct course, a bunch of prickly pear or a stubborn diamond-backed rattler that would not break ground, we sank to the ground so slowly and regularly that the buffalo did not detect any motion. When well down and flat, with our guns closely embraced, we rolled over and over until the obstacle was out of line, and then we used the same precaution in getting up as in sinking down.

There were usually two to four sentinels on the look-out. When they began to get uneasy, we would go down on the ground again with more caution if possible and crawl on all-fours in a bee-line for the herd, and when the sentinels began to get uneasy again, we knew that our time was up. We were usually then at a distance of 200-300 yards. Lying along the ground, we would get our old pizen-slingers to our shoulders and plump the most suspicious sentinel right at the edge of the long hair at the bulge of the ribs. At the crack of the guns we jumped to our feet and ran after the buffalo as hard and fast as possible to save every inch of that hard-earned ground. When the buffalo were running, they couldn't see that their pursuer was in motion. They usually ran 50-150 yards at the first shot, and a good swift hunter who got to his feet right could gain about half that distance on them when they began to slow up. Then, after a little maneuvering, we had our herd at what is called a "stand," when we could sit in one place and shoot as many as we wanted for the day's skinning.

On a warm, still day the buffalo are much more easily handled than on a windy day. For there is not only the drift of the ball to contend with, but the herd on windy days is much more active, and most of them have to be killed on what the hunters call a "run" and is often strung out for a mile or more. There was considerable danger in a run, for the hunter had to pass right by the buffalo that had been shot. The sight of a man so near often brought them to their feet, and at such times old ammunition would not have been a pleasant memory.

My partner was once killing a run, and as he passed a big cow, she came to her feet after him. He gave her a slug and drifted, and then there was a race on. When the cow fell she was so close that she snorted blood on him. The incident unnerved him for the day. He went straight to camp and went into tranquil meditation for the rest of the day. A buffalo can hook a pocket handkerchief to shreads from the ground, which is not at all pleasant to think of when drifting before an infuriated brute with nothing nearer than the North pole to dodge behind.

In the winter season, the old bulls separate from the herd, so that one often encounters a herd of from 25-50, all bulls, a dangerous, ugly-looking lot. I call to mind one particular incident when I had worked up to the desired distance for the first shot, and a big, ferocious bull caught sight of me, shook his shaggy mane and whiskers, came to his knees, and horned the earth. I lay stiff with a nerve born of fear. I was praying to the hunter's god, Mr. Sharp, that the old bull would turn the other way. But no. When he got up, he started straight for me. Not a twig for miles. Nothing but Sharp and a steady aim between me and the divide.

When I was certain my aim was right, I let her go. The old bull humped himself as they always do when shot in the lungs, but still he came straight on. I rammed another cartridge in and slung it into him again. Now he was within 50 feet of me, but at the crack of the gun he stumbled, made a desperate effort to keep his feet, took a header, and fell. I was paralyzed. I couldn't move. I had forgotten I could run.

In the spring of 1877 we sold 6200 hides at one dollar apiece. We had moved our camp from near Signal Peak to Sulphur Springs at the foot of the Plains, a hunter's paradise in those days. When we reached it, night had come on and because of the immense herds watering there, we had some difficulty in getting to the spring. The water came out of the bank of a draw, flowed about a half to three-quarters of a mile, and sank. And this whole distance was worked into a loblolly of mud by great thirsty herds of buffalo that were drinking every hour of the day and night. We stood at the head of the springs and chunked buffalo off with stones until the water cleared so that we could drink and water our horses. It was a sight that overawed us, old buffalo hunters though we were.

For fear of a stampede which might cost us our lives we rode out five miles from the springs before spreading our blankets for a night's rest. The next morning we went back and in a circle of three to four miles in every direction from the spring, the ground was literally covered with buffalo. The wildest dreams of a hunter's paradise must fall short of Sulphur Springs as it was in the winter of '76 and'77. The wolves and the antelope were standing around for a chance to drink. Buffalo, antelope, and wolves seemed to regard us as some strange animal which had come for water. They were all strangely tame. We threw stones at the wolves and they would run after the rolling stones and paw them with their feet like a puppy. This all sounds very "fishy," but it is as true as it is strange.

The buffalo hunters are often blamed for the slaughter of the buffalo. It is true that we each averaged from 4000-6000 hides per season, and that by the close of the season of '77 the main herd was perceptibly decreasing, but it had to be. With the end of the buffalo, the Indian depredations were over. They lived on buffalo, and came in and murdered our women and children. After the buffalo were gone, the Government had no trouble in keeping them on their reservations, and the range was soon settled by thrifty farmers and ranchmen. Now there is a cow where there used to be a buffalo, and the country is dotted over with thrifty, happy homes.

W.S. Glenn getting a stand

Chapter 6

W. Skelton Glenn was, so far as can be determined, a native of Georgia. He was born about 1845 and carried by his father to Miller's Bluff in northern Louisiana. When the Civil War broke out, he joined Mathew's company, and was there when Farragut bombarded Port Hudson on Feb. 22, 1863. He was captured by Union forces, and soon paroled, perhaps due to his youth. In 1864 he broke parole and joined Joe Shelby's cavalry in Arkansas. He fought again at the Battle of Jenkins' Ferry, and he was finally discharged from the Army of the Confederacy at Elysian Fields, Texas.

Apparently he was in Dodge City in February of 1873. Whether he met Henry Raymond or Jim White, who we know were also there at that time, is not recorded. Somehow, he entered the buffalo hunting business, and survived to leave a history of the events he witnessed in 1876-1877, on the Texas buffalo range. We are pleased to read of his encounter with Jim White, because it adds a little to what is known of this "greatest of all buffalo hunters."

Glenn's veracity and accuracy as an observer are borne out by a close reading of documentary evidence and he is perhaps more accurate in dating events than was John R. Cook. Cook's *The Border and the Buffalo* agrees in essence with Glenn's description of the hunter's life, but differs in details on the events of the Hunter's War.

This chapter is based upon Glenn's recollections as written in 1910, when he was about 65 years old. The material was edited by Rex W. Stickland and published in the *Panhandle-Plains Historical Review* Vol. 22, 1949. I have removed all the physical evidence of Stickland's editing, omitting brackets where he indicated his insertion of words or punctuation, and omitting those of his footnotes which are no longer germane. I have expanded on some of Strickland's footnotes where more recent information has become available, and I have added some new footnotes. Altogether, the effort has been made to make the material more readable without removing the author's flavor, nor confounding Strickland's efforts. As Strickland said, "After all, thousands of persons who can write a grammatically correct sentence have never killed a buffalo, much less skinned one."

Buffalo Hunting in the Texas Plains 1876-1877

W.S. Glenn

About this time the hunt had grown to such an enormous business that J. R. Lobenstein, a capitalist of that time, and ram rodder of the buffalo hunt, furnished the capital and contracts were sub-let for robe hides, dry hides, bull hides, etc. Merchants were furnished supplies, equipments, etc., and they in turn furnished smaller men, who kept up with hunters ready to supply them. As they had begun to make money out of it, they would supply any hunter who had a team and wagon. Now all this while the hunter was pegging away and it was not until afterwards that we got it down to a system to make it profitable over a scant living.

There were several methods to kill them and each one adopted his own course and plan. They would get together and while one gained a point from another, he, in turn, would gain a point from him. One method was to run beside them, shooting them as they ran. Another was to shoot from the rear, what was termed tail shooting: always shooting the hindmost buffalo and when a day's hunt was done, they would be strung on the ground for a mile or more, from ten to fifteen yards apart, and in this way the skinner had so much territory to go over he couldn't make wages.

We first noticed that the buffaloes always went around a ravine or gulch, unless going for water straight down a bluff; and as the buffalo always followed these trails a man on foot by a mere cut-off of a hundred yards could cut him off. That is why they were so far apart in tail-hunting, as it was called.

Hunting this way, the skinner and his wagon and team would have to travel to get in a day's work to make it profitable. Another method was to start out in the morning, which was most generally daylight both winter and summer. The hunter would start on horseback and when he came to a high place he would find out the direction of the wind, and would then know which way to approach them. He would then proceed until he came to a bunch of buffalo, and if there was no ravine to get near, he would dismount, hobble and lariat his horse or turn him loose, whatever method he was used to, and proceed to crawl on his stomach so as to get near enough to shoot in the main herd. They would then run off two or three hundred yards, stopping to look back; if they happened to get wind of him at the second shot, they would not halt for a mile, and sometimes not for five. Sometimes the whole running herd would be moving for miles and in this way making his rounds he would often run or walk some twenty-five or thirty miles and come into camp from the opposite direction from which he had left his horse and would have to walk after him. This system was afterwards dubbed "tenderfoot" hunting and did not often pay expenses for either hunter or skinner.

Another method of hunting was to leave your horse out of sight after you determined the direction and course of the wind, and then get as near as possible. If the herd was lying at rest, he would pick out some buffalo that was standing up on watch and shoot his ball in the side of him so that it would not go through, but would lodge in the flesh; as on many times it had been proven by men who were well hid and the wind taking the sound of the gun and whizz of the bullet off, that if a ball passed through a buffalo the herd would stampede and run for miles. A buffalo shot in this manner would merely hump up his back as if he had the colic and commence to mill round and round in a slow walk. The other buffalo sniffing the blood and following would not be watching the hunter, and he would continue to shoot the outside cow buffalo; if there were old cows they would take them as there would be some two or three offsprings following her. If she would hump up, he would know that he had the range, and in this way hold the herd as long as they acted in this way as well as the well trained cowpuncher would hold his herd, only the hunter would use his gun. This was termed mesmerizing the buffalo so that he could hold them on what we termed a stand, which afterwards proved to be the most successful way of killing the buffalo.

It was not always the best shot but the best hunter that succeeded, that is, the man who piled his buffalo in a pile so as to be more convenient for the skinner to get at and not to run all over the country.

Beginning about the first of November and up until the middle of February, we were killing expressly for the robes. At this time of the year, all bull buffalo over three years old were separated from the cows and yearlings, going in herds by themselves, and were classed scrubhorn bulls, scarcely never seeing a cow in a herd of these scrubhorn bulls. The hunter could easily tell a cow herd at a distance from a herd of these scrubhorn bulls.

The hunter was hired by the piece: if robe hides were worth $3.00, he was given twenty-five cents for every one that he killed and was brought in by the skinners — was tallied up at camp. It was the camp rustler's business to keep tally of the number of hides killed each day. If the hides were worth $2.50, then the hunter got 20 cents; $2.00, he got 15 cents; $1.50, he got 10 cents; and $1.00, he got 5 cents.

All the cows shot at this season of the year were not classed as robes, as she would sometimes be poor and had not shed on the hip and flank, thus having a patch of dead hair and classed as a cow hide, and worth $1.50. The young bulls of three years of age were classed as spikes and equal to cow hide. Smaller buffalo, such as small cows two or three years old, were classed as kips and were worth from 75 cents to $1.50, smaller yet from 25 to 75 cents, and were seldom shot except by accident, as a stray shot, or staying with their mother and standing around would be dangerous to leave on a stand.

The hunters began hunting with the army guns which were Springfields, it being the best gun at that day and time, and with the old Henry gun which was afterwards the Winchester. The Spencer carbines were tried by men on horseback, running by the buffalo and shooting them as they ran. The hunters began to complain to the merchants for a better gun and in this way some one proposed writing to Sharps at Bridgeport (Hartford until 1876), Connecticut, to see if they could not make a gun that would kill buffalo successfully. Thus Sharp commenced to experiment, sending out samples to different points where the hunt had begun. They manufactured an octagon shape barrel of various lengths from 25 to 30 inches long, 50 calibre, using 380 grains of lead and burning 100 grains of powder, with reloading outfit including a bullet mold to make bullets on the range. After experimenting sometime, it did not give the satisfaction desired in Nebraska and Kansas, because the wind was much stronger than it was in Bridgeport, Conn.. The merchants wrote that the bullet would catch too much wind and would wind drift, so Sharps decided to make another calibre of smaller size; so made a 44, burning the same amount of powder and lead, but using a bottle-neck shell. After experimenting a long time this one did not give satisfaction, as it leaded too badly, and there was no certainty to the marksmanship. He next went to making a 40 with less powder and lead. This proved like to the others to be a failure, as it would not even knock the buffalo down, not having enough lead. He then began to make a 45, using 380 grains of lead and 100 grains of powder. This took a straight shell, and he thought it would overcome the leading, giving the weight and being a smaller calibre than the 50 and would not wind drift.[1]

. . .At the Doby Walls fight (i.e., the Adobe Walls, June 27, 1874), the hunters used all classes of guns, such as the Spencer, Springfield, Winchester and six-shooters,[2] also all classes of buffalo guns, including a new 45, which Sharps had just sent out, . . . Still some were not satisfied, so went outside and stepped off a 150 yards and commenced to pile dry bull hides ten in a bunch, and began to shoot with all four guns — as they went through so easily, they added more and continued to add until they had shot through 32 hides and one bullet stuck in the thirty-third one and it proved to be from the new gun. All had to have a shot with the new gun and as it gave entire satisfaction, they sent word back that this was the gun for the buffalo, and all of them ordered a gun. Sharps began to manufacture these rifles as fast as they could in various lengths and this gun, as it

[1]Although Glenn's folk history of the development and popularity of various Sharps Rifle Co. cartridges is interesting, and partially correct, it has the bullet weights wrong. The real story can be gleaned from Seller's *Sharps Firearms*, which shows the following from an examination of actual sales records:

Years	Calibers of greatest sales
1870-71	.44-77-380 or 405, .50-70-457 or 500 pp
1872-73	.44-90-450 or 500 pp, .50-90-425 or 473 pp
1874-75	.44-90-450 or 500 pp, .50-90-425 or 473 pp
1876-77	.44-90-450 or 500 pp, .50-90-425 or 473 pp
1878-79	.45-70-400, 420, 500, 550 pp, .45-100-550 pp
1880-81	.40-70/90-330,370

[2]Charles Hanson, historian at the Museum of the Fur Trade, identified the cartridge cases archaeologically recovered from Hanrahan's Saloon at Adobe Walls, and stated, "Aside from revolver cartridges, all the fired cartridges were .50-70, .50-90, or .44-77 (using modern terminology), and they were found in a wide litter of Berdan primers and sprues from bullet casting." (Hanson 1977). According to Bob Cator (Hamner 1943: 30) one of the .50-70's used at Adobe Walls was his Remington R B sporting rifle.

afterwards proved, was the cause of the extermination of the buffalo, as before this they had increased faster than killed out as it took too many shots to get a buffalo.

Meanwhile the hunter would be looking over his dead and wounded and cutting out the tongue, hump, and sometimes the tallow, it being the hunter's business to take these out while the buffalo was fresh, throwing them on some tree or rock where the wolves could not get them. In some instances if the hunter did good work the skinner could not keep up with him. Where the buffalo would be killed one day and skinned the next, they would be called stinkers. A buffalo left with his hide on will sour even in freezing weather; if skinned right after killing would not smell for months if his entrails were removed.

I have seen their bodies so thick after being skinned, that they would look like logs where a hurricane has passed through a forest. If they were lying on a hillside, the rays of the sun would make it look like a hundred glass windows. These buffalo would lie in this way until warm weather, drying up and I have seen them piled fifty or sixty in a pile where the hunter had made a stand. As the skinner commenced on the edge, he would have to roll it out of the way to have room to skin the next, and when finished they would be rolled up as thick as saw logs around a mill. In this way a man could ride over a field and pick out the camps that were making the most money out of the hunt.

These hides, like all other commodities, would rise and fall in price and we had to be governed by the price in the East. This man, J.R. Lobenstein, that run the hunt, has known them to be shipped to New York, then to Liverpool and back again in order to raise the price or corner the market.

We will now describe a camp outfit. They would range from six to a dozen men, there being one hunter who killed the buffalo and took out the tongues, also the tallow. As the tallow was of an oily nature, it was equal to butter; it was used for lubricating our guns and we loaded our own shells, each shell had to be lubricated and it was used also for greasing wagons and also for lights in camp. Often chunks as large as an ear of corn were thrown on the fire to make heat. This (i.e., the removal of the tallow) had to be done while the meat was fresh, the hunter throwing it into a tree to wind dry; if the skinner forgot it, it would often stay there all winter and still be good to eat in the spring and better to eat after hanging there in the wind a few days.

We will return to the wagon man. There were generally two men to the wagon and their business was to follow up the hunter, if they were not in sight after the hunter had made a killing, he would proceed in their direction until he had met them, and when they would see him, he would signal with his hat where the killing was. If they got to the buffalo when they were fresh, their duty was to take out all humps, tongues and tallow from the best buffalo. The hunter would then hunt more if they did not have hides enough to make a load or finish their day's work.

A remarkable good hunter would kill seventy-five to a hundred in a day, an average hunter about fifty, and a common one twenty-five, some hardly enough to run a camp. It was just like in any other business. A good skinner would skin from sixty to seventy-five, an average man from thirty to forty, and a common one from fifteen to twenty-five. These skinners were also paid by the hide, about five cents less than the hunter was getting for killing, being furnished with a grind stone, knives and steel and a team and wagon. The men were furnished with some kind of gun, not as valuable as Sharp's rifle, to kill cripples with, also kips and calves that were standing around. In several incidents it has been known to happen while the skinner was busy, they (the kips and calves) would slip up and knock him over. Toward the latter part of the hunt, when all the big ones were killed, I have seen as many as five hundred up to a thousand in a bunch, nothing but calves, and I have ridden right up to them, if the wind was right.

The buffalo were different than the domestic cattle. While they were traveling or grazing they would go with their head toward the wind, while domestic cattle turn their tails to the wind. Nature has provided the buffalo with an abundance of wool or hair called the fore-top or mane, also mops, and a shaggy mane over his neck and shoulders where the hump properly sets. This hump is the flesh that grows between the bones, commencing at the root of the mane and extending along the back to the loin, being highest at the mane. This upright or set of bones, that goes along with the ribs, varies. A well matured buffalo being eight or ten inches in height and tapering down as it ran back to the loin.

In order to get this hump out in a systematic manner, they would cut the flesh down the side of the blade bone (shoulder blade or scapula) until it would drop down like it was cut off, then they would commence on the ribs and peel the flesh down until they got to the backbone, then skin over the set of bones in the back. When taken out properly the neck part was the largest, being as large as a man's thigh, and tapering as it went to the back, being in a V shape and it was this hump that made such delicious eating when cooked properly.

The best way I ever saw humps prepared was after they had formed a crust by hanging out, . . . to lay them on a flat board. The sinew lying between the flesh and hide scarcely fit to eat, was taken off. It would then be sliced crossways, and salt and pepper it to suit the taste. The tallow was chipped up and dried over the fire in a frying pan, and there being plenty of it, these cracklings were used for fire. With the frying pan about an inch deep in pure tallow and boiling hot, these chips being about the size of an ordinary saucer, were slipped in enough to cover the pan so all could float, the pan boiling all the while and as soon as they were done they were taken out and more cooked, until there was enough for all the men. If we had cornstarch it was used, and if not, flour was made in a batter and poured in this and boiled until thick and then poured over the chips already taken out in some vessel that could be covered up and kept warm till all the meat was prepared. This being on the table was very fine and palatable.

Sometimes the boys would want a change and as turkey and deer were plentiful they would kill some, but one change was enough. Nine out of ten of our meals were of the hump style prepared in the very manner as we have described above.

There was always a boss or head man for each camp, and he was often the hunter. If he was a successful hunter, he would soon run a camp of his own, but if of the Pat Garrett style and gamble his money away would never run one successfully, as the business men soon learned he gambled and would not credit him.

There was also a camp rustler to each camp, and his business was to watch the camp and look after everything about the camp, and prepare the meals, early and late. The boss and cook generally slept together in order to get him up in time to get breakfast, and whoseever time it was to feed the stock, the other would peg the hides killed the day before. As soon as he got his hides in suitable shape, he would examine them to see if any would do to flesh. If the wind and weather were right a week or ten days was all it required; all surplus flesh was removed by him, after they were dry a little, the flesh coming off easily. It usually took from eight to ten days for an ordinary hide to dry so they could be ricked and stacked. Watching these hides, he could tell by trampling over them by the rattle when they were right, and would go out about sundown and pull the pins out of the dry hides, reversing them top from bottom . . . The moisture from the ground would be sufficient to have them encased the next morning. If he had a killing of hides in shape he would attend to this the first thing after getting to the hide yard. If they were robes, kips or spikes, he would double them in the middle with the fur inside, and by then tramping them with his feet to get them smooth, with something to protect them from the ground, as rocks or brush. If neither were convenient, he would use an old bull hide to make his foundation, thus he would begin stacking them with their backs together, crossing them, and thus building until they got as high as he could reach. A cover was then made from an old bull's hide and if rocks were not convenient, he would take his spade and throw sufficient dirt on top to hold it down, also to press them together so they would take less space in hauling. He would pile all the hides together, if there were only a few of each kind, and if they were plentiful, he would pile them separately. His duty was to tally the robes, kips and cows, such as would not make robes on account of not shedding, and would be governed by weight, as a good robe hide had to weigh from fourteen to twenty lbs. If it was a cow or spike of less weight, it was classed as a kip. Even cows were sometimes so heavy they were classed as bulls, ranging in weight from thirty to fifty pounds. The camp rustler had to keep tab on all this so the men could be paid in proportion. He also had to run bullets and look after the meat and tallow for the camp. As he did not get but one meal a day in daylight, he had a potful of boiled tongues also extra bread cooked for the men's lunch, for if buffalo was plentiful, they never got in until dark and after, and often two or three hours later in the night.

The skinner was also furnished with a saw to cut out the best piece of meat, a small grindstone and a good supply of skinning knives with a sixteen to eighteen inch steel to each man hanging to his belt.

The hunter was furnished after it proved to be a success, a .45 Sharp's rifle, costing $56.00, and a double belt with a hundred rounds of ammunition and sometimes more on his saddle also a couple of knives and a steel. The most of them went horseback, but sometimes went afoot. As they had had years of practice they could start in the morning and after taking the bearing of the wind, if they did not succeed in getting a stand, they would proceed to cut them off especially if it were a bunch of scrubhorn bulls. Taking his gun in hand in order to balance himself, he would slap his left hand on his ripper and steel, and start at a long trot . . . Many a time I have had a bunch run down by nine o'clock so that they would have to stop and blow and I have killed the whole bunch, making my round of thirty miles, getting into camp at one o'clock, with my horse in an opposite direction.

We will next speak of the hide busines. There are all sorts of ways to prepare these hides for market but the best method of skinning was to have a stick about the size of a chair post with one end sharpened and the other end with a spike in it sharpened to a point. If the buffalo was lying on his side and if he was a large one, the skinner would have to get down on his knees under the foreshoulder and raise it up far enough until the backbone showed on the opposite side. When he got the buffalo up at the proper height, he would jab the stick in the ground, catching the spike behind the fore shoulder just below the brisket. If the ground was not soft, the buffalo's weight would not force him back more than three or four inches. He would commence at the head on the underjaw, and would run a straight line from the brisket to the root of the tail. Next the foot, running a straight line to the tail. After ripping both, he would commence at the hoof and run over the knee, coming out a little below the brisket. In ripping in this manner, the hide was uniform to stretch, although a great many skinners would rip straight down the foreleg on the inside and the same with the hind leg, but this way would leave a gap and the first way did not do so. He would then begin peeling the hide off, taking the jaws running to the back of the neck. When he had peeled the hide over the backbone, he would go to the other side and skin the two legs down, when about halfway down the ribs he would pull out the prod, that side being in good skinning shape, and if all had been done right, and he had shoved the hide properly underneath, it would all be on one side and he could pull it out and throw it in the wagon. These scrubhorn bull hides were, when green, slippery and slick, weighing some eighty pounds, hard to throw into the wagon, and if he were skinning by himself, would spread it out on the ground, roll the legs under and when each side was properly wrapped, it would be some three feet wide. He would then commence at the jaw and roll to the tail and taking hold of this tail would throw it in the wagon the same as a sack of flour.

Another way of skinning was to skin down the jaws, then take the head off at the neck and place the nose under the buffalo with the horns on the ground turning the buffalo up against it the same as he would a prod but a great many that skinned this way never skinned the jaws. If a man was onto his job he could cut the head off as quickly as you could kill a chicken. Another way termed the tenderfoot way was to skin with the wagon. Take a forked stick of some five or six feet and fix it to drag behind the axle at the same time the fork going around the axle. When the wagon was stopped, any weight ahead would cause it to enter the ground. But this was too bothersome, as the team would have to drive over it (i.e., the buffalo) or else back up with one man holding this stick. So to each hind standard there was attached a rope some eight feet long with a ring large enough for the rope to double through, this ring being used for a slip noose like a lariat. When the wagon was thus backed up, with some man handling the team, the skinner would slip the rope over the hind foot as well as a fore foot, the driver would then drive up, the skinner telling him where to drive and where to stop so as to get the buffalo as near a balance as possible. He would skin the side opposite the wagon first, but could not skin the backbone. He would then skin the other side but could not skin the legs. Now as he could not pull the buffalo farther he would have to take out the prop or shove it (i.e., the buffalo) up by main strength going over and down the backbone to get the hide off.

We will here relate an incident that occurred while skinning this way. A man by the name of Spotted Jack[3] of a mongrel breed was doing the shooting, having an Indian boy of some fourteen years helping him. This boy's duty was to drive, and he had nothing but a pair of Arkansas yearling calves. When Jack made his killing, he motioned the boy to come up. He had made quite a run before killing this bunch of buffalo and after waving to the boy, he walked back and sat down on a big buffalo bull with his feet by his back and while thus seated here

[3]Spotted Jack, Glenn asserts elsewhere, was a Mexican. Jack was killed August 12, 1877, just out of Rath City. He had the reputation of being a horse thief. O.W. Williams, "From Dallas to the Site of Lubbock in 1877," West Texas Historical Association Year Book, XV (October, 1939), 20.

Spotted Jack hung on tight

resting, the boy drove up. As he wanted him to make a circle, he motioned with his hand for him to do so. The boy was not driving to suit him, having pulled out to make the forewheels go over the neck of the buffalo. The calves did not like the scent of blood and broke into a run. As the wagon struck the bull's neck, Jack had thrown his other leg over to see how they were coming, and the bull being only creased, was on his feet before he knew it. He overturned the wagon with his horns and head. Spotted Jack and the buffalo went one way, and the boy and the calves went another. Now buffalo do not run smoothly but go along something like a jack-rabbit. Jack said that all he could do was clench his heals and hold onto the mane. The old bull was about seventeen hands high and at each bound he made, he said it looked like he was fifteen feet in the air. It was down hill and rocky at that so he was afraid to jump off. He said he had not gone far when he made up his mind what he would do. On looking ahead he saw a lake and there was but little water in it, mostly slush and mud. When about half way the bull went to his stomach in the mud, and Jack slid off and made for the bank thinking the bull would come after him. Getting to the bank he said that the bull had come out on the opposite side and if a bull ever ran, that one did. Upon coming back to where he had made the killing the boy was nowhere in sight, so he took the trail and found the wagon scattered for a mile before he found the boy and the calves returning with everything torn up.

We will now describe the method used in curing these hides. A hide yard was selected on some smooth ground. Owing to the number of hides they would lay them in rows, piling five or six in each pile. When thus landed the camp hustler had to take care of them. He made his pegs of wild cherry, hackberry or pecan, sawed off in blocks of six inches then split in sticks all the way from a half to an inch square. One end being sharpened, they were ready for use, it being his business to make these pins at odd times and as we moved along they were hauled in the wagon from place to place and could be used quite often.

These camps were established where there was good drinking water, some five or six miles apart, it being customary for one man not to shoot near the other's camp. Sometimes they would camp together and the two hunters would go in opposite directions, so as not to trespass on the other's ground and in this way, they were strung north and south working west and embracing a country from five to seven hundred miles long, this being called the edge of the herd. If we were in the midst of a herd there was no chance to get a bunch by itself, as all the animals would stampede together.

When we would kill all around one camp, if we did not sell the hides or contracts for them to merchants, we would leave them or move on. This was continued until they were all gone and the buffalo exterminated.

Six Shooter Bill, or Bill Hillman was going into Camp Reymolds during the hunt and stopped at Bud Murphy's camp. The next morning when the cook went to wake them for breakfast he told Bud to get up quick, that there were a lot of buffalo cows right in camp. So he hurriedly dressed and commenced to shoot and made but few shots before he got his stand, and in less time than it takes to tell it, had them all piled in a pile, just as the cook said, "Come to breakfast, it's getting cold." Bud told the fellows to go on and eat and he would see if there were any wounded. He came back in a few minutes and as they sat down to the table he said, "Bill, they say you are about as good a skinner as there is on the range; how many buffalo can you skin in a day?" Bill said he couldn't tell, as he had never had enough to try on. Bud said, "I've got seventy cows out there in a pile and will make a bargain with you, as I want to see if you can beat Mickey Carr. He skinned sixty-five in a day. If you will skin them cows today without cutting their hides, you can have them, and if you don't what you skin is mine. What do you say?" Bill said that he had no knives but if Bud would loan him two or three he would make a trial. Bud told him that there was a pile of knives out by the grindstone, that he was welcome to as many as he needed and that one of the boys would turn out and help him sharpen them, so after breakfast he sharpened them up and went to work, Bud going out on the field to kill more, and the rest of the men following him. The cook alone was left to watch Bill. At eight o'clock he went to work and at ten minutes after four he finished the last one, saying that he had beaten Mickey Carr by five, thus holding the championship. On seeing the sun so high and as it was early winter, he said, "Begorra, I'll see if I can peg them," and before the sun went down he had the last cow pegged and as they were number one robes he went to Reynolds and sold them to W.H. Webb for $3.00 apiece on the ground. Thus he made $210 in one day. He got on a highlonesome and did not leave Reynolds till he had blowed his last cent in on drinks and cards and other evils that always follow a frontier town. He then begged for a job. This was the way of the majority of the men who worked for wages or by the piece, making it easy, spending it in the same way.

Toward the latter part of the hunt, when the buffalo had all been driven back and killed, at the foot of the plains, we came in contact with large outfits of Mexicans who had come from the Pecos and Rio Grande. Their way of killing the buffalo consisted of taking only the meat and destroying the hides by cutting them up to string the flesh on, or leaving them to decay on the ground. Now, as but few of us were taking the flesh, we might have gone into partnership, we taking the hides and they the meat, but we soon saw that we could not get along together, their ways being so different from ours.

When crossing the plains for wood and water, they came into the East side of the plains. Their methods were to come with the bull teams and old wooden axle wagons, eight or ten little Mexican calves to the wagon, with a bunch of well trained lance ponies. There were a number of men along to cut up the meat into sheets and strips, being generally in bands for self defense against the Indians. Sometimes there were as many as one hundred wagons together and when the oxen were turned out, they herded them to keep them from mixing with the buffalo. Their camps usually covered some ten acres of ground. The lance ponies were tied to the wagons with blankets on and groomed like a race horse, as they did not dare to turn them loose until they had run them down in the chase. They carried no guns to kill the buffalo, but some ancient guns to protect themselves from the Indians. These expert lancemen would mount their ponies lance in hand, and all that the men who cut the flesh had to to was to go along on foot or on their ponies, just as they chose.

There was always a boss with each herd and as soon as a bunch of buffalo were seen apart from the main herd, they would start out in two wings, one to the left and one to the right, each wing going in a circle so as to come together at some point from which the wind came, all of them keeping together and some distance from the buffalo, and in case they should stampede, they would close together as quickly as possible, then with a signal, they would make the start, closing in till the men were near enough to keep the buffalo in this circle or corral formed by the men. It was so arranged that these lancemen were equal distance and proportioned among what was known as rounders and when the buffalo began to chase around with the lancemen going at full speed, the lancemen would continue lancing the buffalo, and by keeping his horse to the left or outer edge as they ran by, if his horse was well trained he could lance them every time. The lance he used was ten feet long, with a spear fastened to the end, some eighteen inches in length, shaped like a dagger and sharp as a razor. A hole was bored through the opposite end of the pole, having a small stout cord or hide, and this was tied to the horn of the saddle to save the wood and lance, if by a mis-stroke he broke off the lance. He would make his stroke in front of the buffalo and backwards in order to strike him just behind the shoulder blade. As both buffalo and horseman were running at top speed, this would cause the weight of the buffalo to come against the lance, so the lancer could send it home. But if by chance he hit the shoulder blade, he would either break his lance or pole, and if not this , it would not go in far enough to stick. As he made his stroke if his horse was well trained he would file to the left. If he did not do this, the buffalo would either gore the man's horse, or often kill the man and horse both. If his stroke was successful he would then gather up his lance and go to work again till he neared the line of round-men, or his horse gave out. Whenever the lancer saw fit to fall out, the nearest man took his place, the older lancer taking the place of the man that was in the ring, thus they would continue killing until they had as many as they wanted or the herd was gone.

All hands would them commence to skin, cutting it (the buffalo) up on the ground and hauling it to camp. All the flesh was taken from the bone and either piled on brush or on string lashes of green hide, from wagon to wagon. When it had hung in the wind two or three days the flesh was turned. This was done in the early part of the fall before there was any snow. They would have to work all night sometimes, as this flesh had to be taken off before more was killed. Cut properly and fair weather for it, five or six days were enough to dry this meat. It was called *carne* and commanded from twenty to thirty cents per pound. It was pounded to a dust between two stones and mixed with red pepper and tallow, with other seasonings in proportion, making a great dish. As fast as the meat got dry enough it was thrown in the wagon with a man standing on it, and they would pound it down with a maul to make it take less space.

Now the reader can see why the Americans could not get along with the Mexicans. We will mention one instance concerning this manner of hunting buffalo.

Jim White, a big Irishman, was running an outfit on the Quitaque River near the foot of the plains. One evening an outfit similar in size pulled in near him. Jim was out early the next morning and had succeeded in getting a stand on a bunch of cows, and had just commenced to kill them, having some five or six dead on the ground. All at once they stampeded and no wonder. There was a band of one hundred Mexicans surrounding this bunch of buffalo, and as the ground was somewhat broken, they were forcing them to a more open ground, as they wanted a level ground to lance on. Seeing the Mexicans were the cause of his losing his stand, for when he had a stand he considered them all his, and as he termed it, knocked him out of $150, it made him very angry, and he soon decided how he would get revenge. Some of the Mexicans were in range of his gun and he had been shooting for years and was a good shot, his eye was quick in telling him the distance, and with the first shot he unsaddled a rider, and thus continued till he had shot three horses down. The Mexicans well knew from whence came the shots, and quite a group gathered on a knoll nearly a mile away. On seeing them there he decided that they were deciding what to do for revenge, thinking themselves safe at that distance. Jim threw his sights to the top of the notch, set down his rest stick, made something like a pair of blacksmith's tongs, setting his gun in the rest stick with his left hand to hold it steady, he pulled the trigger and saw another horse fall. To his surprise the whole band broke, and he ran to a high point to see if there were any more in sight. When he did not see anyone, and seeing that the buffalo were moving for miles away, he saw it was useless to hunt any more that day so proceeded to camp to fortify himself, as all his belongings were there. Every minute he looked for an attack, as they were overwhelming in numbers. He had not long to wait when he saw a whole bunch pulling out, and the last he saw of them they were going toward old Mexico and looking back to see if they were followed. After that White Jim, as the Mexicans called him, met some other hunters. There were no other Mexicans in that locality that winter, all going to other quarters to hunt buffalo and from then on he was dubbed White Jim.

The Mexicans soon ceased their occupation of crossing the plains for buffalo meat, the last of the meat being hauled all over to New Mexico and sold at a good price by the buffalo hunters, George and John Causey and Jeffries and Rowdy Joe.

We will describe how the meat was kept successfully. On killing the buffalo there would be a meat wagon, as well as a hide wagon. After the skin was taken off, the hams were taken off at the hip joints, the humps cut out, also the tongues, next the tallow was taken to camp where the butcher or meat man would prepare it. On the side where the most flesh hung, he would commence following down one of the seams, not breaking the flesh from the butt end up to the knee. Thus by pulling with his fingers and cutting but little, if cut out properly, it would in size and shape resemble the ham of a hog, with the big end trimmed and rounded in shape so as to make it resemble a ham. If this was taken out right, there would only be a cut across the lower or larger end. The next piece would be smaller and more flat like the muscles of a man's arm, it also having a coat of skin (fascia) around it. The last and third would go to the bone, being scarred with the knife on one side, and then trimmed so as to make it look nice after curing it for market.

The hump and tongue were already in shape for the cooking vat. These vats were prepared by digging a hole in the ground round in shape, varying in size according to the buffalo hide that was to be used for the hole and in shape would resemble a big salt or furnace kettle. The hides selected were the best that could be found picked from the green hides. Robes were seldom used, but cows, bulls and kips being of less value and only such as had few holes in them from knife or bullet. If it were a bullet it could be easily corked with a round stick. After being stretched these hides would be spread over the holes with the hair next to the earth, one man would stand in the vat, and another pegging all around so as to make the edges of the hides come even to the top of the ground. If there was any holes a pin was made to fit them and driven into the earth through the hole and was now ready for the meat. The meat was salted down the same as pork or beef and when the hole was filled a brine was made by boiling and letting cool till about blood heat. It was poured into this hole till level with the top of the meat, then a hide was stretched over for a cover and was pinned down to keep out dust or grit, a weight put on it to hold it in place and press it to the bottom. This meat was then allowed to stand some nine or ten days before being uncovered.

Next came the meat house. This was made by digging into the bank of some steep ravine and made smoke-tight with hides. A small trench some eight or ten feet long was dug outside and covered with poles and dirt. The meat was then hung in the house and the fire built in this trench so that the heat would not get to the meat and only the smoke going into the meathouse.

All this work was left to one man, the butcher or meat cutter, and it was his business to watch it. He would usually use green wood, and if that wasn't to be had, bull chips, to smoke the meat until it was in shape for market.

As a general rule, three or four days smoking was sufficient and then it was ready for market, commanding from twenty to thirty cents per pound among the Americans and very good to eat. In the same manner hams were cut and fixed, but the Mexicans would not buy it while the Americans would not buy carne or dried meat that was prepared in Mexican fashion.

We will next describe the method used in freighting these hides. The merchants would contract with the hunter, agreeing to give him so many dollars a hide delivered at his camp in a certain number of days, the merchants sending teams to the front and a man to tally the hides. Another way was for the merchant to supply the hunter with goods and ammunition of from one to three months' time with the understanding that the hunter would bring the hides to him and that he would give him the market price for them. By this method the hunter sometimes lost and sometimes made, if the price was governed by delivery and not by contract as he would have to take whatever they were quoted at in the Eastern market with freight off.

Now it was a difficult matter to get a horse or mule team to go to the frontier, as without a guard it was a risky business on account of the Indians either attacking in daytime, or stampeding their stock at night.

The teams that did go to the front to bring the hides to the settlements, that is on the inside of the Indian lines, were ox teams, called bull-teams, while the drivers were called bull-whackers. These trains varied from ten to thirty teams, according to capital and ranged from six to twenty yoke of oxen to a wagon, owing to the experience of the driver. If he were an expert, he was given a long team and a pony to ride up and down his line on, and if his oxen were well trained would haul many thousands of pounds. His first wagon was a very large one and the next some smaller and so on down the line, as many as four being hitched this way. In some wagon of the outfit would be what was called a mess wagon, which carried the grub and camping outfit. This way they saved expenses in the way of hands, one hand handling so many oxen.

A good bull whacker was always in demand, some of them getting as much as $5.00 a day. In the rear of the wagon train would be a herd of extra cattle driven by the day herder to replace those that were crippled or that died, or gave out.

After the hunt in Texas was in full blast, Frank Conrad said to a gang of us hunters one day, that he could look back and see how green he was at the beginning of the hunt.

"It was in the fall of '76, I was engaged in the back end of a storehouse and heard someone ask the boys who ran the shebang, where the boss was. I went forward and met the man. He had on a pair of old greasy overhauls, with grease from his shoes to his hips and his beard was long and rough. He was a big stout red-faced man. He had on a belt partly filled with shells, the longest belt I had ever seen in my life. To this belt hung a steel and knife. The man said he wanted some ammunition, and asked if I had plenty. I told him I did. 'Well,' he said, 'give me three kegs of powder and about four hundred pounds of lead.' It nearly took my breath away. I asked him if he was shooting an artillery and what his occupation was. He said he was a buffalo hunter. I told him that I had only two-thirds of a keg, and as a general thing only sold at keg in three months. The man said if I didn't get it in, that some one else would. By this time I had recovered from my surprise, and told him that I had a telegraph line there and would get it as soon as a driver could bring it. He said he couldn't hunt without ammunition and reckoned he would have to wait. So it was ordered sent by the first wagon. I had a lot of talk with the men and found that he was the fore-runner of a lot of Kansas men coming to Texas to kill buffalo. After thinking the matter over I decided to send to Bridgeport, Connecticut, after twenty-five kegs, and before it came there were men who would have taken twice as much . . ."

Conrad being very liberal with his dealings, having been in business ever since he was discharged from the army, got so careless with his crediting toward the end of the hunt, that he lost quite a bit. The old buffalo hunter had always met his obligations, and Conrad got so he would not size up the men, as he did at first, and got to giving any man credit that came along that had a team and had the appearance of being a hunter. As his store was up on a hill, the rest being down on what they called the Flat, where there was the dance hall and other buildings that followed a frontier town, he was not bothered by the loafers and dead beats. Now the meat hunters that dropped in there became experts in mixing and mingling with the (hide) hunters. They would give the hunter a $5.00 bill to swap rigs, and find some man about their size. After swapping rigs, he would take the man's gun and steel and go to Conrad's store gun in hand. As soon as he got in at the door, some clerk would meet him and ask him what he wanted. "Oh nothing, I just wanted to set my gun down a minute," he said. "Are you a buffalo hunter?" the clerk would ask. The man being posted on the country would next get an introduction to Conrad, he filling the bill. Going back, he would drive up with the hunter's team. Thus Conrad sold thousands of dollars worth of goods and never saw the man again. They would go to the range, trade their powder for hides and go to Fort Worth, Texas, go home and tell their neighbors of it, and they in turn would come out and try their hand, in many instances getting sufficient grub to make a crop on . . .

The Hunter's War

In the spring of 1877 the Indians were raiding the country at every full moon, carrying off the hunters' horses, etc. They made their raids often and returned quickly back to their camping ground beyond the main herd of buffalo.

I decided to move back into the buffalo range, being then camped on Croton Creek.[4] As it took two days to make the trip, the Moody

[4]Croton Creek heads in Dickens county and flows southward across the northeast corner of Kent County whence it turns eastward to empty into the Salt Fork of the Brazos in Stonewall County. The buffalo hunters drank "Croton Coffee" from beans of this member of the Castor bean family.

brothers,[5] who were camped nearby, also decided to move with us. We moved one load, and leaving a man in each camp, sent back after the other . . . The camps were not far apart. One of the Moody brothers stayed at the old camp and the other went to the new one with the other load, leaving at the old camp a fellow by the name of Jim Bermuda or Jim Carlyle, afterwards killed by "Billy the Kid." Jim was the hunter and a man by the name of George Jilds (Giles?) was doing the skinning. Bermuda made a killing and was helping Jilds skin. Jilds, thinking that he could finish the pile by night, told him to go on and make another killing . . .

. . . He (Jilds) had been in the country but a few years. When he started from the skinning he thought that he started in the direction of the camp, it being a mile away. It had been misting but by now the rain had turned to sleet, and he saw that he was lost. He spent the night in a gulch or canyon. Having no matches and as the country was so rough he decided to cover himself up by digging the dirt down with his knife. There he lay until day. When daylight came, . . . he could see that he was not more than a mile away from camp, so he got up and made for camp, half froze so that he could hardly walk. He came to a pile of hides that he and Bermuda had skinned the day before, throwing off the tops he came to one that had the animal heat in it and rolled up in it and went to sleep, not waking until the middle of the evening, taking him until dark to get to camp. He stayed for some time, as his nose was frost bitten, rubbing on liniment.

Something had gone wrong with Jim's gun and he had taken it to pieces. They were camped in a gulch for protection from the wind. He went out of the gulch and down to see about the horses. As he looked up there he saw an Indian, another unhobbling Jilds' horse and one already on his. So he went back, hollering to Jim that the Indians had their horses, and getting his six-shooter. Jim hurriedly put his gun together, and when he went to shoot found that the breach block was gone and so he ran after it. Jilds' pistol fell short of its mark and the Indians rode off, and by the time Jim came back with his gun they were out of sight. Jilds going with him they soon came up, one Indian was down, wearing a linen duster, cinching up his saddle. Jim fired three or four shots, but without effect, and all they could do was to walk back to camp. When the Moody brothers returned they related

[5]Strickland suggests the Godey brothers.

the loss to them. They remarked that they were glad they were not there with the mules, as they might have lost them.

Now, while Jilds was shooting at the Indian who had unhobbled his horse, the Indian had dropped his lariat. This was made from tanned buffalo hide and one could see it was not a white man's work. Jilds was setting by the fire very late that night, cracking pecans and lamenting the loss of his horse. It made him mad to think that the others could sleep so sound with the country so full of Indians. So he kept planning some scheme by which he could get even with them. As he had not shown the lariat to the boys he got it and went to the top of the bluff and laid it down, then went back to the fire, hollering: "Indians! Get up boys ! The country is full of Indians." Out they came, grabbing their guns. While they were getting in shape and their eyes open, he ran down the canyon to the place he had shot from and returned firing another shot. So he told the boys that they (i.e., the Indians) were gone and he guessed that he would get a little sleep and "you boys can watch." Thus they sat all night, talking about Indians while Jilds snored away.

In describing it to the boys, Jilds said he saw a lump of dirt fall and looking to the top saw an Indian trying to lariat some one and showed the rope saying: "Here is the lariat and he would have got some one if it had not been for me." This made the excitement worse. On my going over there the next day they had a terrible tale to tell me and showed me the lariat.

The excitement was made worse by Jim Smith,[6] "All Weight" (Alf Waite), Jim Melligan and "Spotted Jack" coming into camp trailing Indians. They said that the Indians had killed Marshall Sewell and scalped him.[7] He was running a buffalo outfit and had made a stand near his camp, shooting his ammunition all away and leaving several buffalo still standing. The Indians were on the watch, and when they saw him start for camp, they knew he was out of ammunition. They shot him in the thigh, breaking it, he trying to get to camp where he had plenty of ammunition. He got within twenty yards when they killed him and scalped him, taking his gun.

[6]There were at least two Jim Smiths in the buffalo country; Limpy Jim Smith, bartender at Rath City, and Hog Jim Smith. The latter is the Jim Smith of this episode.
[7]Sewell was killed February 20, 1877.

Alexander Gilbert, Louis Keys and Joe Jackson were working for Sewell, and at the time were skinning buffalo across a ravine about a mile from camp; this all happened in full view. They had been watching Sewell shoot, and seeing that he quit shooting, looked up to see the cause, saying that they reckoned that he was out of ammunition and was going to camp for more. In a few minutes more they heard loud yelling, and looking up, saw a band of Indians scalping him.

Billy Devons with his outfit had just come in sight. As he was an old U.S. soldier, he ordered the driver to drive on a high point where there was some cedar.

As the Indians had seen (Sewell's) boys skinning, they did not wait to plunder the camp. There was a fine pair of mules to the wagon that the boys were with, and, seeing the Indians coming, they ran the team into the gulch and went down the bed of the creek; but they had not gone far when they broke the neck yoke, and having nothing but common wagons, they decided to make their escape and never stopped running until they got to Camp Reynolds.[8] There raising the alarm, it was soon noted all around. Those that escaped the reds all pulled into Camp Reynolds with their stock.

As the Indians had discovered Billy (Devons) and his outfit, so while they were chasing the others, he drove in a different direction . . ., striking some other hunters. He told them what he had seen and they all pulled into Reynolds, and later it proved to be only two or three Indians the men had seen. This he learned from Montachenia after the opening of Oklahoma.[9]

After this news, the Moody brothers did not sleep for several nights, as there was fresh Indian news every day, and the hunters were pulling in (from) all over the country. Some of the more timid ones decided it would be safer to go to Ft. Griffin and they stayed there for some time, trying to get some one to haul their hides. Bill Criss (Mortimer N. "Wild Bill" Kress) claimed them as his hides and had traded Jilds a horse, bridle and saddle, and it was after this that he told me how he had made the Moody brothers lose their sleep. Jilds went east and we have never heard from or seen him since.

[8]Glenn commonly refers to Rath City as "Camp Reynolds."

[9]Montechania, or Montachanna (Our Child in Common) was a white captive of the Comanches. His name was Rudolf Fischer.

While this was going on, they gathered up a crowd of some 40 men and going back to the ground buried Sewell. Marshal Sewell was afterwards taken home for burial.

Pat Garrett was in the Moody camp. Not a man would go with the trailers. As they passed several camps they got no men. After several days' trailing, one morning they saw an Indian alone and on foot and they gave chase; all at once he disappeared down a bluff. On nearing the bluff they saw a few wigwams, so hurried back to a little gulch a few steps in their rear and dismounted. There was nothing to tie to, but Jim Smith had a well trained pony that would stand. All he had to do was to throw the reins over his head. So all hitched their horses to his saddle, then went back to where they could see the wigwams. They had Sharps guns in plenty, also plenty ammunition and began to shoot every Indian in sight. In a few minutes, with a few guns and bows and arrows, the Indians were giving the hunters a warm reception and the lead and arrows came thick and fast. As a great number of the wigwams were built of sage, when the Indian had run into camp he had reported that the soldiers were coming from all directions, so they fired their camp. Thus raising such a cloud of smoke that the hunters could see nothing to shoot at.

By this time Spotted Jack had received a ball in the thigh but not breaking any bones. The Indians were gathering their horses, and, seeing these four horses in the ravine and knowing that the men were not far off, sent a volley of arrows into Smith's horse, stampeding them, running in all directions. This left them with only a small amount of ammunition, the rest was tied to the saddles of the horses; to their surprise there were some 100 Indians, so they began to retreat, carrying Spotted Jack.

Luckily it began to snow about the time the Indians fired the camp. During the excitement, before the Indians could see their strength, they made good their escape, the snow blotting out their trail. After a six or seven mile walk Jack began to get very lame, and at the first suitable place, which was at the head of the gulch, under a shelving rock to protect him from the snow, they cached him, one man being on the lookout. As they had their canteens, one man went for water, and the others piled rocks in front of him to make a barricade in case the Indians attacked him. After this had been done, they said they would go to Camp Reynolds and bring a wagon after him, just as quick as they could go there and back.

During this excitement all the hunters had pulled into Camp Reynolds from the adjoining country, so they commenced to organize a company either to kill these Indians or drive them from the country. There were many men there of Pat Garrett's style who knew full well that they could not get no drop on "Mr. Indian." Pat had already pulled out of the country as fast as he could go for the settlement. We were some two days getting a company and out of 500 men, all frontier men, only got 48 men and four wagons to haul the grub and bring back the wounded. With 26 men on horseback, we left Camp Reynolds on the 4th day of March, 1877, to go after Spotted Jack, as well as to punish the Indians for killing Marshall Sewell.

Jim White, who was captain of the company, bled at the lungs the first day and night out. While making up the company there was plenty of bad whiskey and the men were drinking heavy. Now, this excitement and drink was the cause of Jim White's bleeding at the lungs. The second night out from Reynolds we persuaded him to go back and we elected limpy Jim Smith captain of the squad. Jim White continued to bleed all that night, and the next morning Bill Bronson took him back to Camp Reynolds. After the hunt, Jim went to the Black Hills and continued to drink heavily, and, whenever, "tanked up" became quarrelsome and was shot and killed by a miner somewhere in the Black Hills and died with his boots on.[10]

As we now had forty-six men, we decided to have Jim Smith for captain and Hank Campbell was elected lieutenant; Smokey Hill Thompson, wagon master; Bill Beldon and George Holmes agreed to do the cooking; if exempt from guard duty, fighting the same as the rest, if necessary when it came to a showdown. Beldon had been cooking in a restaurant and was going without a gun, as no extra guns were to be had, saying, he would use the gun of the first man shot.

Early the second morning . . . we met Spotted Jack, on foot, hobbling his way along. Some of the hunters had his horse; he was an Indian horse with his tail cut smooth off, thus disfigured the Indians thought no white man would have him. After the boys left Spotted Jack he lay there until the second day. Late in the evening, getting so hungry, he crawled out, found some water, shot an old buffalo, cooked, ate and drank until he was filled up. He traveled the greater

[10]The death of Jim White is accurately recorded by O.P. Hanna in this volume.

part of that night, and, as he was on a divide, he decided he had better lay up during the day. . . He lay there all day and at night continued his march until he met the hunters who were going after him.

The next day we began to strike the main herd of buffalo. We had got out of the hunters' line, as there was a brisk "norther," the buffalo were all feeding north in a solid body . . . we had not traveled far before we found out why the Indians always made for the main herd of buffalo, as they would tramp out their trail . . .

The company consisted, when all together, of 26 mounted men, four wagons and horses and the rest on foot, keeping pretty well closed up we would make a string of some 200 yards. The buffalo seemed to care as little for us as for rabbits. Why it was we could not tell, unless it was because we did not fire a gun for fear of alarming the Indians. These buffalo simply gave way leaving a space of some 150 yards.

We had struck the trail where Spotted Jack was wounded, and the scouts and trailers would run back and forth to the wagons keeping us posted as to their general course. These scouts would generally be in advance some six miles, that being about the distance of the range of our field glasses; we soon learned to detect our scouts and Indians if there were any in the country. Going to some high point we could see the buffalo working and tell where Indian or man had disturbed them, the buffalo giving way to let them pass. To cross this vast herd took us three days, and, at that time, we thought they would never be exterminated.

Smokey Hill Thompson was the man appointed by Lee, Rath, Reynolds & Co.[11] to lay out the trail from Dodge City to some place in the neighborhood of the Double Mountain in North Texas, to select some place on the flat and where there were plenty of buffalo. So it was selected 15 miles southeast of the Double Mountains. A cistern was built big enough to hold water for the town, filling it from soft water holes or lakes; adjoining this he built a restaurant and sent a

[11]In ascribing the establishment of Rath City (Camp Reynolds) to Lee, Rath, Reynolds and Company, Glenn may be more accurate in his recollection than at first appears. Charles Rath and Robert Wright had been associated in the store at Ft. Elliott (Mobeetie) in 1874. Lee and Reynolds were hide merchants operating out of Dodge City. Quite possibly Lee, Rath and Reynolds combined to make the establishment near the Double Mountains. It will be noted, that Glenn always referred to Rath City as "Camp Reynolds.' '

man back to pilot the outfit down. The saloon men, dance hall outfits, with some 40 women, hotel keepers and hunters all came down and started to Camp Reynolds the 24th day of December, 1876, right in the heart of the buffalo country. When the news spread around that the outfit had got in, W.H. West, who was sent by Lee, Rath, Reynolds & Co. to "ramrod" the hunt, did not have time to build the stores, so they commenced to sell from the wagons while the men were building adobe stores. They continued to buy and replenish their stock, sending their teams back with hides and to return with more goods. The train consisted of twenty-six mule teams, forty bull teams ranging from ten to twenty yoke to the team with trail wagons. It has been estimated that during the last winter of the hunt there were at least 5,000 men in the field hunting buffalo. Smokey thus stayed around Camp Reynolds until the buffalo hunt had ceased. I had left my outfit in his charge, and the last that I heard of him was that he had taken it and gone to Dallas and was running a restaurant.

The Indians got quite sharp, using all kinds of strategy after they left the place that Spotted Jack was wounded. All hands have stopped for hours before he could find the trail and at other times it could be followed at a lope. Next it would disappear as if going in the ground. We at least learned the trick. They had a place selected and when some two miles in front they would turn back on their trail, taking up their tepee poles, lash them to their ponies and commence dropping out, thus making a complete circle right and left, scattering some 200 yards apart and go clean around their camp. And if they were traveling west would be traveling east when they came into their camp, and when they went out in the morning would do the same thing and come together afterwards.

We followed the trail to the Yellow House Canyon. Then they changed their course to a left angle, seeming to follow the draw. The Mexican who was helping us trail, Jose La Vacas or "Hozay" as he was called by the hunters, McKinzie[12] having given him this name when he was scouting for him. "Hozay" had lived with the Comanches two years before captured by McKinzie and was supposed to know nearly all the water holes on the plains. He said he thought they would be on this stream somewhere, and for fear that we run on to them that

[12]General Ranald MacKenzie had been summoned up from Ft. Concho following the battle at Adobe Walls; in Sept 1874 he cornered the Comanche in Palo Duro Canyon.

evening we had better camp, so went in to camp at the foot of the plains. No one was allowed to speak above a whisper and we were up bright and early the next morning, the trailers and couriers going up the canyon and the others up on the plains, taking the level ground. About nine o'clock a courier was sent back and long before he got to us we could tell by the way he rode that there was unusual excitement. On coming up he said to get the wagons under cover as quick as possible, that the Indians were shooting buffalo not far off. So we got the wagons under cover and by this time could hear their guns, either stolen or captured from the hunters. After getting our bearings we could see them going to and fro packing buffalo meat to their camp. "Hozay" said they were preparing meat for their squaws while they were going on another raid.

After holding a council we decided to lay there all that day and make preparations to go for them that night. "Hozay" saying from the direction that they were taking they were camped in the Yellow House Canyon. So we laid there and tried to sleep, which no one could do on account of the excitement. Judging from the signs and lodges where they had slept, "Hozay" estimated the Indians as 90 or 100, which afterwards proved that he was right as to their numbers.

The Captain and Lieutenant counted out, it made an even 44, so they commenced at the head and numbered one, two and so on down the line. In case of surprises No. 1 was to follow the Captain and No. 2 the Lieutenant and be governed subject to their orders. After tramping and walking all night, some times sitting down, as "Hozay" had got tangled up and took the wrong draw, when daylight came we were out at the head of this draw, not a tree or brush in sight. He was somewhat in advance and from the head of the draw turned due north. Some one came galloping up from the rear, saying that the men in the rear said to hold up, they were about played out. So the Captain sent a courier to "Hozay" to hold up until all hands were together. The interpreter had to explain why he was making such a turn, and learned that he had lost half the night by taking the wrong draw and now we had marched all night when he had said that we would get there by midnight. The men were hungry and footsore and began to want their coffee, with none nearer than the wagons. He said that he was turning back for fear that he was running onto the Indians, and did not think it was more than two miles to the canyon where they were. He said that it was dangerous to stand there in the broad daylight, as the Indians had about 500 horses and could run them all off. We did not go far before we struck their trails where they had come and gone with the meat. On getting into the canyon "Hozay" thought it best for us to stop and let him go forward. As he rode to the bend, which was some 300 yards, we saw him halt and sort of peep around, as if he saw something, and the next instance was leaning back as if he was trying to keep from being seen. On coming back he reported that when he first went there he saw a loose horse or two and knew that they were Indian horses and was satisfied that they were around the next bend. On talking it over, we decided to go slow from there, in case they were on the lookout. It was then about sun up and we had planned to round them up in the night. But it was sun up before the first gun was fired.

I had been in numerous fights in the Civil war, but never a better or more picturesque one than when those big buffalo guns were cracking, the bucks, such as had horses began to run for them leaving the squaws to surrender. By this time they had run up the white flag, in token of surrender, thinking that we were soldiers. Some of the braver squaws had gone to the top of the bluff and were shooting arrows and six-shooters at us. At this juncture, Smith ordered every sixth man to take the horses back to a place of safety. As they started back it looked like two men to every horse; the squaws on the lookout took it for granted that we were retreating, so began to chant a song, the bucks coming back. The lieutenant, being a natural born coward, ordered all his men, which included me, to fall back into the canyon.

By this time everything was in confusion and I could see nothing to shoot at, but on looking around the point, the first thing that my eye fell on was a lot of tents, with a banner or flag sticking up, which was their medicine. Outside stood one lone Indian, acting as if he were bullet proof, so I got down on one knee and turned loose at him, my first ball fell short, the next one I shot too high. As I was aiming for the third shot, I looked up and saw three Indians on the bluff shooting across at me. They would bob their heads up and shoot at me. I was shooting as fast as I could load, and as I was shooting black powder, every time I would shoot there would be considerable smoke. Being on sort of an incline I had lain down and was shooting from my back; whenever I made a shot I would roll over and down the hill, they popping up shooting at the smoke. I being on the lower edge, as they would show up I would crack away again. These Indians were to the north and the first thing I knew a ball just missed me from the east. I wondered if some Indians had got behind me, but my attention was to those directly over me, they appeared all to be young Indians not over twenty years old, each doing his best to get me first. As they had been a little reckless in showing their head I had killed one, this put sort of a quietus on the others showing themselves, and they did not pop up as fast as before.

In a few minutes another bullet came from my man to the east and from its sound I knew it was from a buffalo gun. As I looked over my shoulder I could see the smoke from the fellow's gun, some nine hundred yards away on a little ridge. Not a soul could I see between me and him, it being an open flat. I knew that he was shooting at me through mistake or ignorance. At the same time I held my gun toward the Indians and jerked off my hat and motioned him to shoot no more. By this time the Indians were coming down the canyon, riding one way and the other. Every time they made a circle they came some ten feet nearer to where I was lying. In looking over my shoulder I could see no one in sight. The buffalo hunter who had been shooting at me had disappeared. I said to myself, "This is a damn close place, and it is a pretty officer that would desert his men in this shape." I was afraid to get up for fear the Indians would see me, so concluded to slide as far as possible. Thus I slid along for some distance. As no bullets or arrows fell around me I decided I had not been discovered, so I kept on going with my gun toward them. As their horses were going at full speed I could see that they were fast gaining ground. Looking over my shoulder I could see a level spot of ground of some 800 yards. Thinking now that the only chance was to get up and run and probably the boys would see me if I was shot down, and the reason that I ran was because I could not fly. All at once I came to the boys as I was running east, and looking in a small gulch there the whole gang lay, like wild hogs holding the dogs at bay.

I was so mad that I was not excited, to think that my own men were shooting at me, and when I saw them all huddled up there it made me madder than ever. I said, "You are a pretty set of officers to run off and leave your own men. I heard no order to retreat." John Cook, George Holmes, as well as two or three others spoke up, saying, "When we saw you motion your hat we thought you were wounded and were motioning for help. Some five or six started to go and bring you in, but Hank Campbell ordered us to come back, saying that one life was better lost than a half dozen." I remarked that I had been four years in the army and never saw an officer refuse to let volunteer comrades go to his assistance and that he was a pretty specimen of an officer. John Cook then asked what I was motioning for. I said, "Some ————— was shooting at me and if you will show me the man I will finish him right here." As I had shot the bigger part of my cartridges away, I asked some of the men with filled belts to divide with me. In front of me sat a fellow by the name of Luther Duke, who had once been a partner of mine. He had his belt on the outside of his coat with his gun between his knees, leaning against his shoulder. I was shooting what is called a short shelled 50 (.50-.70). I said to Duke, "Suppose you swap guns with me, that is my gun anyway, and as your belt is full, I see that you have not fired a shot, and what have you been doing? When we were making up Camp Reynolds I asked you why you did not go, you said you did not have a gun, but if I would let you have mine you would go. Now," I said, "you either get up and shoot Indians or let me have it." At this juncture I walked around and looked down the muzzle of his gun and said, "Men, sure enough, he has not fired a shot, not even smoked the muzzle of his gun." I said, "If any man in this outfit will go with me through this crowd we will see who has been doing the shooting, that I do not think this is the only one showing the white feather." In an instant there was some man on his feet, but I do not remember who it was, but going through we found some ten men who had not fired a shot, and as many more who had fired only one or two shots. All this time we were out of sight of the Indians, sort of hid in the canyon. I said, "If we do not do something these Indians will go around us and be flank shooting us."

I neglected to say that Joe Jackson offered me his gun as he was wounded and in a bad shape. The Indians had one rifle which we thought must be Sewell's gun. Jackson was wounded in a peculiar way. While falling back a bullet from the .44 (Sewell's stolen Sharps) struck one of his cartridges driving its ball into the flesh, the speed of the ball checked, both balls lodging in his body. This was some two hours before and Jackson was sore and stiff by this time. When he handed me his ammunition I merely filled my belt and handed him his belt back.

By this time someone said that the Indians were going around on the south side. I said, "Let five or six men go with me. That will be over half the fighting men." We would go to the draw on the opposite side, and while they drawed their fire, I would crawl out of the bluff and that would make the wind just right to burn them out. This would compel the cowards to fight or die. At my request Billy Devons and Jim Gratehouse said they would go with me. I think John Cook and George Holmes also went, five in number. I asked the men if some would get up and draw the Indians' fire while we made the run. So several of the boys got up and began to fire from a bluff over their heads. I asked the interpreter to ask "Hozay" if the creek was boggy. The answer was that there was so much rush grass there would be no danger, so we got across successfully, not a man wounded while we made this run, some 400 yards under heavy fire.

The Indians seeing that we were rallying sent their warriors from their camp which was hid from our view, so I told the boys to poke the lead into them. Soon I saw the boys shooting too fast to do any damage to them, and as the Indians came out one at a time I saw that it was just a ruse to get us to throw away our ammunition. They were wobbling their shields and not firing. I crawled up the bluff and laid down with my back to the wind and tried to fire the grass. The wind being so high I burned my entire stock of matches and did not succeed in firing the grass.

As the boys ceased firing the Indians ceased to come out. Those who had been circling also turned back, and as nothing could be done there I said we might as well go back to the main gang, also made it back safe. By this time the Indians had commenced circling to the north to see what could be accomplished on that side. So we decided we had better fall back down the canyon on the south side. Being in such shape that they could not cross fire from the opposite side of the canyon at us.

I afterwards learned that some of the hunters had been rounding up Hank Campbell for shooting at me and they thought that he had crippled me. On seeing me so vexed at him, he thought that I thought it was him, and begged the men not to tell till we got off the raid, so I never learned of it until afterwards. On meeting Bill Belden in Colorado a number of years afterwards, he said: "You remember the boys called me the long range shot, as I had no gun but a pair of field glasses. I was standing in 10 feet of Campbell, looking on, taking the whole situation. Hank said, 'I came very near getting one — — — —and knocked the dirt up on each side.' I threw my glasses down and told him who it was, that I saw you go there and was shooting at those

Indians on the bluff. Then he asked, 'What is he motioning for?' I told him I guessed you were wounded."

We retreated to the large gulch without the loss of a man, the Indians not following us up but holding their first battle ground. As they could do no good, some five or six were doing all the shooting, the other lying in the gulch sleeping. We piled up rocks, making a sort of port hole, as this Indian who had the gun (Marshall Sewell's .44 Sharps) was continually pecking at the top of the bluff. Although it may sound strange to the reader, being so used to each and every gun we could tell what caliber each gun was by the sound, as easy as we could tell one man's voice from another at a distance.

As soon as the Indians discovered us, they commenced sending warriors out again, but keeping them at a greater distance. The first rider came out on an iron grey horse, one after another followed. As we were shooting from rest we were taking more pains. This same Belden had a hole watching our shooting, telling us where to place the balls. We estimated it at 1200 yards. Finally Amos Kemp hit a brown horse just behind the saddle. As Hank Campbell and Jim Smith had both taken a back seat we payed no attention to them, every one shooting as he saw fit. I said, "Amos what was the range?" He said, "1100 yards." I said, "Boys, drop your sight down about 100 yards." As this Indian had lain down behind the horse we put them in through the horse's flank. Bill said, "You are getting them right, I can see the fur fly every time. Some of you try him about the heart and may be you can find a place there you can get through with your bullets."

We had not long to wait. The horse was shot down. The Indian jumped up and running, the boys all yelled. I hollered to them to raise their sights to 1100 yards and right quick. He ran about 50 yards, stopped and put his hand to his hip, stopped there a second or two, then managed to run out of range. This put a stop to their sending out warriors from this point.

While thus coming out one of them was a greater dare-devil than the rest, and was working his shield to perfection. Just as he came to a ridge, knowing that he would soon disappear, he had the audacity to change it from the elbow and run it up on the point of his finger over his head as much as to say, "You can't hit me, look at that."

After the opening of Oklahoma, Bat Carr, Jim Dobbs, Neal, N. York and myself were sitting in front of a hotel in Lawton . . . This was the first time the gang had all been together since the breakup of the hunt.

We were all sitting down except Montachana, who was also present. We were telling our ups and down on the frontier. Neal, Dobb and myself were all in this Yellow House fight. I said, "Dobbs, do you remember when we were shooting up that last bunch of horses? Belden was telling us where to shoot and you remember how Kemp knocked down the brown horse, and how at last we wounded the Indian, and old man Jackson always claimed that shot. Well, I always thought that Amos done it, as he had made the other crack shot." Montachana had not spoken a word up to this time, but walked a few steps closer, saying' "I remember; that was me. I have got that ball in my hip now. Us Injuns always thought that you were soldiers, but now I know that you were buffalo hunters by them remarks. You couldn't tell them things in that way if you weren't there, for I know you are telling the truth."

It was about one or two o'clock in the evening by this time and I saw that about ten of us had to do all the fighting, the rest sleeping, and as most of our ammunition was gone, we began to think of our wagons. "Hozay" said it was some 12 miles to them, but as there was a Mexican trail on each side of the canyon, and as the Mexicans could not get down with their wagons, the road followed straight on down. By following this road it would take us straight to the wagons in the canyon where we had left them the day before. We now began to plan to get out again. We decided that some 10 men would go to the level flats, some 800 yards, sort of dividing the crowd so as to leave some that would shoot in each squad, we would hold them at bay until they got back in case they were attacked. The field glasses were divided so that each squad had a pair of glasses, and thus fighters and cowards well divided we accomplished our aim.

By the time we got out it was two or three o'clock. We could see a group of Indians watching us, which showed they also had field glasses. We were surprised on getting to the wagons to find them still standing, not a soul having been there. We put out our pickets, as we could see the Indians following us at a distance, seeming to be in no hurry to overtake us. We decided that they were going to make a night attack. The boys that had shot most of their ammunition away went to reloading, while the rest went to feeding the stock and getting a meal. They were in groups and bunches discussing our situation. I had but little to say, as I was still mad at the lieutenant; but I told Smokey Thompson, Jim Smith and a fellow by the name of Benson that if they would turn the outfit over to me that I would get it out and insure all to go O.K. They said if I would make my plans known and they thought them advisable they would turn it over to me. I told them in the first place I would have everything ready to snap together after dark, and would get all the wood and combustible matter that would burn as if we were going to camp all night. Then as soon as it was dark a detail would pile it on the fire as rapidly as possible, running in and around the fire to magnify their numbers. While this was going on we would get out on the north side opposite the Indians, where "Hozay" said an old trail was, and by traveling east between the trail and the canyon we could not get lost. As there was no moon it would be a hard matter for the Indians to trail us over this carpet grass. When I thought they had got sufficient distance ahead I would come on and overtake them.

All agreed and said that I could take charge, and that they would not let the other boys know but that we were going to stay all night. As Smith was Orderly and kept the roll, he would make a detail of two men to go with me and get wood for breakfast, saying, "We won't make breakfast before day in case the Indians attack us." He made his detail to go on guard and then arranged with the wagon drivers to lay the harness on the horses getting everything ready. When this was all done I was to tell the detail that had been helping me to get wood to help me build a fire, so that the Indians would shoot into it and they could tell where they were. I would come to the front and take charge of the outfit and pilot it throughout the night until we went into camp. Everything went well until we were building a fire. By the time that half the fuel was on, the Indians were dropping lead in thick and fast. The boys who were with me stampeded and ran for where they supposed the wagons were. On arriving there they saw they were gone but heard them a short distance from there. When they overtook them they wanted the roll called, as they were satisfied that some one was killed, and the majority of the men insisted that they would not be moved until it was called. I said to Jim, "Nothing will do but call it, and the quicker the better." Running to the wagon, I grabbed a pair of blankets and told Jim to sit down and I would strike matches under the blankets while he called it, as Jim knew it almost by heart it took but little light for him to call the names, as every man answered they were satisfied and went on.

We will now call the roll as well as we can remember:[13]

Capt. Jim Smith	Lt. Hank Campbell
Jack Leack	Amos Kent (Kemp)
Sol Reese (Rees)	Bill Criss (M.N. "Wild Bill" Kress)
Nick Ross (Mick Carr)	John (R) Cook
Tom (Doc) Neat	Limpy Jim Smith
Harry Harrest ("Deacon" Forrest)	George Homes
High Biggedite (Hiram Bickerdyke)	Bill Beldon
Ben Jackson	Dick McLoughlin
Joe Jackson	Billy Devons
Smokey (Hill) Thompson	Lander (Alexander) Gilbert
Jack Matthews (Matthias)	(Charlie) Emory or Squirrel Eye
Bill Benson	Whiskey Jim Gratehouse (Greathouse)
One Eyed Mexican Joe	W.S. Glenn, The Writer
"Hozay" or Jose Lavacas	Luther Duke
Bill Hillman or Sixshooter Bill	Lewis Keys (Louis Keyes)
Buckskin Bill, John Godie (Godey)	Jim Dobbs
Ben Freed	Jim Harvey
Spotted Jack	Dick Wilkinson
Ben Milligan	Alf Wright (Al Waite)
Big Infant	Willis Atchison
Dick Hughes	Billy Dickson (Dixon)
Tom Skemon	

The other two names we have forgotten.

So I got in the lead, and we travelled until about 11 o'clock. I turned due north as we had been traveling due east about two miles as the country was level. I took my bearings telling them we would go into camp and leave our wagons in the shape of a corral, tying a lariat from wheel to wheel. Each and every man unsaddled, teamsters likewise. Smith put his pickets out about two hundred yards, so it would give room to picket the horses, and two men on camp duty to awaken the men, it being dark. There was some confusion at first over blankets, but in an hour's time everything had settled down.

Before daylight we had started east, not having as yet found the Mexican trail. "Hozay" saying that it was five or six miles from the canyon and thought we could go down most anywhere and strike it.

[13]The names or nicknames that appear in the parentheses are Strickland's emendations for the sake of clarity or explanation. In the manuscript the names were arranged in two columns in order to distinguish the two details that respectively followed Campbell and Smith.

So I told Smokey to follow the Morning star until daylight, but I had business behind the outfit to look after.

It was about the middle of March and the wind generally came up at that time of the year from the south or southeast and would be in full blast by sunup. So I told two of the boys who had good horses to fall back with me and we would fire the prairie, as it was a perfect mass of mesquite like a perfect carpet. We made a V shape. In getting on our route the wind and smoke would go in that direction behind us. I told them to each take a box of matches, one to go to the right and the other to the left for a half mile or more, and leaning over their horses to strike the matches and let them fall in the grass, making this circuit as fast as possible, coming back to the wagons as day was fast approaching. I would drop back to the rear and follow until daylight to see the effect of the burn. And I was not long in seeing that we had completely obliterated the trail. The sun was up by this time, also the wind, and the fire burning as fast as an ordinary horse could go, and the smoke was so thick that I do not think they could see 100 yards. At any rate it was a success; we lost all sight or trace of the Indians during that trip.

We went off the plains without further trouble and came back into the main herd of the buffalo. So we each killed a buffalo, each taking his choice piece, selected a place where the horses would be out of sight and every man went to cooking his piece of buffalo. So we stayed here until the following morning. We could see the foot of the plains some five or six miles away and kept watch that night, the buffalo were so thick the Indians could not find us after dark.

The second day the boys began to scatter and look for buffalo camps. They run into Pat Garrett and another fellow skinning buffalo. They taking them for Indians ran and hid in the gulch and when they got to camp the men were busy cooking their meals and had about cleaned up the camp of grub.

We were gone 23 days from the time we left Camp Reynolds until we got back to our camp. Captain Lee, who was stationed at Ft. Griffin, on hearing of the fight went in pursuit of the Indians, and with him went some 40 Tonkawa Indians as trailers. They took up the trail from the site of the Yellow House fight.[14]

After this expedition returned to Camp Reynolds, Tom Lumpkins had been drinking heavy until he had the "jim jams." With his six-shooter in hand he started out to kill a man as he wanted to start a graveyard. He tried to pick a fuss with everyone he saw. There was no one on the street, as there was scarcely any one in town but the gamblers and dance-hall people. He finally rambled into Jim Smith's saloon and pointed his gun at Jim, saying that he was going to start a graveyard. As Jim's pistol was in another part of the house, he kept dodging behind the bar; Lumpkins, standing in the door, finally saying: "You ain't worth killing anyway, I'll hunt another man." As soon as he went out the door, Smith grabbed his pistol and ran to the door, laying it up beside the casing, took good aim, and at the crack of the gun shot him in the back of the neck, so Lumpkins started his own graveyard. With a buffalo skull for a tombstone some of the boys had marked: "A graveyard started by Tom Lumpkins at his own suggestion."

[14]Glenn does not give the exact location of the Yellow House fight in this extract from his manuscript. However, in another portion, as yet unedited, he says, in relating the experiences of Bill Benson in connection with Nolan's famous Dry March, August, 1877, that, "The place where he struck the water was at the present site of Lubbock and also the site of the Yellow House fight." In another section which deals with Quanah Parker, he writes, "Now after our fight at the Yellow House, where the city of Lubbock now stands, being the 18th of March of the year of 1877, . . . Captain Lee of Fort Griffin went to the head of Yellow House Canyon . . ." This seems to fix the location of the Yellow House battlefield with sufficient accuracy.

Nothing is known of P.C. Bicknell except that he had just begun in the hide business when he wrote a letter dated December 30, 1876, from the North Concho in Texas. A contemporary of Glenn, Dixon and Jim White, he shared the latter's desultory attitude toward Mexicans. His letter was found among the Sharps Company records, and was first published in Sellers (1978) and then in Conger (1981).

Head of North Concho,
Sat. Dec. 30, 1876

Dear Dave: I have not heard from you since I last wrote — nor from anybody else. I suppose there are letters for me, somewhere, but they have not yet reached me.

I have reached at last a primitive and wild country. It is part of the old Comanche hunting grounds. We are camped 60 miles up the North Concho from the Post, & close by another camp of Buffalo Hunters. I have degenerated from a would be sportsman to a man who hunts for a living. Cas will tell you all the particulars I have not time now. I traded off my pony for a black pony & that pony I trade at the Post for a Sharps Carbine .50 cal. & 16 cartridges or 14 I have forgotten which. I could get no more in town — by town of course I mean Fort Concho. I have done no hunting yet having no ammunition. My partner does the hunting & I help skin & do the staking & cooking. I shot two buffalo out of a herd that came on while I was skinning. There are lots of buffalo on all sides. The hunters are a different class of people than you have met in Texas — not akin to the cowboy —they are men who have hunted and trapped all over the west from the Black Hills south to Texas. The gun they swear by is Sharps .44 cal. just like yours they shoot 90 gr. powder — some use the 50 cal & 120 grains. The best gun in this part of the country is a Sharps 40 cal with 90 grains of powder, the ball weighs 420 grains. The hunter who has it, says he can hit & kill a bull as far almost as he can see it. It holds up wonderfully. The 44 cal day before yesterday, loaded with 85 gr. 420 gr. lead shot through several bulls in succession at 500 yds. My partner shoots a Maynard 40 cal-ring ball 70 gr. powder 340 gr lead. He shot a bull last week just to one side below the tail — the ball

lodged in the tongue. The bull was 250 yds. distant. Shooting from one side the balls mostly go through & frequently kill two at once. The Maynard seems to do as good work as the .44 cal. Sharps. The only objection my partner has to it is that it ought to shoot a patch ball. Shooting 20 or 30 shots inside of half an hour leads the gun & probably wears it out sooner. That 40 cal. Sharps must be the Boss gun. You see it shoots the same amount of powder as the 44 with a longer ball. The Winchester is a laughing stock among these men —they would not take one as a gift if they had to use it. These hunters ought to be pretty good authority for most of them have killed the Grizzly, the Cinnamon Bear, which they say is about as bad — the Elk the Blacktail Deer, the Panther the Indian the Greaser &c&c. They are the company I have been in since I came to Texas, not excepting your own. If I cannot make a living in any other way I shall turn hunter & in the spring if I have enough money to get an outfit that is wagon horses &c. I shall start north through the Territories & hunt perhaps in the Black Hills. There will be a great deal of money in meat there, selling to the miners and new Forts which are to be built. We have up to this evening 52 hides — bulls sell for $3 and cows for 4 1/2 at the Post. Bull hides dry average from 35 to 55 lbs cow from 15 to 30 lb.
No more time to write now — must make bread for tomorrow. My partner goes to town for ammunition & provisions — taking 30 hides — all that are dry. I hope he sells them for enough to pay for what we want to buy, for we have no money. I have written this letter by the light of a piece of cotton cord hanging out of a plate filled with Buffalo tallow. Love to all
Yours very truly

P.C. Bicknell

P.S. We have a comfortable wigwam or Tepe built with poles & 10 hides — fire in the middle — very comfortable.

Bicknell wrote from just south of what is now Big Spring, Texas. Two hundred miles to the northeast lies the town of Jacksboro, where in the spring of 1873 began events which have become legend in the classic song of buffalo hunters. The version recited here was that sung by old-timer, Slim Critchlow, and serves as an appropriate end to this chapter on getting a stand in the southern herd.

THE BUFFALO HUNTERS LAMENT

as sung by Slim Critchlow

It was in the town of Jacksboro, in 1873
when a man by the name of Crego[15] came stepping up to me
and says he "My fine young fellow, how would you like to go
and spend one summer season on the range of the buffalo?"

With me being out of employment, to Mr. Crego I did say,
"This going out on the buffalo range depends upon the pay,
but if you will pay good wages and give transportation too,
I think sir I will go with you, to the range of the buffalo."

"Yes, I will pay good wages, and give transportation too,
provided you will go with me and stay the summer through.
But if you should grow homesick and come back to Jacksboro,
I won't pay transportation from the range of the buffalo."

It's now our outfit was complete — seven able-bodied men,
with Navy six and needle gun — our troubles did begin.
Our way it was a pleasant one, the route we had to go,
until we crossed Pease River, on the range of the buffalo.

It's now we've crossed Pease River, our troubles have begun.
The first damned tail I went to rip, oh how I cut my thumb!
While killing the damned old stinkers, our lives they had no show,
for the Indians watched to pick up off while we skinned the buffalo.

He fed us on such sorry chuck I wished myself 'most dead.
It was old jerked beef, croton coffee, and sour bread.
Pease River's as salty as hell fire — the water I never could go.
Oh God! I wished I had never come to the range of the buffalo.

Our meat it was old buffalo hump and iron wedge bread,
and all we had to sleep on was a buffalo robe for a bed.
The fleas and graybacks worked on us; O boys, it was not slow.
I tell you there's no worse hell on earth than the range of the buffalo.

[15]According to Mrs. Ella Bird (Lee 1964) a Mr. Crego ran a hog ranch near where Croton Creek empties into the Wichita River.

Our hearts were cased with buffalo hocks, our souls were cased with steel.
And the hardships of that summer would nearly make us reel.
While skinning the damned old stinkers, our lives they had no show,
for the Indians waited to pick us off while we skinned those buffalo.

The season being nearly over, old Crego he did say
The crowd had been extravagant, was in debt to him that day.
We coaxed him, and we begged him; but still it was no go —
So we left old Crego's bones to bleach on the range of the buffalo.

Oh, it's now we've crossed Pease River, and homeward we are bound.
No more in that hell-fired country shall ever we be found.
Go home to our wives and sweethearts, tell others not to go
For God's forsaken the buffalo range and the damned old buffalo.

Oliver Perry Hanna in rodeo rig. Photo courtesy Charles Hanna Carter

Chapter 7

Oliver Perry Hanna was born May 10, 1851 on a farm near Matamora, Illinois. He was ten when the outbreak of the Civil War left him "bound out" as a farm hand to his brother-in-law, a stern taskmaster. "I didn't take kindly to the whippings he gave me." Hanna wrote. He determined to escape and seek adventures like those he read about in Beadle's Dime Novels. To young Hanna, characters like Louis Wetzel, Wild Cat Joe, and Indian Dick were the greatest men living. His ambition was to become a trapper and Indian fighter. By 1867, his ambition had been realized.

Hanna escaped and joined a wagon train which took him all the way to Bozeman. He worked on a farm for two years, invested his earnings in a horse and a Henry rifle, and joined Ben Walker and Bill Hamilton, experienced trappers. They took him up the Clark's fork of the Yellowstone, and taught him how to trap and how to stay alive in Indian country.

In 1870, he explored the area now called Yellowstone National Park. In 1871, he prospected for gold in the Big Horns. He returned to the Yellowstone area as a member of the F.V. Hayden survey party in 1872. 1874 found him in the fire fight on the Rosebud. He was a member of the hazardous Sibley Scouting party in 1876. In the winter of 1876-1877, he was on Louis Swan's payroll to provide wild meat for the Chug Ranch cowboys. He was similarly employed by the Army to supply Ft. McKinney in 1878, when he met Jim White.

Hanna's story is told here in his own words, dictated to his son-in-law in 1926. Parts of it have appeared in newspapers but, for the most part, it has not been previously published. I became aware of Hanna's association with Jim White through a footnote in Wayne Gard's *The Great Buffalo Hunt*. Hanna's manuscript was in the Wyoming State Archives in Cheyenne. In reading the manuscript, which told only of Hanna's life from 1878-1880, I

Oliver Perry Hanna in Sheridan for the 50th anniversary of the Custer battle, 1926

Photo courtesy University Wyoming Archives.

discovered that he had given his Sharps rifle to his grandson, Charles Hanna Carter, who was born in 1917. Hoping that Mr. Carter might still be alive, I asked Elsie Spear Byron, octogenarian historian of Sheridan, if she knew him and his whereabouts. She thought that he might still be practicing law in southern California.

I located Mr. Carter and found, to my delighted surprise, that he not only still had O.P. Hanna's Sharps rifle, but he also had a fairly complete autobiography his grandfather had written eight years before his death in 1934. It is with deepest appreciation that I acknowledge Mr. Carter's kindness, and encouragement in presenting this part of O.P. Hanna's story.

To preserve the old-timer's flavor, only a little editing has been done; a few footnotes have been added for clarity.

My Life as a Hunter and Scout 1874 - 1880

O.P. Hanna

In the winter of 1874-75 Ben Walker, George Graham and I were engaged in hunting buffalo, trapping, and poisoning wolves. We were very successful and had a fine lot of dried buffalo meat, hides and furs. Not being able to sell them for what we thought they were worth, in the spring we hired a bull team and freighted them to Fort Benton, a large government trading post, situated at the head of navigation on the Missouri River. During the high water the steamboats would get up that far loaded with all kinds of supplies for the miners and the cities of Helena, Bozeman, Butte and Virginia City.

The Diamond River Company had the largest train of bull teams in that country, consisting of fifteen teams with twelve to fifteen yoke of oxen to a team. There was a Murphy wagon, which held almost as much as a box car, and the trailers were smaller. The Broadwater Company had a long string of mule freight teams, and there were many smaller outfits which visited Fort Benton for supplies.

Outside of the government post was the small town of Fort Benton. The saloons, dance houses, hurdy gurdies, and gambling halls there were in full swing. Many a fellow lost all he possessed in one night in the gambling dens.

At Fort Benton we bought lumber from T.A. Powers & Co. with which we built a flatboat. We loaded our meat, hides and furs onto the flatboat and floated them down the river to Bismark, Dakota Territory, a distance of about nineteen hundred miles. The hides were piled around the sides of the boat and our bedding was in the center. We had a small sheetiron cook stove to make our coffee on. The Indians took several shots at us on our way down, but the high piles of hides afforded us protection.

There were millions of mosquitos. At times they were thick enough to cut with a knife. We used yards of netting around our heads, but even so the little ones would get through and many nights we could not sleep at all.

We often camped along the shore and were able to get all the fresh meat we needed; buffalo, elk, deer and one bear. We watched as they were swimming across the river and killed them as they landed.

At Fork Peck, a distance of perhaps six hundred miles from Fort Benton, we stopped over for a day. I met some of the Indians who had fought us miners in our scout of the Rosebud the year before. Fort Peck was the Agency for Sitting Bull and his tribe. Several of the Indians came to see us; they talked with us through an interpreter and admitted we were good Indian fighters. Unwittingly, through Fort Peck the Government furnished all the ammunition and supplies to the Indians for the Custer battle.

We arrived at Bismark about the first of August, sold our hides, meat and furs at a big price and divided the money. We separated and I never saw George Graham again. He went back East and Walker went down to Omaha on a boat. The railroad had reached Bismark from Chicago and I was glad to see it. I decided to go back to Illinois to see my people, and boarded the train for Chicago.

After I saw my people and had a good visit I began to be restless and in May of 1876, my sisters, Linda and Laura, went with me to Denver. At that time there was great excitement over gold in the Black Hills and thousands were going there by way of Cheyenne. I was one of the thousands. I arrived in Cheyenne to find the town full of gold-seekers on their way to the Black Hills and there was no place to sleep in the town. I rolled up my blankets and slept on a floor. I read in the newspaper that an expedition would leave Fort Fetterman, Wyoming, situated on the Platte River on the old Bozeman Trail. They would head for the Big Horn Country under the command of General Crook.

I decided to go with that expedition rather than to the Black Hills and so I traveled one hundred sixty miles to Fort Fetterman. I bought a good saddle horse and in four days I was at the Fort. I had spent eight years in the Big Horn mountain country and in the Rosebud country, where General Crook was going, and I knew all about it, the haunts of the Indians, the trails, etc. I told General Crook of my experiences on various expeditions, and he took me on as a Scout, along with others.

The expedition included fifteen troops of about one thousand cavalry. Major Noyes had five of the 2nd Cavalry; Colonel Evans about ten of the 3rd Cavalry and three hundred infantry. They were all under the command of Colonel Wm. B. Royall of the 3rd Cavalry.

General Crook was an officer of wide experience. The object of this expedition was to bring Sitting Bull, Crazy Horse and their followers back on to the Reservation. They were thought to be up in the Rosebud country, and Crazy Horse was posted as to the movements of General Crook by Indian scouts. There was an abundance of transportation, a big wagon train, and four pack trains, which proved to be of great value in the battle of the Big Bend on the Rosebud sometime later. About the 25th of May, 1876, the march north on the Bozeman Trail began, by way of Fort Reno, which had been deserted. Around June 10th we reached Tongue River, near where Goose Creek empties into that stream, and just below where Sheridan is now located.

We camped on the south side of Tongue River, and the first evening we could see the Indians at a distance. They were attracted by our camp fires and began to shoot at us from a long distance. They kept up a steady fire for some time, but they did very little damage, killing only a few horses and wounding some others. That night about one hundred fifty Crows and Shoshone Indians arrived at our camp. We had been expecting them, because they were enemies of the Sioux and Cheyennes, and they were eager to help the government conquer them. The Sioux soon disappeared.

On the morning of the 16th of June General Crook left the wagon train with the infantry to guard them and, with the cavalry and pack train, he crossed the Tongue River and took up the trail of the Indians. Before we made camp two Scouts, Frank Grouard and Little Bat, had ridden in advance and discovered Crazy Horse and his band at the Big

Bend at the head of the Rosebud, forty miles north. They returned and reported to General Crook. The trail led straight to the Big Bend of the Rosebud. During the day our Indian scouts ran into a herd of buffalo and couldn't resist the temptation to slaughter a number of them.

On the morning of the 17th we were up and moving early. About ten o'clock we stopped to rest our horses while the Indian scouts went ahead. Soon they came galloping back, yelling "Indians, the Sioux, the Sioux." Soon the Sioux Indians came dashing toward us, being careful not to venture too near. They would circle back into the hills and then charge down toward us. They had congregated in a narrow valley from two to five hundred yards wide, known as Rosebud Canyon. Here they had made preparations for battle, piling up rock and hiding on either side of the valley, hoping to entice the soldiers into the canyon where they could slaughter them.

Frank Grouard, the Chief Scout, was a South Sea islander by birth, but he had lived for many years among the Sioux. He knew their tricks and warned the officers not to follow them into that canyon. The Indians and soldiers were keeping up a constant fire, the Sioux galloping to and fro, yelling and shooting from their horses, raising a dust and making a lot of noise but doing little harm.

In the meantime the Crows and Shoshones had fallen upon the flanks of the Sioux, but with little success. Every one on the field was busily engaged and the firing was fast and furious. The Indians seemed to be as thick as blackbirds. If one fell from a shot a dozen appeared to take his place.

In one of these charges Captain Henry was shot through the face and badly wounded. He reeled in his saddle as the bullet passed through both of his cheeks; still he kept on the battle-line and held the left flank. It was his duty to be there. But eventually he fell from his horse, and it was a shock to his soldiers. They fell back and the Sioux went charging over his body, but his men rallied and rescued him.

Old Chief Washakie of the Shoshone showed splendid bravery during this fight. After this struggle the Indians picked up their wounded and all but about a dozen of their dead and retreated down the canyon, leaving behind some dead horses, blankets and trophies. There were a number of soldiers and friendly Indians killed. We camped on the battleground and during the night we buried our dead. Next morning we had to contrive some way to get our wounded back to the supply train on Tongue River, a distance of thirty-five miles. We tied long poles from one mule to another on both sides, then we nailed our canvas across these, making stretchers, and upon these we put our wounded men. Those who were not wounded too badly to ride did so. We led the mules into camp and from there they were taken in ambulances to Fort Fetterman, a distance of one hundred fifty miles, where they received medical attention.

Thus ended the battle of the Big Bend of the Rosebud, which was the forerunner to the great tragedy that occured eight days later, resulting in the massacre of General Custer and his command in the valley of the Little Big Horn.

We scouts expected that General Crook would go over into the Little Horn (Little Big Horn) where the Indians were congregating, but instead we pulled up Goose Creek to the mountains, in an opposite direction. I understood later that General Crook went up there to wait for General Merritt's command, which was on its way from Fort Fetterman.

On the 25th of June, the day of General Custer's battle, General Crook, some other officers, Frank Grouard and myself were up in the mountains fishing on what is now called Teepee Creek. We returned in the evening, never dreaming of the terrible tragedy that had overtaken General Custer.

Sibley Scouts June, 1876.

I will tell you of the "Sibley Scouts," as I was a member of that expedition. It was considered by old Indian fighters as one of the narrowest escapes from savagery.

The battle of the Big Bend of the Rosebud had just closed in June, 1876, and General Crook sent out a posse of thirty mounted men under the command of Lieutenant E.W. Sibley, to reconnoiter and see where the Indians were and what they were doing. As a scout I was ordered out with that posse; Frank Grouard was Chief of Scouts. Sibley was a young, inexperienced officer from West Point, and General Crook warned him to take the advice of the scouts should an emergency arise. Away we went to explore the country along the base of the Big Horn Mountains. We were instructed to go as far west as the Big Horn River or Fort C.F. Smith, an old, deserted fort.

We had been west to Tongue River and knew there were no Indians in that section, so we decided to go that far in the day-time and, after a good rest, make a night ride to the Big Horn River, about fifty miles farther on. We arrived safely on a little stream called Twin Creek, flowing into Pass Creek, and then into the Little Big Horn River. We had unpacked and eaten supper, when the pickets came running in, yelling "For God's sake, pack up and get out of here." They had seen the Sioux Indians, thousands of them, coming up the creek, ignorant of the troops being in that vicinity. In a short time they discovered our trail and saw us. We knew then that there was a fight on for our lives, and the mountains were our only refuge. We packed up and lit out, with Grouard in the lead and the Indians after us. We would stop and fire a volley and they would return it. We were getting to the mountains as fast as our horses would carry us, and on came the Indians whooping, yelling and firing.

It was understood that we would not surrender; we would take our own lives rather than fall into the hands of the "Red Devils" to be tortured alive. They were out for vengeance, blood and scalps.

We did not think that we could escape, but no one seemed disheartened although fear was in our hearts, for the thought of a mutilated body, scalped and left for the wolves and vultures to feed upon, was not very good food for meditation. On we rode and on the Indians came. With the yell of the Indians growing stronger, and the shots hitting nearer every moment, the Indians divided, trying to surround us. We were ordered to fire and keep up a noise, even if we didn't aim at the enemy, for the shot of a gun made a noise like a cannon among those hills. We had the best horses and reached the foot of the mountains first. We began to climb as fast as we could and the Indians were right after us.

We had gone perhaps five or six miles into the mountains when we came to Tongue River canyon and could go no further in that direction. We stopped in some pine timber where there were plenty of rocks, a good place to defend ourselves, and prepared for the "Last Stand." We battled away for four hours. We were so well fortified that not a man was killed but many of our horses were killed and wounded. It pleased me to see a man shoot a chief right through the heart. We had no way of knowing how many Indians we killed, for when the

Indian is shot his comrades get him out of sight. That was four hours of hell. Our only chance was retreat, and that chance was becoming less each minute. We kept up our defense, praying for night to come and, when darkness finally descended, Lieutenant Sibley decided that we must abandon our horses and the "retreat" was ordered. In the excitement of the moment many of the soldiers forgot to go to their saddle bags for rations. These became very weak before the expedition was over.

The only way to get out was to go down into the canyon. There was a square jump-off of fifteen feet. We had ropes, so we tied a rope to a tree, Grouard took the lead and we let ourselves down one at a time. Then Grouard took a long rope and went ahead, the rest of us following, holding on to that rope, for it was darker than a "stack of black cats." Finally we reached Tongue River, which we were forced to wade. The river was high and the water cold. It was a fierce struggle through that canyon and across the river in total darkness.

I remember that there was some thunder and lightning, which once in a while gave a ray of light to us.

During the night we could hear the Indians firing at our horses, not knowing that we had retreated. When daylight came we got out on a point of a hill overlooking the valley and could see the Indians camped along the Tongue River valley.

We didn't dare go down to level ground where it was smooth walking; we had to stay among the rocks up in the canyon where the Indians could not get to us on horseback. We could see them riding along the mountains, half a mile or more below. Some of them had uniforms on and were riding grey horses. They were coming from the "Custer Massacre," but we knew nothing of the Custer fight at that time. After a day and night with little or no food for the men, we came in sight of some soldiers from General Crook's camp. We attracted their attention and Grouard got to them and told them our troubles. Lieutenant Sibley sent them into camp to ask for an escort to go as far back as Big Goose Creek and get the two men who had refused to cross because they could not swim. Most of Sibley's men dropped to the ground, too fatigued and hungry to go any farther. Within two hours the men returned with horses and cooked food. It was a tired and sick-looking bunch of men who rode into camp and were greeted by those who had remained.

That was the end of the Sibley Scout Expedition. We told General Crook about seeing the Indians in government soldiers' uniforms and riding grey horses, and said there must have been a big fight somewhere.

On the night of July 9, 1876 Buffalo Bill Cody and Jack Crawford, two scouts, came to our camp and told us of the Custer fight, which was the first news General Crook had of the "Custer Massacre." The next day General Merrit came to our camp with his whole command, about six hundred men.

We camped on Big Goose Creek for a time and then went over onto Tongue River, but the Indians had scattered to the four winds. They knew that the United States Government would be after them in full force after the Custer battle. Sitting Bull took his tribe and lit out for Canada.

John Finnerty, who was with General Crook as a reporter for the Chicago *Times*, wanted to go to the scene of the battle, so General Crook detached about one hundred men to accompany him. I was one of those and Buffalo Bill Cody was another. We took a pack train. I knew that country like a book; I had hunted and trapped all over it years before and in 1874 I had gone with the Bozeman-Rosebud Expedition. Bill cody had a big name at that time and was riding with officers at the head of the command as Chief Scout. I will admit that I was a little envious, for I knew that I was better acquainted with that country than Buffalo Bill, and I should have been leading them.

Cody had never been up in that country and he did not know the trails through the rough Wolf Mountains. Pretty soon they passed the Old Sioux Trail which they should have taken. I had dropped back in the rear and they had traveled perhaps two miles when the Commander stopped them. I said nothing, but I knew what was the matter. Soon an orderly came back and asked if anyone had seen Hanna. I rode up to meet him. He said, "Major Baldwin wants to see you up in front." The officer said to me, "Young man, do you know this trail through the mountains?" I replied, "No Major, I don't know this route, I guess Cody knows this route." Then he snapped back at me, "Do you know any route through these mountains?" I said, "Oh, yes, I know two or three trails. We passed by the Old Sioux Trail about two miles back. We should have taken that but I thought Cody was going to take you on a nearer and better route." The officer called Cody back and said, "Cody, I think this young man knows this country better than you ever did." We retraced our steps for about two miles and took up the Old Sioux Trail.

Years later, I met Cody many times at his hotel, the Irma, in Cody, Wyoming. We became good friends and he often told that story and acknowledged that he did not know the country and was so glad that I did and that I could lead the command to the Custer battleground.

We reached the scene of the tragedy about twenty-eight days after the battle. The dead horses were lying all along the ridge; the men had been buried in shallow graves or rounded out holes by Reno's and Gibbon's men. We could see an arm here or a foot there, protruding from the little mounds of dirt where the coyotes and wolves had pulled them out.

We could follow the trails of Custer, Reno and Benteen plainly because their horses were shod. Finnerty, the reporter of the Chicago *Times*, took some pictures and made a map of the surroundings, and then we were glad to get away because the stench was something terrible.

At the point where Reno made his retreat there was an old creek bed, which had a natural breastworks, and he could have done some great execution had he taken advantage of it, for the Indians were camped out on a level flat to their disadvantage. In my opinion, had he done so there would have been a different tale to tell of the Custer Massacre, because Reno could have mowed them down by the thousands.

Most of us went back to camp where Crook and Merritt were. Cody, John Finnerty and some others continued down the Rosebud and caught a boat down the Yellowstone to civilization. General Crook, with his men, went off into the Powder River Country and the Black Hills. Frank Grouard went with them. I went with a bunch of soldiers back to Fort Fetterman by way of the "Bozeman Trail." So ended my involvement in the campaign of 1876.

Sam Stanton Expedition

In January, 1878, there was a Government expedition that left Cheyenne to carry supplies to Red Cloud Agency, Nebraska, where many hostile Indians had come and surrendered their arms.

This expedition consisted of 80 men and 112 wagons loaded with supplies for the starving Indians who had surrendered. There were over 400 work oxen drawing the wagons and all of these were to be turned over to the Indians, according to a treaty, if they would give up their arms and cease all hostilities. I heard of this expedition and decided to join them because I was always interested in the Indians. I left the Swan Brothers ranch and rode to Cheyenne to investigate if there was anything worth while in a financial way, in case I should decide to join the expedition. In Cheyenne, I met my old friend Billy Larkins who had been stock inspector for some time and I had helped him arrest some men the past summer. The first thing he said to me was, "Hanna, how would you like to go with the Stanton Expedition?" I told him I wouldn't mind going if there was anything in it. He said there would be about one hundred men; they would travel across the country where there was plenty of wild game and that they would need a hunter to furnish the fresh meat. He said he had told Major Nash at Fort D.A. Russell about me. He then took me out to the Fort and introduced me to the Major, told him I was an experienced hunter and dependable. Major Nash said he would put me on the payroll as a hunter for the expedition and also as his private detective to see that no Government goods were stolen during the trip.

Sam Stanton had charge of the property. He was quite a politician and had influence with the "powers that be," but Major Nash didn't have much confidence in him. I accepted the position and Major Nash gave me a letter of introduction to the commanding officer at Fort Robinson near the Red Cloud Agency, to whom I was to report.

The expedition left Cheyenne about the middle of January and it was bitter cold. We reached what was called Goshen Hole. There were thousands of antelope around there and we camped for a few days so I could hunt and lay in a supply of fresh meat. I killed over 20 antelope. The other men dressed them and packed them into camp.

Stanton was much pleased with my success as a hunter. That night he invited me to his tent. He had plenty of good things to eat and to drink; in fact he was a tough old cuss and tried to put on airs. I told him of many of my adventures in the Yellowstone country, which he enjoyed very much. He invited me to his tent almost every evening and I could see he was an old crook. We had traveled about one hundred miles and were camped on the Niobrara River when he asked me if I would like to make a little easy money out of the government. I replied, "Oh, I wouldn't mind it. What's your scheme?" He said that just over the hill was a big freight outfit; that they wanted to trade oxen, offering fifty dollars a yoke between their old and our young oxen and that he (Stanton) must have someone to help him make the change and it must be somebody he could depend on to go out and tell the herders that he said for them to come into camp and that I would watch the oxen. When they came in, he would come out and we would make the exchange. I did just as Stanton told me because he had charge of the expedition. As soon as the men got into camp, he was out where the oxen were. It was getting pretty dark. We ran thirty six head over the hill to the freighters and they gave us as many of their old oxen. The next morning we went on our way. Stanton also disposed of several sacks of sugar and other provisions. I was the only one who knew what he was doing.

Finally we reached White River about eight miles from Fort Robinson and went into Camp. I had to make a report to the commanding officer and I was ashamed of the part I had played, so I thought I would give Stanton a chance to get away. I rode past his tent and called to him. I said, "Stanton, did you ever suspect that I might be along with this expedition for some other purpose than just a hunter?" "No, no, no, what's the matter?" I replied that I came with the expedition as a secret service detective and I must make my report to the commander at Fort Robinson and he knew what it would be.

I rode on into the Fort and made my report. I had made a list of the property disposed of and I had over two hundred dollars which Stanton had given me which I turned over to the commander. The officer sent some soldiers out to the camp and pretty soon in they came with Stanton and put him in the guardhouse. He sent for me. I went down to see him and he said, "Hanna, I wouldn't have thought you would treat me this way, after I was so kind to you." I said, "I think I treated you pretty well when I gave you a chance to get away. Why didn't you go?" He said, "I didn't believe you, I thought you wanted me to leave so you could get charge of the expedition." The United States Marshal came and took him to Cheyenne.

It was reported that the Indians had gone on the warpath again and we were ordered to unload all the 112 wagons of supplies and put the goods in the warehouse at Red Cloud Agency, and to wait there until further orders. The men were all to go except enough to take care of the oxen, to herd and look after them, about a dozen men in all. This was in February and we remained there until July.

On June 1st 1878, Charlie Ferguson, Gus Terry and myself were subpoenaed to appear in Cheyenne as witnesses in the Sam Stanton case. It was 200 miles across an uninhabited country. I knew nothing about law and so we decided that if they wanted us they could come after us. We weren't very eager to testify against Sam Stanton anyway, so we did not go. One day there appeared on the scene Deputy United States Marshal Schnitger who put us under arrest for contempt of court for not appearing in Cheyenne. Deputy Marshal Schnitger came for us in a Government ambulance and on our way down, I told him about my experiences fighting the Indians and so forth.

When we got to Cheyenne I had on an old dirty buckskin suit and hadn't had a shave for some time nor a hair cut. I wanted to go and have a bath and clean up before I appeared before the Judge, but Schnitger said I would make a better impression if I went just as I was. I had never been in court in my life and I appeared before the Judge without any misgivings. The Judge looked stern at me and said "What excuse have you for not obeying the Supreme Court?" I replied, "Well Judge, I was two hundred miles away and had no way to get here except to walk and I didn't feel equal to the occasion." I could see sort of a smile on his face as he told the marshal, Schnitger, to take me to a hotel and get rooms for us. We felt pretty good to go to a hotel instead of to the jail. This was the old Dyer Hotel, popular with the cowboys at that time. Well, we testified at Sam Stanton's trial. He was convicted and sentenced to the pen for three years. He served a year and was then pardoned on account of old age and the political pull which he had.

Buffalo Bill, Jack Crawford, Doc Carver and several other men who were celebrated marksmen were in Cheyenne at that time and they had advertised a shooting match out at Major Talbert's in the suburbs of Cheyenne. I was a good shot. I had had much experience in hunting and fishing and at the time I was in excellent practice. While we were waiting at Red Cloud Agency I had little to do and every day I would put up a target the size of a dollar one hundred paces away. I got so I could shoot it all to pieces every time without ever missing it.

So, without saying anything to anyone (I did not want to enter the contest because it cost $50) Charlie Ferguson and Gus Terry, the boys who went down to Cheyenne with me and who knew I had been practicing, entered my name in the shooting match.

There were nine entries. I won the match and divided the money with the boys who put up the entry fee for me. Then Bill Cody challenged me to shoot alone with him for $100, and Ferguson and Terry put up the money for that. We were a tie on the first and second shots and I won the third.

The Cheyenne papers gave quite an account of it. I did not drink or use tobacco any in those days and I had a steadier nerve than any one of them.

When court was over, we were ordered back to Fort Robinson, and the Government furnished us the transportation. The Indian trouble was over and we took back a lot of men to help load up the provisions and supplies and they went on to the Pine Ridge Agency and turned them over to the Indian Agent.

Trip with Charlie Ferguson to Fort McKinney. Summer of 1878

During the summer of 1878, Charlie Ferguson and I had about decided to go over into the Black Hills and try mining for awhile. About that time the report came to Fort Robinson that the Big Horn country had been thrown open for settlement. I had declared when I was in that country in 1876 with General Crook at the time of the Custer Massacre, that if that country was ever thrown open I was going to be the first settler. I had been telling Ferguson what a wonderful country it was and I knew it would soon settle up, so he decided to go with me. We had riding horses and bought a pack horse and were soon on our way. It was about 450 miles across an uninhabited country. We traveled one whole day, twenty four hours, without striking water. This was on the Dry Cheyenne.

I was riding ahead and about 2 a.m. when my horse began to pull on the bit, I said to Ferguson, "There's water ahead. I can hardly hold my horse." Within a quarter of a mile we found a hole of water. There had been a thunderstorm that day and I can see the picture of those horses drinking at that water hole now. They were famished. We went into camp, rolled down our bedding and we were soon fast asleep.

The next day we continued our journey, arriving at the Dry Ford of Powder River and then we came on to the Bozeman Trail, the first sign of a road that we had seen for four or five days. We started down the Dry Fork and soon heard a voice, "Whoa, haw, Baldy." We found a man with six yoke of oxen teams, loaded with foods for Fort McKinney. His name was Charlie Rounds. We certainly were pleased to see him and camped with him that night. He told us all about the Government building at Fort McKinney and how it would be but a few years until the country would all be settled up with ranchers. The next day we rode into Fort McKinney on Clear Creek. The soldiers were busy laying foundations and hauling logs from the mountains for the buildings.

We made camp near by and noticed that just above us there was a camp of three men and a covered wagon. They seemed to be having a pretty hilarious time. One was singing German songs, another was singing "We are the boys that fear no noise." The other one was turning hand springs. After supper I walked up to their camp and discovered the cause of all the hilarity. In the end of the wagon they had a keg of whisky on tap and were certainly celebrating. These men were Tony Yetzer, Jack Coates and A. Sonnesberger, who all became prominent in the early history of northern Wyoming.

The trip had been pretty hard and so we remained there for a day to give our horses a rest. On the morning of the second day we resumed our journey along the Bozeman Trail. As we were riding down onto Piney Creek we discovered a cabin. Pretty soon we saw an unfamiliar object moving around the yard: I exclaimed, "By thunder, Charlie, I believe that is a woman." I took a look through my binoculars, and it was.

We soon came to the cabin and there we found Mr. and Mrs. T.J. Foster, commonly known as Jeff Foster. They certainly made us welcome. They had raised a fine garden and had plenty of green vegetables. How we did enjoy a meal cooked by a woman, and to think we were eating on a table spread with a tablecloth! I noticed the beds had sheets and pillow cases on them, all of which I called to Ferguson's attention. After a pleasant visit, we bade Mr. and Mrs. Foster goodbye and next morning started on over Massacre Hill, made famous by the Fetterman Massacre in 1866. We looked the ground over and found many relics; cartridges and shells, old muskets and caps as the Indians used muzzle loading guns at that time. That day we traveled along the head of Prairie Dog Creek. We ran into plenty of prairie chickens and sage chickens and ducks. The grass was knee high. I gazed all about and thought, what a wonderful country this is going to be.

I decided when I got to Goose Creek, right there somewhere I was going to build my future home, and so I did. Charlie Ferguson was not as enthusiastic as I was over the country, but he stayed with me until the next spring, when he said goodbye and departed for a more civilized country. He said it was too lonesome. I didn't mind it so much because I was used to that kind of life.

We arrived on Little Goose Creek in August. We looked the valley over for two or three days and I finally laid some logs for a foundation where Sheridan, Wyoming, now stands. That would hold the land for a short time. I wrote a notice that I claimed that land and I tacked my notice on one of the poles. That was at the fork of Big and Little Goose Creeks. Later I decided to move up Little Goose Creek just above where Big Horn City is situated. I expected to hunt, trap and prospect and that business was much better near the mountains.

On August 11th, 1878, with the assistance of Charlie Ferguson, I began to build the first cabin that was completed by a settler in what is now Sheridan County. We didn't have any teams to haul in the logs for my cabin. We cut small logs and peeled them of the bark, then we tied a rope around one end of the log and fastened the rope to the horn of the saddle and dragged them in.

We worked hard but we only got a few logs to where we were going to build the cabin the first day. We felt very discouraged. That evening I looked down the valley and saw a yoke of oxen. I went down to where they were and under a hill I saw an old man in camp and I soon learned that he was an old trapper named Jim Mason. He was on his way to the Upper Yellowstone. I told him that I was trying to build a cabin up the creek, but I had no team to haul out the logs. I asked what the chance would be to get him to lay over a few days and drag in the logs with his oxen. I told him I would pay him well and he consented to help me out.

In short time we had a comfortable little cabin, with a small fireplace and stone rock chimney built on the outside. We had no lumber for a door, so we made a frame out of small quaking aspen poles and then nailed a bear skin over it, and it made a good door. At one of General Crook's old camps, we found a lot of pickle bottles. I cut out part of a log on the west side of the house and placed these bottles in for a window, plastering in where they didn't fit close.

Mason was a carpenter and had a set of tools which certainly came in handy, for Ferguson and I had started to build the cabin with only an axe and a hammer. We found some old boxes at a deserted Army camp and made a table from them. These boxes were probably from the camp of Crook and Merritt because it was near there that we had camped in 1876. Our bed was built in the corner of the cabin of quaking aspen poles.

I had talked Mason into the notion of taking up a ranch, and he wanted to know where I would advise him to settle. I told him that my next choice would be down at the forks of the two creeks. We went down there and he decided to locate a ranch there on the land where Sheridan now stands.

Ferguson and I helped him build his cabin and that was the first cabin where Sheridan now is located.

After I had completed my cabin I had only six dollars and seventy-five cents left. That was almost enough to take me through the winter; in those days we had no rent to pay, no electric lights, gas, telephone, or taxes. When I wanted meat I went out and killed deer, elk, or wild chickens, and caught fish. I killed a bear to get oil for lighting. I would fill a tomato can with bear's oil, twist a rag or string for a wick and pull it through a hole in the top of the can and this made a fine light. I used the oil to cook with and I used to drink a half pint of it on a cold morning before I started out.

If we needed clothes we tanned deer hides and made garments from them. If we needed boots we killed a buffalo, skinned the hind leg from the knee down, without cutting the hide. A man's heel would fit in the hock, and all we would have to do would be to sew it across the toe and put it on while green and let it dry on the foot. There were no seams in it to leak, except around the toe, and it made an excellent boot. When we wanted a cap we trapped a beaver and made one; a coat from a buffalo skin; and bear skins covered the floors for warmth. It was not expensive living in those days. We had an abundance of wild fruit which we enjoyed in the summer and dried for winter. Later on when the settlers began to arrive, the women canned the berries in beer bottles, secured from saloons, for jellies and preserves. They used a hot iron with a handle which they put around the bottle when hot, then stuck it in cold water, when the neck would crack off even and smooth, then with a file the sharp edges would be taken off. The beer bottles were in great demand.

I wanted to do something to replenish my finances so I decided to go over to Fort McKinney and see if I could get a contract to furnish wild meat for the soldiers. Captain Pollock was Commander at the Fort. I had heard that he was a mean, disagreeable old man to deal with and he wouldn't let any one take up a ranch within twelve miles of the fort. I had gotten me a small team and wagon so I hitched up and drove over to the fort. There had been a lot of horse thieves around the fort and they had stolen some mules the day before, so the Captain had no use for any strangers.

When I drove up I asked to see the Captain and was told that he had gone up Clear Creek Canyon. They said he was riding a little sorrel mule and soon I saw him coming on the little mule. I went out and said, "Is this Captain Pollock?" He replied, "Yes, what do you want?" I told him I was a hunter and would like to get the contract to furnish the wild meat and game for the soldiers. He looked at me for a moment and said, "You look to me more like a horse thief than a hunter, and I will give you fifteen minutes to get out of this fort or I'll put you in the guard house." I didn't dare to say anything for he was the whole thing around the fort and would do just what he said he would do. so I got into my wagon and, as I left the fort, I said to myself "You old devil, I'll catch you on my ranch some day and I won't give you more than one minute to get off." When I arrived on Piney Creek, I stopped at the T.J. Foster ranch. I told them of my reception at the Fort. They had a good laugh at my expense. I hadn't had a hair cut or shave for a month or so, and I asked Mrs. Foster if I could take a look at myself in her looking glass. Well, after a good view of myself my feelings kind of softened toward Pollock. I decided I did look pretty tough. Foster said, "Had you consulted me, I would have told you of the reception you would get from Captain Pollock."

There was an old green "Yankee" by the name of Kinney, from Vermont, a regular green-horn, stopping by Foster's. He wanted to go with me to my ranch to see how we trapped and killed game. Charlie Ferguson had gone to work at Fort McKinney and I was alone, so I told Kinney it would be all right if he wanted to stop with me for awhile. I had a lot of traps set for beaver and the old man would follow me around as I was looking after the traps. Occasionally I would kill a deer or some other wild game.

One day we went to the upper end of the ranch where there was some thick brush. There had been a little snow that night. We saw where three bear had come out of the brush and gone over to a stream which was later called Jackson Creek, about one-half mile away. We saw where they had gone down into some thick brush, so I went up on a knoll overlooking it. I was satisfied that they were in that brush, because there was no trail of them leading out. From the knoll later I could see one old bear and two others about half-grown. I told Kinney to stay at the foot of the knoll and to lie behind some rocks and when I whistled to him he was to throw stones into the brush. When the bear would rear up to see where the noise came from, then I could get a shot at them. I got on the knoll and gave a whistle. Kinney had gone down into the brush and began to shake the willows, yelling at the top of his voice, "Shoo, shoo!" Pretty soon one of the bears reared up about fifty feet from him and I put the lead into it. In a minute they were all roaring and I kept a string of bullets flying until I got the last one. Kinney held his ground, yelling "Shoo, shoo, shoo" all the time. When I had killed them I went down to where Kinney was and said "My God, man, didn't you know better than to go into the brush where those bears were?" "Oh" he said "I knew you wouldn't let them hurt me." Well, he had more confidence in me than I had in myself. (Once, years later, I was telling this story, to my three children; Merle, Jesse, and Laura. They were very much interested. When I had killed the third bear I hesitated as though I was going to kill another one, and Merle exclaimed, "Hold on, Papa, don't kill any more, you have them all dead now.")

A man by the name of Charlie Farwell had a good team, so I decided to get him to haul the bear to Fort McKinney for me and to take chances of Captain Pollock putting me into the guard house. We arrived at the fort and put the bear in an old shack. The soldiers were busy looking them over and while I was skinning one of the cubs I was thinking about the Captain and that he might put me in the guard house. An idea struck me and I immediately put it into action. I cut off a ham from the little cub, wrapped it in a paper and said to one of the soldiers, "Will you please take this to Captain Pollock?" He said he would, and I sent a note with it saying "Compliments of O.P. Hanna, to Captain Pollock. From the man who looked more like a horse thief than a hunter."

Soon I saw Pollock coming across the parade ground. I thought to myself, "I guess I am in for it," but I kept on skinning the bear. When he came up I paid no attention to him. When I did look up he was standing near, looking at me. Finally he put out his hand and said, "Shake, I owe you an apology, and you can furnish all the meat you want to for the fort." We were the best of friends after that. He often stopped at my ranch when he was in that vicinity and he gave me enough government lumber to put a floor, a door and several other things in my cabin, which I greatly appreciated. The lumber I used had been hauled 150 miles from Fort Fetterman, by government freight teams.

Buffalo Hunt with Jim White, Noted Hunter 1878 - 1880

One day in September of 1878 a man drove up to my cabin with two big span of mules and two wagons and made a camp near by. He came to the cabin and asked if my name was Hanna. I said, "Yes." He said "My name is Jim White, I'm a buffalo hunter from Texas and I am hunting for a good place to locate and hunt buffalo. I was referred to you as you had roamed over this country and could advise me where to locate." That evening I went down to his camp and could see by his outfit that he was a real hunter and, I decided, a good one. He had three sixteen pound Sharp's rifles, seven hundred pounds of lead, five kegs of powder, and other hunting paraphernalia. He had an old buffalo skinner with him by the name of Watson. I told White my trouble, that I had a contract to furnish five thousand pounds of wild meat every week at Fort McKinney, and offered to take him in as a partner. He finally decided to join me, as it was getting pretty late to establish a buffalo camp that winter. White was about fifty years old, a big, stalwart, rawboned Missourian, weighing about two hundred pounds and six feet two inches tall; a good natured, easy-going fellow.

We decided to hunt first for blacktail deer on a small stream flowing into Tongue River, now called Young's Creek. The deer were very plentiful there. We arrived on the hill overlooking Young's Creek and discovered on the other side a band of about twenty blacktail. I was driving the head team and saw them first. I motioned to White and he said "We better take a shot at them before we go into camp." They were four or five hundred yards away and I was figuring which was the best way to get closer to them, when I saw White preparing to shoot from that long distance. He got out one of his big sixteen pound rifles, fifty caliber, that consumed one hundred grains of powder. The first shot hit under the belly of one and the next shot killed one. Most every shot after that I could see one fall. Pretty soon White turned around and said, "Why don't you go to shooting?" He had nine down then, so I said "Go ahead, White, you're doing fine." The deer soon passed over the hill and we pulled into camp. We took a mule and dragged the deer to camp. I said to White, "You have taken all the conceit out of me as a hunter; I can't kill deer at the distance you killed these." He replied "Throw that little popgun of yours into the wagon, use one of my big guns and practice shooting at long distance. In a short time you can kill them five hundred yards as easily as you can kill at two hundred yards. Being so far away they can't see you and run away." I took his advice and used one of his guns after that and soon could kill at as long a distance as he could. We hired two men to haul the meat into the fort while White and I did the killing. Sometimes we would load the teams in less than a day.

I remember one time we were hunting elk on Soldier Creek. I struck a band of elk and killed eleven. I said to myself "I guess this is once White will not get the best of me." When he came in , his sleeves rolled up, blood up to his elbows, he asked me how many I got. I replied with great pride "Eleven, how many did you get?" He said calmly, "Seventeen." I never tried to get ahead of him again.

We were busy all that winter filling the contract at the fort. We kept two men busy hauling the meat. That winter Jim White located land that is now the famous Polo Ranch owned by Malcolm Moncrieffe at the head of Hanna Creek.

During the summer of 1879 he left the Big Horn mountains and went north to the Yellowstone country to locate a buffalo camp for the winter. We had an understanding that if he found a good buffalo country I was to join him. Time went on and I heard nothing from him. I had about given up the hunting for that winter when, along in December, I got a letter from him, written in October, saying he had established a camp on the head of Sunday Creek, right on the divide between the Yellowstone and the Missouri Rivers, 225 miles from my cabin and 55 miles north of Miles City.

Although the snow was deep and the weather cold and stormy, and I would have to cross the Wolf Mountains, I decided to go. I had two good ponies; I packed one and rode the other. After crossing Tongue River I traveled north toward the Wolf Mountains. The snow got so deep I could not go any farther, it was belly deep to the horses. I then rode down a draw or gulch that led me into the Tongue River canyon. I started down the canyon but the snow was so deep and there was so much big sagebrush that I began to think I would have to give up the trip. Then I got the idea of traveling on the ice, as my horses were shod, and I rode two and a half days on the ice before I got through the canyon. I had nothing for my ponies to eat, so I climbed cottonwood trees and chopped out the tops for the ponies to browse on until morning. It was thirty degrees below zero, but there was plenty of wood. I scraped off the snow and built a big fire and dried the ground so it would be nice and warm to make down my bed. After getting through the canyon I ran into a bunch of buffalo and killed one, for I was out of meat. This supplied me through to Miles City.

Miles City was built in a big cottonwood grove at the mouth of Tongue River and, in the morning, the buffalo would be roaming through the streets. I put my ponies in a livery stable and went to Savage's store to inquire if they knew Jim White, the buffalo hunter. They knew him and said one of his men was in town. I hunted him up. He said White had almost given me up. I went out with White's man and it took us two days to get to camp, miles from Miles City.

When we arrived at White's camp he was certainly glad to see me, as he was about worn out getting his camp established. It was a beautiful place for a hunting location: there were thousands of buffalo, as far as the eye could reach. This was a very dangerous Indian country, but they did not frequent it so much in the winter on account of the many hardships they would have to endure. It was cold, bleak country; no wood or water. White had made a dugout in the side of a hill. It was made from poles and thirty feet square, and he had nailed buffalo hides inside and out and dug a fireplace in the hill. There we cooked our meals. We had skins for a carpet, piles of buffalo robes for a mattress, and we were fairly comfortable. After I joined him we sent a man back to Miles to get more buffalo skinners and a cook. We went into the business on a big scale, having six men to skin and take care of the hides.

When you hear a man say he was a buffalo hunter on horseback you can put him down as a "fake" as far as real buffalo hunting is concerned. Buffalo are restless animals. One day they will be traveling north by the thousands, the next day they may be going south, or some other direction. Two experienced buffalo hunters go together. We had three sixteen-pound Sharps, fifty caliber rifles, and the reason we had such heavy guns was because in those days we used black powder and when we would get what we called a "stand" on them, the small guns would get so hot in a short time they would be useless.

I will explain how we get a "stand" on them. As I said before, they travel in large droves and when we would see a drove coming we would hide in a gulch or somewhere, and when they were in good range of our guns we would both begin shooting rapidly, always shooting the leaders. When we had shot the leaders the drove would stop, for they always have a chosen leader.

Then we would wound two or three; they would walk around among the others which, smelling of blood, would begin milling around. That was what the buffalo hunter called "getting a stand" on them. From that time on only one man would shoot while the other cooled the guns with water, cleaned and reloaded them, taking turns at shooting. Every little while one buffalo would start to take the lead and we would get him. Sometimes we would get forty or fifty, all the men could skin in one day.[1] We did not wish to leave any, for they would freeze so hard by morning that we could not skin them.

We used the softest lead that we could buy and when the bullets hit an animal they would flatten out like a one-cent piece, tearing a hole in the buffalo and generally stop on the opposite side against the hide, where the skinner would extract it and save the lead to remold. Lead was very expensive and we reloaded all of our shells.

After we had killed all that the boys could skin in one day we went back to our shack and reloaded enough ammunition for the next day. Some of our men were experts and could skin twenty-five or thirty buffalo in one day. They began first by skinning the head, then they would cut it off, laying it aside, then turn the body on the back with legs straight up, using the head under the side to keep the body from falling over. They would then skin the legs and half way down the sides, leave the animal and pass on to the next one. A man with a mule and a chain would follow up, hitch the chain to the buffalo's tail and pull the hide off, thus saving a lot of time. When they got all that the mules could haul they would load the hides on a sled and take them to camp, where a man would stake them out and, when dry, pile them up in stacks ready for the bull freight teams, when they arrived, to haul them to the Yellowstone River. There they would be stacked again, waiting for the boats to come up the Missouri and Yellowstone Rivers in June, during the high water. On the trips up the boats brought supplies for all the buffalo hunters.

We saved most of the extra good meat, built a smoke house out of rock, and smoked and dried some of it. We also placed tons of the choice meat under a bank where snow would drift over it. It would keep perfectly there for two or more months, when we would send it in by ox-teams and sell it to the soldiers and people around Miles City. It was cold-storage meat and the choicest. We saved all the tongues, which were worth fifty cents each.

There was a vein of lignite coal near our camp, but it would not burn very well, so we saved all the suet from the buffalo and mixed it with the coal and it made a fine fire.

[1]Several documented stands have been recorded.

YEAR	HUNTER	CALIBER	SHOTS	KILLS/ STANDS
1882	Chambers	.40-90	35	16
	Hudson	.40-90-370PP	32	29
			64	32
			71	45
1875	White	.50-90	47	46
1883	Hudson	.40-90-370PP	79	49
1882	Chambers	.40-90	79	54
	Hudson	.40-90-370PP	108	58
	Maguire	.40-90-340	98	61
	Andrews		115	63
1873	Light	.50-90		74
	Edwards			75
1872	Reighard	.50-90	91	79
	Zahl			85
1876	Mooar	.50-90		96
1873	Jordan			100
1873	Rath			107
1882	Smith			107
1873	Nixon	.50-90		120
1879	White	.50-90		120
	Zahl			120
	Collinson	.45-100		121
	Nixon	.50-90		204

A record was set and broken for the most buffalo skinned by one man in one day. Mickey Carr's record of 65 was broken by Bill Hillman, who skinned and pegged out hides of 70 buffalo cows in less than 10 hours.

RECORD KILLS IN ONE SEASON OR TOTAL CAREER BY HUNTER/YEAR

PERIOD	HUNTER	KILLS/SEASON	CAREER
35 days in 1873	Tom Nixon	2173	
season of '73-'74	Zack Light	2300+	
1872	Tom Linton	3000+	
Sept '73-Apr '74	Bill Tilghman	3300+	
season of '77-'78	Joe McCombs	4900	12200
	Vic Smith	5000	
60 days in 1876	Brick Bond	5855 300 one day	
1872-1875	Jim Cator	4000/yr avg.	16000
1872-1880	Jim White		19000
1872-1878	J. Wright Mooar		20500

We had been hunting about two months and had about twenty-six hundred hides, when something happened. Although we knew that we were in a dangerous Indian country, the weather was so cold and the snow so deep that we had become careless. We did not think that the Indians would come up into that bleak country. We were camped at the head of Sunday Creek, on the divide between the Yellowstone and the Missouri Rivers. It was about one hundred miles from one stream to the other. We had made some branch camps out five or six miles from the main camp. When the buffalo would shy around the main camp, we would go out to one of the other camps for a day or two. We were out at one of these camps and had killed about forty buffalo; the skinners were behind with their work, and White told me to go back to camp and start supper, (the cook was taking a vacation) while he helped the boys to get the hides to camp. We had eleven head of mules and horses and when I arrived at our little dugout they were peacefully grazing on the flat above. I started a fire and was busy getting supper when White came in, about dusk , and said "Did you see anything of the horses?" I told him they were up on the flat when I came down. He said that he did not see them, so I told him to look after the supper and I would go up and bring them back, as I thought they had started for the main camp. I took my gun and hadn't gone more than seventy-five yards when I discovered Indian moccasin tracks. I shouted to White that the Indians had our horses and mules. He came running out and we followed the tracks to the top of the hill. Not more than half a mile away we could see them driving our stock through a herd of buffalo. We fired several shots without effect, so we returned to camp. The next morning we discovered that they had been hiding in the draw waiting to steal the stock. When I came down to the dugout we found where an Indian had hidden behind a rock, to kill me if I had come outside before they got away with the horses and mules. Had I gone outside I wouldn't be telling the story now.

The next day we made some sleds out of the sideboards of our wagons, hitched ourselves to them and pulled down to the main camp, where we found everything all right. Later, we learned that the Indians were a band of Sioux from Poplar Creek Agency on a horse-stealing expedition.

Our camp was fifty-five miles from Miles City and some one had to go there. I was the only one who was tough enough; I was only twenty-eight years old, and White was fifty. I volunteered to go. I filled my pockets with bread and meat, mostly dried, took a good supply of ammunition and, bidding the boys goodbye, started for Miles City after dark, in the deep snow, through the hills, with not a sign of a trail. I could see the stars when I started and the North Star helped me keep my direction. I knew there would be no wood for at least thirty miles.

Well, talk about a hard trip! I certainly had it that time. Part of the time the snow would hold me up and often I would break through, and it would be knee deep. I ran into several herds of buffalo and the wolves were howling on every side. About two o'clock in the morning there came up a chinook wind, which melted the snow, as it blew against me, wetting my clothes, but in a short time the wind changed to a northwester and it began to get colder and to snow. I was warm from walking and did not dare to stop for fear of freezing, although I was very tired. I kept hoping that I would strike a gulch or draw leading toward the Yellowstone that I could follow and it might lead me to where there was wood and water and I could make a fire and dry my clothes. I was getting so cold and tired that I often stumbled and fell. I felt like lying down and going to sleep, then I would think "Brace up, or you are a goner." At that time I was traveling down a draw but no sign of wood. At times I imagined I could hear some one talking, but soon realized it was only my imagination. Pretty soon I smelled coal burning and all at once I could see smoke. It was a burning coal bank that had been burning for years. It was daylight and still snowing. The fire from the coal had burned back under the rocks for a hundred feet or more and the ashes, which were six inches deep, were warm. I crawled under the rocks, with a rock at my head, lay down and was soon fast asleep. I had slept about two hours when I began dreaming of snakes. Suddenly I awoke to find I was in a den of rattlesnakes that had gone in that warm place for the winter and they were investigating me while I slept. I'll bet I jumped ten feet to get out of there. Well, I was warm, my clothes were dry and I was rested. The sky was clear and the sun shining brightly. I decided that the snakes hadn't bit me, so I ate some lunch and continued on my journey. I arrived at Miles City twenty-two hours after I left our camp, tired, oh, so tired. It makes me tired and shivery now to think of that trip, when I sometimes broke through the snow up to my waist.

The next day after I arrived in Miles City, some hunters came into town from the mouth of the Rosebud. They had seen some Indians with a bunch of horses and mules across the Yellowstone, near the mouth of the Rosebud. I felt sure that it was our stock and I tried to get a horse, but there was none to be had that was fit for the trip. I went up to Fort Keogh and there met a noted scout, Yellowstone Kelly, and had a talk with him. General Miles was in command at the fort and so I went to him and told him my troubles. In those days the government was always willing to help us because they wanted to get the buffalo killed off, for as long as the Indians could get plenty of buffalo meat they would go on the war path and not surrender or give up their firearms. The government wanted them to stay on the reservation and be furnished supplies. I asked General Miles for some horses, telling him I wanted to follow up the Indians and rescue our stock. He said he could not let me have government horses but told me to come around in about an hour and he would see what he could do for me.

At the appointed time I went over to the General's quarters. He greeted me and said "Some of the boys are anxious for a little trip, so I have detached ten soldiers with ten days rations and two packers to accompany you." We started about 2:00 o'clock p.m. and traveled twenty-five miles when we discovered tracks where the Indians had crossed the Yellowstone on the ice. I knew the tracks because the mules were shod. We took the trail up the Rosebud, the same Rosebud that Custer had followed to his last battle and the same on which the Bozeman-Big Horn Expedition, of which I was a member, fought for their lives in 1874.

All night we followed their trail but we did not overtake them. When daylight came we stopped for breakfast and slept while our horses were grazing. In about three hours we saddled up the horses and continued on the trail. We were going directly south and about sundown we saw them in rendezvous in some pine timber above the mouth of Lame Deer Creek. We held a consultation and decided not to molest them at that time but to make camp under the hill, get some supper and some sleep, and to attack their camp about three o'clock a.m., while they were sleeping, and clean up the whole bunch.

They had been stealing horses from other hunters who had joined us in the chase. The Indians had about forty head. We unpacked and were getting supper when one of the guards came in and said, "Boys, they've discovered us and are pulling out toward the Little Horn." We were tired and hungry and decided to have some supper and a little sleep. About midnight we saddled our horses and continued on their trail. When daylight came the Indians were in sight but several miles away. They turned down Tullock Creek and were headed north for the Missouri River from whence they came. We followed them and would occasionally get a shot at them. We must have wounded some, for there was blood on the trail. Finally they dropped out a pair of mules and soon they let another pair drop back. The mules were contrary and hard to drive and we were gaining on them. I felt pretty good to get those mules back, for they were big fellows and worth $400.00 a span. It was here that I took the last shot at the Indians on this trip. An old Indian was riding "Bones," my mount. I fired at that Indian but did not get him. That night we were back on the divide of the Yellowstone and the Missouri Rivers. The Indians were passing around Sheep Mountain, the mercury down to twenty below, and there was deep snow. The soldiers decided that was as far as they wanted to go. I didn't care very much, because I had the mules which were worth more than all the rest of the ponies. I think we were about ten miles from our main camp. We had been traveling in a circle and, although I was very tired, I decided to ride into camp that night. The soldiers started for Miles City, expecting to camp when they found wood. I returned the horse the General had loaned me and jumped on one of the mules, bade the soldiers good bye and "lit out" for Jim White's camp. It was much farther than I thought and I was so stiff and tired when I got there that I could not get off the mule. I called to White, who came and helped me off and hugged me as though I was a little child. He carried me into the shack, got hot coffee for me and prepared supper. I then told him my story. White said "Hanna, you've more pluck and endurance than any one I ever knew." They all thought I had perished in the storm the night I left.

The thieving bands of Sioux became so bad that we had to give up hunting buffalo. We couldn't get the skinners to work because it was too dangerous. We kept the men there on salary for about a month to guard the hides and along in March there came a chinook and caused a big thaw, the snow disappeared and we were able to get a lot of freight teams to come out to the camp. We loaded the hides on their wagons and they were hauled to the Yellowstone near Miles City, where we piled them up along the bank and placed guards over them, to await the steamboats which would come up in May or June. There were no roads and, in order to cross the gulches and draws that had drifted full of snow, the men made a bridge of buffalo hides on top of the snow, three or four deep, and the teams would draw the wagons across on the hides. In this way they would not break through the snow and ice. The steamboats brought up supplies for the buffalo hunters and bought their hides, dried meat, tongues and furs. There were also many skins of wolves which we had poisoned and shot. I have seen a dozen steamboats going down the river loaded so high with buffalo hides that one couldn't see much but the smoke stack.

It was estimated that there were over two hundred thousand buffalo killed along the Yellowstone during the winter of 1879-1880.[2] The hides were piled along the river for miles and miles, waiting for the boats. That was about the last of the buffalo hunting.

In Miles City there were many saloons and each dispenser of liquid refreshments had a formula for making "tangle foot," a quantity of boiled mountain sage and two plugs of tobacco, steeped in water; if any one got low on whiskey he promptly manufactured some. Saloons, gambling houses, and public dance halls (hurdy gurdies) ran wide open. A dance at one of the hurdy gurdies cost $1.00 and, as each

[2]*The Yellowstone Journal* states that Custer Co., which then comprised the entire southeastern corner of Montana, shipped 180,000 hides in 1882. In May, 1881 the *C.K. Peck* alone had 10,000 hides on board (Brown and Felton 1955:75).

He lit out barefoot through the sagebrush

dance wound up with an invitation to visit the "bar" where drinks for self and partner were expected, the cost of a waltz, schottische or quadrille was usually $1.50. Dances continued all night and every sort of gambling was indulged in.

After we came in from the buffalo range we had nothing to do until the boats arrived for the hides. Some of us would take a hand at the gambling table and I got to thinking that I could play poker a little. Of course there were plenty to play with me and I generally lost. One night I was sitting in a game with an old fellow and a real gambler; his name was "Flick." There were also several others in the game. Pretty soon "Flick" had all the money, so I went to my room. "Flick" boarded where I did and pretty soon he came in and saw me sitting in there reading. He came up to me and, taking out a roll of bills, extracted $15.00, the amount he had won from me, threw it on the table and said "Hanna, here is the $15.00 I robbed you of." I said "No, I will not take it; if I had won I would have kept it." He said "You had no show to win my money, and any old woman could beat you gambling. I could look in your face and tell what you were holding. For God's sake, Hanna, make me a promise that you will not try to gamble again." I made that promise and I have always kept it.

"Flick" was a good fellow, as far as a gambler goes; when he had money all of his friends shared it with him. One day I was standing behind him, watching him in a Faro game, and he finally lost his last cent. He scratched his head and said "By thunder, a man who has gambled as long as I have and hasn't anything, the Government should give him a pension." I laughed heartily at such a speech. He looked around and said, "Hanna, give me a dollar." I gave him $5.00 which he put on a card and doubled it. He never left the table until he had won $700.00.

White was a man who sometimes drank and when he did he often would go the limit. After we quit hunting buffalo he got on a spree in Miles City. I was quite disgusted with him. We had sold our buffalo hides, received the money for them and, when we paid our men and settled our other bills, we had very little left, but plenty of experience.

One day White suggested that we go back to the Big Horns, and I was willing. He had two wagons and two spans of mules. He drove one and I the other. He had been drinking pretty hard and I knew he would have to have some to sober up on, so I bought a quart of whiskey and hid it in my wagon. We slept together, and one morning about daylight he jumped out of bed and let out, barefoot, through the sagebrush, shouting "No, you don't; no, you don't." I knew that he had the *delirium tremens* and I started after him with the whiskey, telling him I was his friend. Pretty soon he sat down on a rock and began to cry. I gave him a drink and got him back to camp.

He was soon over the DTs and while we were eating breakfast he said, "Oliver, I know you are a friend of mine and I want to tell you something that I have never told a living soul." He said, "I was born in Missouri. When I was thirty years old I fell in love with a nice girl and we were married. After a few years we drifted down into Old Mexico. An old rich Spaniard won my wife from me and I killed him. I fled to the mountains and stayed there for six months, eventually getting to the southern part of Mexico. I walked 700 miles. There was a $5000.00 reward for me. Since then I have just drifted around from place to place and that is the reason I get to drinking and when I do I imagine they are after me."

We finally arrived safely at my ranch in June and found the Benefiel family still there and taking good care of everything.

White gave up his ranch and located another on Soldier Creek, 160 acres, a part of what is now known as the P.K. Ranch.

I spent the remainder of the summer with a party of English nobility hunting in the mountains and that fall, Jim White and I decided to cross the mountains into the Big Horn Basin. We went around by Pryor's Gap and established a camp on Shell Creek at the base of the Big Horn Mountains on the west. We built a cabin and were fixed up very comfortable. We planned to hunt wild game and to trap. Beaver were plentiful and there were thousands of elk and deer. Our object also was to poison wolves for their hides.

The country was a rendezvous for all kinds of outlaws. One day three men came along and camped a short distance below us. I went down to their camp and talked awhile with them. They did not seem very friendly and I did not feel comfortable with them. That night something seemed to tell me to go back over to my ranch, and the next night I had the same feeling, but much stronger. So the next morning I told White that I wanted to go over to the ranch. He said "What for, why do you want to go?" I told him that if I didn't go then the snow in the mountains would get so deep that I would not be able to cross until the next June. I told him I would only be gone about a week. This was the last of October.

I packed my pony and rode another. It was seventy-five miles across the mountains, by short cut. In two days I landed at my ranch and found everything all right. I didn't have that strange premonition any more and thought to myself, "What a fool I was to let a thing like that cause me to take that long, hard trip through the mountains." In a couple of days I started back and made the trip in good time.

On my arrival at the cabin I received a great shock. I found that White, wagons, mules and everything were gone. I thought it so strange that White would go away like that, and I began looking around. I found fresh dirt under some pine trees. Scraping away the snow I saw that there had been something buried there. I thought "Could it be possible that those tough looking fellows had killed Jim White?" I found an old shovel, dug down about two feet and found him, rolled up in a buffalo robe. He had been shot in the back of the head, which proved that he had been shot by some one behind him. If I had not gone away they would have killed me also. They wanted our good outfit of four guns, three big sixteen-pound Sharps rifles, mules, wagons, bedding, buffalo robes, hides, furs, etc.

Jim White was the greatest buffalo hunter the world has ever known. One day I asked him how many buffalo he had ever killed. He went to an old box that he carried his things in and took out an old greasy book and said "I have most of them down here. I killed so many on the Panhandle in Texas, so many at Fort Hays in Kansas, and so on." I kept account as he read until I had counted sixteen thousand.

About twenty-seven years later I was in the Big Horn Basin, which was all settled up with stockmen and ranchers. I was having my horses shod at a blacksmith shop in a little town named Hyattville. I saw an old Sharps rifle in the corner and, as I looked at it, I said "Hello, here is an old gun that looks like my old buffalo gun." I examined it and exclaimed, "By George, it is my old gun! Here is my initial 'H' on it." The murderers of Jim White had taken all of our guns.

I dug down and found him rolled up in a buffalo robe

Hunting with English Lords

In the summer of 1880 two wealthy English lords, William and Morton Frewen, from London, located a big stock ranch on upper Powder River. They at once proceeded to build what was considered then a "mansion" out of logs for the purpose of entertaining their friends from England. Lords, Ladies, Dukes, Earls, and other members of the nobility, came over from England to hunt in the Big Horn mountains.

Soon after my return from the Big Horn Basin, where I found Jim White had been murdered (October, 1880), I received a letter from Frewen saying I had been recommended to them as a responsible guide and hunter. He wanted to know what would be the chance of employing me to go out with their party on a trip in the Big Horns. I did not wait to write but jumped on "Buster," my riding pony, one of the best in the country, and in twenty-four hours I was at the Frewen ranch, a distance of ninety-three miles. On that trip I really learned what a fine piece of horse flesh Buster was. He was my prize saddle horse for twelve years after that.

I had a talk with the Frewen brothers and told them that I had at one time been with Lord Dunraven in the Yellowstone National Park. They looked up Lord Dunraven's report of that trip and found my name. They employed me at $10.00 a day. I at once began to get the outfit together, provisions, bedding, etc. There were twenty-one riding and pack horses. In three days we were ready to start. There were, as I remember, four Englishmen in the party besides Lord Frewen; Lord Rodney; Captain Ashton of the English Army; Lady Ashton; and a man by the name of Wise, an officer in the English Army. Then there were other hunters, cooks and packers in the party.

Every evening the Englishmen would go out riding to get toughened up for the trip. They generally ran a race back to the corrals. One evening they were going out for a ride and the officer, Wise, was having trouble in getting a horse to suit him. I said to him "Take Buster, my riding horse" and I pointed over to him. "What" he said "That rum little horse, do you think he can carry me?" I told him I thought he could, because he had just carried me ninety-three miles in twenty-four hours. So, he decided to ride Buster.

Now Buster was a race horse, and a good one, too. When he wanted to run he would take the bit between his teeth and keep going until he was tired. I had to have a special ring bit made for him later on. This particular time, when they turned to race back, I saw them coming and told the boys to look out for some fun. Here they came, Buster one hundred feet ahead of the others, the Englishman pulling on the bridle with all his might and yelling "Whoa, whoa." Buster paid no attention until he got to the stable, when he stopped so suddenly that his rider went on over his head and lay on the ground for awhile.

When he got up I said "Well, do you think that 'rum little thing' can carry you?" He replied "By Jove, he's a great little beast to run. I'd like to buy him." I told him that Buster was not for sale.

In about three days we were on our journey. We traveled a few days and stopped on top of the Big Horn mountains at the head of Powder River, where elk, deer, bear and mountain sheep were very plentiful. We had been hunting about two weeks and had killed ten bear, a lot of fine elk and deer, also mountain sheep. The party saved several fine heads to have mounted to take back to London. There were good cooks, camp tenders and other hunters with the party, but the Englishmen took turns hunting with me.

The way we hunted for bear was to kill a deer or elk and hang it in a tree where we thought bear were likely to come. When the venison would begin to rot, a bear would scent it a mile away and would soon be around it until it was all eaten. We would go out about sun rise, find Mr. Bear, and begin to put the lead into him. The bear would often come for us and we had several narrow escapes.

There were many funny things that happened. One day I was out hunting with Captain Ashton, who was not a good shot. He had wounded an elk and had been following it for some distance. I got tired and was sitting on some rocks overlooking a little canyon about three hundred yards across. Over there I saw his wounded elk. It was a pretty shot for me, so I fired away and the elk fell dead. I went around to where the Captain was and found him looking pretty sober. I said "By golly, Captain, that is a pretty pair of horns." He replied, "Yes, but I wouldn't give a damn for them; I didn't kill the elk."

He also informed me in pretty plain words that they weren't paying me $10.00 a day for my own amusement. He said "In the future you wait until I tell you that I need your assistance," and I said "All right."

In a few days I was out hunting again with the Captain. He wounded a bear and it had gone down into a brushy swamp. Pretty soon I saw the bear lying in the mud. I was not to shoot until I was told to do so, and I called to the Captain "There he is," and he went down after him. I dropped back behind some pine trees and soon I heard the brush begin to snap and crack and here came the Captain and the bear close behind at the pony's heels, the Captain whipping his mount at every jump. I could have killed the bear, but I knew the pony would outrun him. Pretty soon the bear turned and went back into the brush. In a few minutes the Captain came back looking as white as a sheet. I said "Captain, that bear gave you a pretty close shave." "Yes" said he, "Why didn't you give me a hand?" I replied "Why, you told me a few days ago that when you needed my help you would let me know, and I was waiting for the signal." "Well, I want some right now." he said, and we soon finished Mr. Bruin.

There was one Englishman in the party whom none of them liked very well. One day I had been out hunting with him and we had poor luck. He was not in a very good humor and kept complaining until I was getting rather sick of it. He said he thought we had better go back to camp. It was almost sundown as we started and I was jogging along at a pretty good pace when he said "I say, hadn't we better get back to camp?" I replied that I was going to camp as fast as I could. He said I was going in the wrong direction, and kept talking as he followed me. We came to a ridge. It was nearly dark and as I turned to the left he turned in the wrong direction. I was soon in camp and they all wanted to know where the Englishman was. When I told them that he would not follow me they said it would do him good to have to lie out in the mountains for a night. It wasn't long until we heard some shots. I was going to answer them but the others said "No, not yet." The next time the shots were farther away, and then we began to answer them. He was a sorry sight when he finally arrived at camp about eleven o'clock. They told him there was no one to blame but himself.

One morning about sunrise I went out with Captain Wise to get bait for bear. About three miles from camp there was a big cinnamon bear, as large as a horse. He had eaten all that he wanted of the bait and was covering up the remainder of the deer with dirt. We crawled up within a hundred yards and gave him two or three shots. He was badly wounded but got away. We trailed him by the blood for a mile or more when his trail led down into a quaking aspen grove. Captain

O.P. Hanna, Sheridan merchant
Photo courtesy University of Wyoming Archives.

Wise wanted to go in after him, but I refused to go. I told him "That old fellow will be on the fight" and I felt sure he would go no farther. I proposed that he go around the brush to the right and I go to the left and try to locate him without getting into the brush. We started and I was up on a small sagebrush hill when the Captain called "Here he is."

He didn't wait for me to get there but fired away with his English express rifle, which shot an explosive ball and was not a good gun for bear. The brush began to crack and the bear's howls fairly rent the hills around. I knew he was coming. The Captain whirled and ran with the bear at his heels. I fired and knocked the bear down. Captain Wise had time to get behind a bunch of brush, but I was standing out in the open where he could see me and, with a roar that made the mountains ring, he started for me.

When the bear was within fifteen feet I fired at him. I was trying to shoot him in the head as he was running toward me, but I shot a little too high. I whirled and ran and was trying to reload my gun when it caught under the sagebrush and I dropped it.

I stumbed and fell and ran my head in the sagebrush. I jerked out my six-shooter, but the bear jumped on me with one big paw on my head and the other on my side. He grabbed me by the left arm and, although I had on two heavy buckskin shirts, he chewed my arm up to the shoulder. I finally got my six-shooter against his side and fired several shots into him. He released his hold on my shoulder and fell over dead on top of me.

It was a lucky thing I had fallen down, for the bear mashed the sagebrush down over my head protecting it.

He was a big cinnamon, so old that his tusks were broken off. That is what saved my arm from being crushed. Had I been standing he would have struck me with his paw and probably killed me.

Captain Wise had got on top of a hill and was firing the lead into the bear and was just as liable to hit me as the bear in his excitement. I finally got him to understand that the bear was dead. That was an exciting time for us.

The Captain got a pole and pried the bear off of me. I came out of it with a broken rib, several gashes in my head and with my arm badly chewed up. I was beginning to feel pretty bad by the time Captain Wise got the horses.

It seemed that my horse, Buster, knew that something was wrong with me. The Captain led him up to a rock where I could get on him.

The Hanna-White cabin at Old Trail Town, Cody
Photo courtesy Randi Gilbert.

He stood very still and walked quite carefully all the way to camp, letting Captain Wise lead him; he was usually very nervous and excitable.

The Captain gave me the credit for saving his life. If I had not knocked the bear down when it was after him it would have killed him in another jump. I was black and blue all over in addition to my wounds. The Englishmen fixed me up in a nice tent. One of the men was a good doctor. He dressed my wounds but it was ten days before I could walk, and a long time before my arm was well. They certainly took good care of me.

The next day the Captain and some of the other men went to get the bear but they could not find him. When they returned I made a map for them and then they had no trouble in locating him. They brought his skin and head back to camp. It was about eight feet long and seven feet wide.

A few days after our bear experience the party was all out hunting. I was lying in my bed on the ground. I could hear an elk bugling. I put my ear to the ground and could hear him plainly. The men had no luck and did not stay out very long. I called one of them to the tent and told him that if they would go out northeast about a half mile they would find a band of elk. They went as I directed and brought back two fine heads. Later, I heard the men talking in another tent. One of them said "Hanna can lie in bed and beat the others locating game."

As soon as I was able to ride one of the men started with me for the Frewen ranch. We got down to the famous Hole in the Wall country, the rendezvous of road agents, cattle rustlers and other notorious characters. We stayed all night in one of their cabins. I was so worn out that we could no farther. The next day we went on to the Frewen ranch, where I could have better care. The hunting party did not return for a week. In about twenty days I was able to ride over to the T.J. Foster ranch and then on to my own ranch.

When the English party returned to London they took the bear skin and head with them, had it mounted and presented it to the museum in London. Captain Wise wrote the history of it and while I was ill, he paid me $10.00 a day and made me a present of $400.00 for saving his life.

I used that money to buy wire for fencing my ranch. T.J. Foster bought the wire for me in Cheyenne. It cost me sixteen-cents a pound, freight and wire. The next year I had letters from a party of

Englishmen, sixteen in number, wanting me to go with them on a hunting trip in the Rockies, as well as in the Big Horn. I refused, as I had made up my mind to improve my ranch, and it was too risky a business, hunting bear under the dictation of inexperienced parties.

Nineteen bars of lead were recovered from the site of the Hanna-White cabin on White's Creek in the Big Horn mountains. This specimen weighs 6.5 ounces, is .2 inch thick, .54 inch wide, and 10.5 inches long. It is a convenient size for melting in a small, handled crucible. Such small bars were purchased in sacks of 25 pounds. Lead bar courtesy of Bob Edgar, Old Trail Town; photo courtesy of Tony Silveus, Silver Images Photography, Flagstaff.

Chapter 8

Robert Loren Chambers was one of the very few buffalo hunters who invested the profits from his hunting. He invested in his education, graduating from Wesleyan University in Bloomington, Illinois. He taught and became principal at Morgansville, Kansas. He homesteaded, took out a timber contract, and studied law. Eventually he practiced law in Kenneth, Hoxie, and Colby, Kansas, before moving to Colorado Springs in 1895. He composed the following narrative in 1939 at the age of 80. Very little editing has been done, and that only to make the reading a bit smoother.

Forty Days on the Montana Buffalo Range

Robert Loren Chambers

During the time that I had spent in Miles City, I met many professional buffalo hunters, and I always talked with them about the money to be made in their work. They told me about the increasing difficulty of making big stands, but even so a hunter could average about fifty head a day. With the price of hides and tongues together at about $2.75, the money to be made as a professional buffalo hunter seemed to me to be pretty good.

I teamed up to help one of them, Jim Grimmit, and learn the business, planning to get into shooting for myself eventually.

He was a long, lean, lank Missourian, and taller than me. He stood in well with the soldiers at Fort Keogh, and through their friendship he was able to obtain bargains in horses and mules that the army officers wished to sell. He purchased a magnificent pair of dapple gray horses and a pair of very large mules that had been condemned as runaways. Grimmit wanted the horses and mules to use hauling hides.

After purchasing the stock, he was afraid to drive them himself. So, he hired me to drive them to Jackson's Ranch, about 200 miles away on Horse Creek, a northern tributary of the Yellowstone River. I took the job because I was eager to learn as much as I could about buffalo hunting.

We loaded up the wagon with loose hay and boomed it down from the top with a couple of spring poles.

The first difficulty of the trip was in fording Tongue River which was in flood. We took the horses over first, then the mules. Next we hitched to the wagon with long ropes from across the river, and finally ferried everything across.

I took up the lines and started driving these four condemned runaways toward Ft. Keogh, with Grimmit accompanying me on horse back. Everything went well until we neared the fort where the road was good and hard. The team spurted into a run and I tugged at the lines, clinging to the boom pole on top of the load of hay. The four runaways ran faster and faster right to the fort. A company of soldiers was drilling, and seeing the dilemma I was in, they swung a line across the road, grabbed the heads of the lead team, and finally brought us to a stop.

We travelled on from the fort for several days along the north side of the river without any incident of note, except that occasionally the Indians would shoot at us from long distance. We knew that our gravest danger from the Indians was that they would try to steal the horses and mules. Stealing stock was their principal occupation in those days. They would fight only if cornered, or if they had all the advantage.

One night after a long and tiring drive we made camp and had some sow-belly and coffee. Making certain that the horses and mules were securely fastened, we went to sleep, concealing ourselves as best we could in the brush near the wagon.

We had four stout leather-covered chains tied around the stock animals, the other ends secured to the wagons. The Indians wouldn't be able to cut through these. Several times during the night we were awakened by the snorting and stamping of the horses. We fired into the air to scare away whatever had bothered them. Next morning we found where the Indians had tried to cut through the chains.

When we were about half way to the Jackson Ranch, we noticed that there was a band of Indians on higher ground, and we became genuinely alarmed. Grimmit suggested that he ride ahead to get some help at the ranch so that we would not be out alone on the road with the wagon and provisions another night. I heartily agreed, and he hurried off, saying that he would be back before dark.

I drove along feeling very uneasy, because I could see Indians dodging behind rocks on the high ridges above the road up ahead. I was sure that they were only waiting until dark to attempt to steal the horses and mules. I determined to drive as fast as possible to reach the ranch before dark, if possible.

Although the wagon was heavily loaded, I kept the team to a good trot until about five o'clock when a dark cloud rolled up from the northwest. In a few minutes rain and hail pelted down in torrents. Wet, cold, and uneasy, I resolved again to keep going as long as possible, hoping that Grimmit would come with help.

All at once I came to the ford at Horse Creek. It was impassable. The rain had flooded the stream from bank to bank which no doubt explained why Grimmit had not come back for me. I did not see how I could get across that swollen stream either. Getting down from the wagon and taking a long pole, I measured the depth of the water. It was swimming deep to the mules. Discouraged, I climbed up on the wagon just in time to see several Indians coming through the dusk!

They were not sneaking along and hiding as they had been; now they were confident of their success.

The stream was fully fifty feet wide and running like a mill-race. But whatever the risk, I was determined now to try to cross before the Sioux caught up to me. The horses had been hitched as the lead team with the bigger mules behind, and now I circled them fully a hundred yards away from the bank, then yelling lustily, I headed them straight at the roaring stream.

As they went over the seven foot high bank, the horses seemed to fall right on their heads, the mules right behind. As the wagon lurched over, I uttered a short prayer and hung on, fearing that the wagon would turn over as we drifted rapidly toward the Yellowstone only a hundred yards away.

I seized the whip and the lines, guiding the team across the stream. They swam powerfully and eventually the horses found a little footing and struggled up onto the bank, the mules following them out of the stream. Now, though, the wagon was tipping under and the load of hay swept below the water line as the front wheels hit the bank. It was a straight up pull to raise that water-logged load up the bank. Cracking the whip and yelling at the team, I urged them to pull and pull hard.

Each team settled down to steady pulling with every ounce of their combined strength. They never wavered, and my excitement seemed to bring out an added effort from those magnificent animals. Slowly, steadily they pulled and pulled. The front wheels raised and water began pouring out the back of the wagon, lightening the load. It seemed like an eternity to me, but finally we were out of danger from the swollen stream.

I looked back across what I had feared would be my watery grave, and there stood three big savages. I knew that they wouldn't try to catch me now, since they were afoot. I kept the team going toward the ranch at a slower pace, and arrived there about midnight.

Grimmit seemed greatly surprised and relieved to see me, and he was highly elated that I had not lost the horses and mules. When the storm started, he gave up the idea of returning to help me. To this day, I do not believe that he expected to ever see me or his team again.

While at Jackson's ranch I met many professional buffalo hunters who made the ranch headquarters for their own protection. From them I learned a great deal about buffalo hunting. They had a very definite code, and since there was no law on the hunting grounds except that which the hunters enforced themselves, it was well that I had the opportunity to learn their unwritten law before becoming a buffalo hunter myself.

The punishment they imposed for hide stealing was the same as for rustling: hanging. Each hunter had his own camp-mark which was placed on the hide. This camp-mark indicated ownership, and the hide could be marked and left to dry anywhere without danger of theft except by the Indians.

Another thing I learned from these professionals was about "trail hunting" or "Texas hunting." This meant shooting an animal out of a bunch but letting the others run off, then catching up with them and shooting another and so on until the bunch was run clear out of the country. The hunters would warn anyone they found guilty of this form of hunting by shooting between the offender and the herd. Then if the hunter did not desist from trail hunting, the next shots would be at the guilty hunter himself.

Another law which I distinctly remember hearing discussed was that there should be no running of game or buffalos with dogs. Anyone had the right to kill any dog caught running game on the open range. Running buffalo from horseback was also frowned upon by these professionals.

Before going out with Grimmit, I had met an Englishman named Frank Van Alstein who was eager to go on a hunting trip with professionals, and we had agreed to try to go out together. The best hunting I had heard about was north of the Yellowstone River where I had gone with Grimmit once to pick up his hides from an earlier kill. It was in the area of Porcupine Creek.

The names of so many of the creeks were derived from some incident or some person or the presence of something in great quantity. Custer Creek was named for Longhair, General George Custer. Muster Creek was so-called because of the roll-call and mustering out of soldiers that had occured there. Harris Creek was named for the only man who had returned from a group of three that had been hauling buffalo hides. A dispute had arisen among them; Harris shot the other two, claimed self defense, and since there were no witnesses to testify against him, he was cleared. Cedar Creek had banks covered with cedars; Cherry Creek and Sand Creek were named for obvious reasons as well.

Porcupine Creek was named for the abundance of porcupines. Their quills were stout enough that they would pass through a leather boot.

When I went to the Little Porcupine country with Grimmit, I met "Dutch" Henry, who agreed to stay as cook for the hunting party I was arranging. Henry trapped beaver as a sideline to make extra money. Because he had had a great deal of experience with hunting parties on the open range, I felt that we would do well to have him for a hired cook to attend to our camp for us on our professional buffalo hunting expedition.

While I was away on the trip with Grimmit, Frank Van Alstein and Wes Morris had been getting the outfit together for the hunt. By the time all our arrangements were completed, we discovered that we would have to use a sled to get through to the campsite I had selected on the Little Porcupine. We loaded kegs of powder, bars of lead, empty shells, Sharps Old Reliable .40-90 rifles, a great quantity of food supplies, and our bedrolls. Our hunting suits were made of white mackinaw blankets and we even had white caps so that we would be less visible against the snow. Felt boot packs and overshoes completed the outfit.

With two ponies we sledded through about two feet of snow for over a hundred miles out from Miles City. Along the way we frequently came upon the carcasses of buffalo lying in bunches as if they had been shot while in a corral. The hides all had camp-marks on them, and under some of the hides the hunters had left buffalo tongues to freeze and thus be protected until they were picked up with the hides. Then the tongues were dried and shipped to dealers.

After we arrived at the Little Porcupine, we looked over the locality for some time and decided to make camp on a piece of flat bottom ground near the back of the stream. The ground was littered with large cottonwood trees and plenty of dry driftwood. We cut about 20 poles, each from 25 to 30 feet long and we set them in the ground teepee fashion for a framework. Borrowing some raw buffalo hides from some hunters nearby, we soon finished a very comfortable and warm home for ourselves. Our shelter was about 20 feet across at the bottom with a smokehole in the center of the top so we could build a fire inside. The fire gave us heat for the whole teepee, as well as a way to cook. We used the teepee much as the Indians did: sleeping with our feet to the fire. We rolled up our bedrolls of government blankets and buffalo robes and stored them against the sides of the lodge during the daytime to make room for cooking and eating. We had bought the government blankets from soldiers for a fraction of what they had cost the government.

After spending some time hunting, we found that the buffalo were indeed scarce in the vicinity of camp, so we moved upstream about four or five miles. To save our ponies from being stolen by the Sioux, who were another 20 miles upstream, we sent the stock back to Miles City with Grimmit.

We decided to build ourselves a substantial sort of shelter in which we could protect ourselves in case the Indians attacked. We found a place which the river had washed out, leaving a large horseshoe-shaped embankment about fifty feet high. We took our shovels and picks and started cutting a path about twelve feet below the surface of the top of this bank. We cut along it for about seventy five feet at the height of a man for an entry way or walk. Then we went up on top of the bank and laid out the dimensions for our dugout, about 12 by 30 feet. Then we cut through the wall a distance of five or six feet and dug out our room, digging out the ground from the top. We framed it out with large logs, roofed it with buffalo hides and brush and finally with dirt. At the back end of this room we dug a fireplace with a chimney running up to the ground surface outside.

We covered the doorway with buffalo hides. The door admitted light and air, but it was always somewhat gloomy inside unless there was a bright fire of dry wood burning in the fireplace. Then our cave-like home was quite a cheerful place. Except for the smoke coming out of the ground level chimney, we were well concealed and we felt very safe and comfortable. We always kept a good supply of wood and water on hand.

We settled into our new home. Our food supplies included a few pieces of sidemeat, several sacks of flour, a few cans of tomatoes, dried apples, raisins, peaches and a supply of seasonings. Our guns were Sharps .40-90s. With these we had powder, lead, caps, reloading tools, our warsacks and bedrolls, a small supply of bandages and medicines. We were ready for the winter hunt.

The first morning after we were settled, I was up early to start on my first hunt. Wes and Frank were to follow me in about an hour and be the skinners. I saw a small herd of about fifteen approximately three miles from camp. Several of the older hunters had advised me against attempting to take a large herd at first, and seeing this small group seemed like a good omen to me. I got my white clothes, rifle, belt of cartridges, and told Wes and Frank which direction I was headed.

The snow was deep and it was hard plowing through it. When I was within a half mile of the band, I discovered a deep ravine that led up the slope to the herd. After about half an hour stalking up the ravine, I felt that I must be near the buffalo. I made an effort to climb up the almost perpendicular bank to get a shot at the buffalo. The bank was about 12 to 15 feet high. Poking my gun over the top while holding onto some sagebrush, I found myself within 20 feet of a nice large cow buffalo. In fact, I was surrounded by the little band. Holding on firmly to the sagebrush with my left hand, I took deliberate aim at her just behind the forelegs and fired. My foothold gave way, the sagebrush pulled out by the roots, and I rolled to the bottom of the ravine still holding to the sage.

Remembering the instructions that the professional hunters had given me, that I should hold my position and shoot the leaders of the band, I struggled to get back up the bank to continue shooting from that excellent position. After 15 or 20 minutes of vain efforts, I sat

The sagebrush pulled out as I shot

back panting, sweating, and discouraged. It was hopeless to get back up to the top of the bank. I retraced my steps to where I had entered the ravine, climbed out, and saw that the band had moved on about a mile further. I immediately ran after them, and they ran over a ridge out of sight. Finally I worked into position to shoot again.

This time I had the satisfaction of seeing a buffalo fall at my shot. The rest of the band circled the ridge as they trotted away. I cut across to try to intercept them for another shot. As I pursued them, a shot rang out. Indians, I thought. Indians! And I was alone. The bullet from my unknown assailant whizzed between me and the herd. I stopped dead in my tracks, but there was no more shooting. Then I realized that there wouldn't be unless I continued hunting as I had been, trail hunting. Unintentionally, absorbed as I was in getting my first days' kill, I had been trail hunting. That shot was not from an Indian, it was a warning signal.

On my way back to camp, I counted the buffalo I had killed. To my surprise, there were nine. In shooting these, I had them scattered over a distance of almost nine miles! Frank and Wes had become discouraged when they could not locate me, and they had returned to camp. Upon my return we all sat down to the dinner that Dutch Henry had ready. While we ate our buffalo meat, beans and dried apples and drank our coffee, I told them of my experiences.

The next morning they went out with me to find the kill. When we came to the place where I had first been tumbling into the ravine. I found that my first shot had been successful, and I took pride in this. Although I had unwittingly transgressed an unwritten law of the buffalo range by trail hunting, my first day's hunt was a decided success. We found and saved the hides of every one of the nine buffalo I had killed.

It was very interesting to watch the professional skinners handle these large buffalos. Each skinner would usually work alone, following along after the hunter. Immediately after the hunter had made his kill the skinner would start to work. He would rip down the skin along the legs and sides and then turn the hide back from the top side. After pushing the hide well under the buffalo, particularly at the hump where the hide is often as thick as a man's hand, he would twist the buffalo's head around and turn it up so that it rested on its horns. Then a pole was pushed under the bottom-most foreleg and between it and the other, thus levering the animal over as far as possible on its back.

Next the skinner would take hold of the under front leg, and standing on the carcass, swinging his own weight forward and backward, the skinner would balance the animal so that it would be turned over on its hump and fall to the other side. The second side was then skinned and the hide spread out, flesh side up in the snow, and the camp mark was put on it. At first, we were not skillful enough to work alone, but with two of us working together we managed to get the hides off in excellent condition.

We often put the tongues under the hides to freeze, although sometimes we took them for ourselves to vary our monotonous diet. The other parts that we took were the hump steak, the heart, the brains, and some fat. We took the hump steaks from young cows. Hearts of the very young buffalos made a favorite dish with us when baked with slices of bacon in the dutch oven. We used the brains for butter. From the buffalo fat we obtained a soft, yellow, rich oil that we used for seasoning our gravy. The remainder of the carcasses, thousands of pounds daily, were left out by the hunters for the coyotes and gray wolves that followed the herds in great numbers. We did not often waste ammunition on these scavengers because it was expensive and not to be used unnecessarily.

The day after my trail hunting, while the skinners were working on the nine I had killed, I walked on ahead and entered a narrow valley. I was determined to get a stand if I could get within range. Looking down the valley, I saw a band of 50 to 75 buffalo coming toward me on a dead run. They were evidently stampeding. I did not then know the danger I was in by being in their path. I thought that they would turn off in another direction when they saw me. But, they do not easily change direction once started in a stampede. As they drew closer on thundering hoofs, I concealed myself directly in front of them, expecting to stop them and make my kill. I failed entirely.

As I fired directly into them, I discovered that they would not stop or change direction, but were going to run right over me. I dropped into a ditch to avoid being trampled to death. Many of the buffalo leaped right over me as they jumped the ditch. I did not make a single kill, but I learned another lesson about buffaloes; never stand in their way or expect to turn them away.

On the following day I killed fourteen bison, shooting first the oldest leaders in the band. I shot one and immediately without moving from the spot I reloaded and shot the next leader. At each shot, the buffaloes acted like a bunch of sheep looking for a barking dog. They would all run together and hold up their heads as if trying to locate the direction of the noise. Apparently they were unable to determine where I was because I was downwind from them.

Each time I shot, the band would rush together, and in a few moments a new leader would start out with the others following. I would quickly shoot it down. Sometimes this was very hard to do if the new leader was on the far side of the band and going away from me. I learned to do some stunts in order to keep the stand, like the older, more experienced hunters did. Since I could not always get a clear, killing shot at the leader, I found that a shot in the shoulder would often cause him to turn about, so that I could aim a killing shot. In this manner the leaders were killed first. When they were all felled, the younger stock with no leaders to follow would just mill around. That day I succeeded in holding two bands long enough to kill nine from the first band and five from the second.

One evening after four or five days of hunting, I visited Grimmit's camp some four miles down the Little Porcupine. Several of the old time buffalo hunters were there spinning yarns and swapping stories of exploits in hunting. A discussion started as to the number of shots required for a good hunter to bring down a herd. In considering buffalo hunting as a profession, an important item was the amount of ammunition used. Our evenings were usually spent in cleaning our guns and in reloading shells. The spent primers were taken from the shells with an extractor and new primers were placed in them. They were loaded with 90 grains of powder, then a wadding was pushed down on top of the powder, then a bullet was forced in on top of the wad. We melted and poured our own bullets from bars of lead. It was work requiring skill.

Hunters watched the amount of ammunition very carefully. The fewer bullets used in getting a hide, the greater the profit. I was a skilled marksman, and for a beginner, I had made more than a fair record on each day's kill. The older men asked me how many shots I had been using for each buffalo killed. I did not know. I had just been going out with two belts of cartridges and I shot until my ammunition was gone or I had enough buffalo for the skinners to keep busy. Naturally, I became interested in seeing what sort of record I could make.

Bright and early the next morning I started out over practically the same route I had taken on my first day's hunt. I reached the uplands where, in the distance, I saw the vast herd from which we had all been killing smaller bands. It is almost impossible for me to describe the sight of that huge herd of black-brown shaggy animals as they appeared against the stark whiteness of the snow. They seemed to be an endless, unlimited army moving slowly in one general direction. Definitely, though just perceptibly, they were moving south. After gazing for some time at this breath-taking scene, I began looking for a small band at closer range that I could get a stand on and try to make a record, using a minimum amount of ammunition.

Nearby was a band of more than a dozen. With great caution I approached until I was within a hundred yards of them and I concealed myself behind a rock on a snowy knoll. Selecting an old bull who from his looks might have been on the plains a hundred years, I shot and he fell. Without moving from my position, I instantly reloaded. The band was rushing about in a confused mass, but in an instant an old cow started out as leader with the whole band following. Peeping through the sights I shot again. She halted suddenly, then plunged forward with blood spurting from her nostrils. I had struck her in the lights, but a little too high for a death shot.

Without moving from my position, I loaded and fired, loaded and fired. Then I shoved the ramrod with a piece of flannel up and down the barrel of my gun, cleaning and cooling it while the band huddled together again. I loaded and fired until I had killed them all. I counted my shots; 32. I counted the buffalo; 16. But, one big cow was still up on her front feet, her haunches on the ground. I was about to fire when it occurred to me that I could kill her with my knife and establish my first record as a buffalo hunter: two shots per buffalo.

Believing that the cow was crippled and could not get up, I walked deliberately over to her with my rifle in my left hand, my knife in my right. I came up just behind the cow and made careful aim for her heart. At the moment I was about to strike, she let out a half-mew, half bawl, and suddenly wheeled around to make a charge at me. I was so close that there was nothing to do but turn and run for my life. Running was not easy in eighteen inches of snow! The buffalo was so close that as I ran, my gun would tick her horns on the left, and my

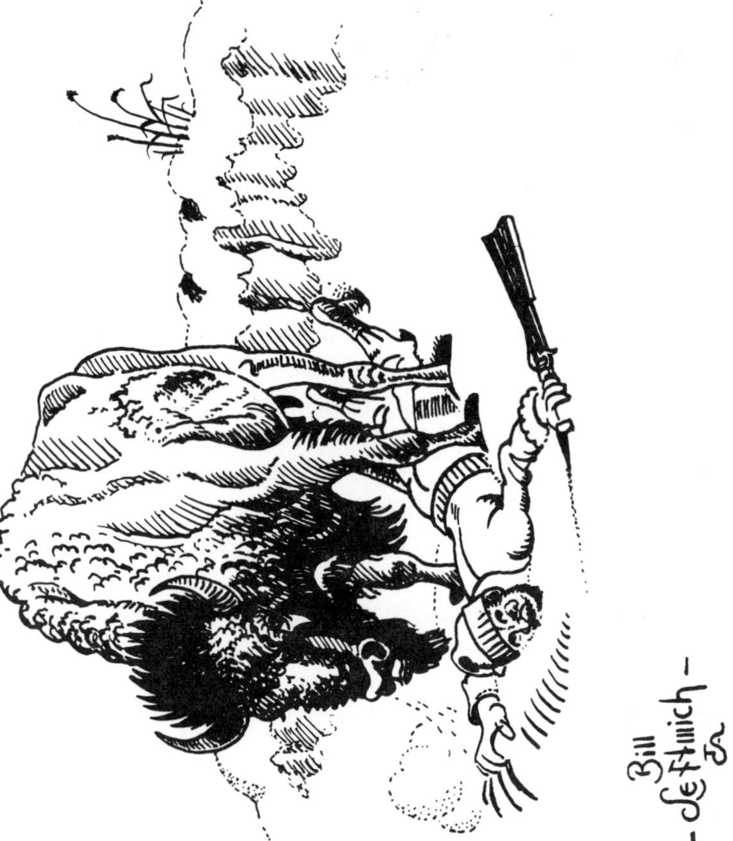

I felt her hot breath on the back of my neck

knife on the right. I ran for my life, thinking every moment that her horns would gore me.

I was almost exhausted and the cow was still close behind me when I fell into a little ditch. The cow tried to jump over but she fell right in on top of me, straddling me. I felt her hot breath on the back of my neck. I cautiously drew my knees up under me and shot out from under her, starting another race for my life. This time she was not so close, tiring from the wound I had inflicted when I shot her earlier. I had dropped both gun and knife when I fell in the ditch, so I circled back that direction.

Redoubling my efforts, I reached the ditch, cleaned off my gun and fired three shots into her before she fell dead. That was the last time I tried to make a shooting record. Still, sixteen buffalo with thirty-five shots wasn't too bad.

One day shortly after this incident, I located a band of about twenty buffalo, grazing and laying down close to the top of a high rock wall. The wall was about a hundred feet high, and almost perpendicular. At its foot was a quagmire of mud, water and quicksand. I maneuvered for a couple of hours to get downwind and still be near enough to shoot. Creeping, crawling, climbing, I finally located a small ditch that would bring me into range. I lay almost flat and dragged myself along, knowing that the ditch did not afford much protection but feeling that it was better than in plain sight.

After reaching the spot from which I thought I could pick off the leaders I found that I could not move without being seen. Studying the herd for a few minutes, I selected an old bull that I thought might be a leader. He was standing broadside and I shot him. The rest of the band jumped to their feet at once and began running confusedly, until another leader started out, only to be shot. This happened three times, then three old cows started out together. When I had shot them, it was practically over. The rest of the band milled about until I had shot them all.

I started forward from my cramped position to count my kill when the huge bull I had shot first came out of the gully into which he had fallen. He was about a hundred yards away, but facing directly at me, and he saw me. I ducked back into my little ditch waiting for what seemed an eternity. Nothing happened, so I looked up again. He was still facing me as he stood over a dead buffalo, smelling the blood. He saw me again, lowered his head and charged, circling his tail in the air.

Taking deliberate aim, I fired squarely at his head. He went down on his knees. But, the soft lead bullet of my .40-90 did not penetrate that heavy mat of thick brown hair on his skull, even though it did stun him temporarily. He got up and came for me again. I shot him in the head again. He went down on his knees, and came up again. What was that skull made of? Two shots directly into his head and he was still coming! I turned and ran down the ditch. When the bull was about forty feet away, I turned and shot again, hitting him in the side, but a little too high. We always tried for a shot through the lights, but in my excitement, I hit too high.

Seeming confused, the bull stood for a moment and I quickly reloaded. He leaped the ditch, landed stiff-legged, and two great streams of blood gushed from his nostrils. He jumped to the top of the rocky wall, and then over the precipice and into the bog below. I followed his course up to the top and looked over. All I could see was a circle of water and mud closing over the place where he had landed. I lost that hide, and I got one of the worse scares I ever had.

A maddened buffalo fights by horning, butting, and hooking, by rearing slightly and then butting with his head and horns, or by pawing and trampling. I have seen maddened buffalo butt, charge, and trample a skinned carcass with such force as to churn it to dust.

We often used a carcass as a shield behind which to conceal ourselves while making a stand. If a wounded or maddened animal sensed our direction, he would charge at the carcass behind which he believed we were hidden. It was not a pleasant sight to see the huge creatures rear, butt, horn and trample the supposed enemy. In that small ditch with no protection, I realized that I was in one of the gravest dangers of my hunt when that injured bull came after me.

There were many entertaining incidents, as well as dangerous experiences on the range. One morning as I crossed a cedar covered ridge, I heard a great commotion in the valley below. I crept carefully through the brush until I could see down into the arena of activity. There was a small herd of cows and calves huddled on the far side of the little valley, while nearest me was a double fight of old bulls against young bulls. The old bulls were strong and stood their ground, scarcely moving except to keep facing their younger antagonists. The young bulls were putting on a real show, butting, hooking, trying to get an advantage on their older opponents.

Occasionally one of the old bulls would meet the younger one head-on, and a real push-of-war would take place. With locked horns, they would try to overcome each other by superior strength, shoving first one way, then the other. I was close enough to see their bloodshot eyes roll in one of these clinches, as the younger bull forced the older one to his knees. Breaking quickly away, the younger one circled and rammed viciously into the older one's side. It was evident that the younger bull was winning this battle. I looked over to see how the other pair was doing just in time to see the older one butted over an embankment. The young bulls joined together to chase the remaining old one up the trail after his comrade. Together they would wander until some hunter shot them or they died of old age, isolated from the herd.

The young victors trotted over to the herd, circled it a few times snorting, and then started it out in the direction opposite that taken by the old bulls. I was so fascinated in watching this battle for supremacy that I completely overlooked the opportunity for a kill.

Some days later when I was hunting near this locality, I saw four old bulls in a deep gully. One of them was very lame. He was evidently one of the old ones in the fight I had witnessed.

Due to the depth of snow, which was three to four feet in places, and to the crust which formed after each thaw, it was impossible for game to cross some of the low valley lands. Thus they were compelled to stay on the higher, windswept tablelands and ridges. We improvised a sort of Norwegian ski to travel on. These were rather rudely fashioned by splitting long, thick boards from cottonwood trees. With these improvised skiis, which we called snowshoes, we were able to cross the low places with comparative security, ease, and speed.

One day when I was returning from a good day's hunt, I noticed a herd of antelope caught on a small hillside, trapped by the deep snow. The next morning, while the skinners were catching up with my previous day's kill, I buckled on a forty-four Colt revolver and took my Winchester with me. Returning to the place where the antelope were trapped by the deep, crusted snow, I found an ideal spot from which to shoot them. When I fired into the herd, they ran to the point of the ridge and jumped over a deep ravine which had served as one boundary of their prison. I shot fifteen of this herd. Four fell into the ravine, crippled. I shot them. The rest escaped, in spite of the treacherous footing, over the hardened crust of snow.

One morning as I was crossing the bottomlands to hunt a ridge that lay beyond, I witnessed another entertaining and interesting performance. A band of about 75 buffalo had left the ridge and started down to cross the bottomlands. They were traveling slowly, in single file. Six large bulls were in the lead, the one in front making a pathway by swinging his head from side to side, lowering it into the snow, brushing and pushing his way through. After breaking trail in this tiresome fashion for a few minutes, he stepped aside and the next bull in line took over. The bull which had been in the lead waited till all the others had passed, then he stepped back into line ahead of the cows and calves. Thus taking turns, they fought their way across the valley. I was so attracted to the systematic regularity of their work I made no attempt to shoot them.

Day after day we worked at our hunting, tramping through the deep snow, shooting and skinning, cleaning our guns and reloading shells. Our meals were also monotonous. Buffalo meat, beans, bread with buffalo tallow or brains for butter, dried apples, occasionally buffalo tongue or heart, or more rarely, sowbelly. We drank coffee with all our meals. It was good food, but the sameness caused me to frequently talk about foods I'd like to eat, and how well I could prepare them.

One evening while we were reloading ammunition after I had shot 54 in one stand, I bragged about what a good cook I had been at home. Since the boys had plenty of work coming up from the stand I had made, Wes and Frank challenged me to stay home and cook them a "real meal."

When all had left next morning, I looked around, trying to plan a meal that would make good my boast. I ransacked the supplies to find something with variety that I could fix to please them and myself. There was no hope of any material change in the menu unless I could get some game. The thought of another meal of buffalo meat made me determined to try to get some other game meat.

There were several likely places to find deer close to camp. Taking my Winchester I crossed over a ridge onto a bench above a creek. Twelve inches of new snow had recently fallen into the well-timbered spot. I had not proceeded far when I saw a large mule deer buck within forty feet. It took but a single shot to drop him. At the crack of my gun, a doe jumped up and ran. Two shots brought her down. Now I knew that I could make good my boast of a "different" meal. The menu was shaping itself in my mind as I set to work to skin and butcher the deer.

It was still early. I decided to walk on a little further before taking the saddles of venison back to camp. A short distance further through the brush, I was surprised to find that the snow had been packed solid like a sheep pen. Following up the little valley which was about a half mile long, I found that a herd of antelope was corraled here by the deep snow. They had apparently been here for several weeks. My first inclination was to open fire on them, but I decided that I had better wait. They would freeze before the others could come back with me to skin them. The hides would be worth about two dollars apiece, and there were at least forty in the herd. The snow would keep them prisoners until I could return with the skinners, so I returned to camp.

I remembered some canned apples we had buried under the snow, and I dug them up. They were in perfect condition, as well kept as if they had been in modern refrigeration. I would make apple pies; that would please everybody. I used buffalo tallow for shortening, and put baking powder in the dough to make it light. I used an old tin can for a rolling pin. Then I filled every one of our tin plates with pies, using the apples and some English raisins for filling.

The dutch oven made an ideal baking place. I heaped hot coals on the big iron cover and baked a fine pie for each member of our camp. Then I made a big pot of venison stew, putting in canned tomatoes, and chopping some potatoes into it. The savory odor of the stew mingled with the spicy fragrance of the pies and filled our dugout.

Usually we didn't quit work until dark, but that evening the men were curious and came in early. They all sat down and I produced the pies. Frank ate his without stopping, but the rest of us saved some for dessert. I served the stew and received high praise for my ingenuity.

The others had a successful day, too. The big dinner over, we lazed before the fire and they told of the small herd they had killed after skinning the 54 I had left for them. Dutch Henry, always good company, was even more jolly than usual, for he had found a beaver in one of his traps. I told about the antelope herd trapped in the snow close by, and how I planned to get their hides.

Next morning, taking the Winchester and Colt revolver, we started out to find the antelope. They were peacefully grazing on the sunny side of the little valley. Wes and Frank walked down on the ridge where the brush was thickest, while I took my place at the end of the corral-like place that nature had made by piling the snow up along the north side. The snow was in a sort of cleft between the rocks, too deep to cross, and too wide to jump over. After resting a few minutes to get my wind, I stepped out in plain view of the antelope and fired into them.

Knowing that antelope usually run in circles, and were forced to in this situation, we kept them running past each group of shooters. They were beautiful creatures. The sun shown directly on their black horns and brown sides, their white rumps glistened against the snowdrifts around them.

Today, in 1939, I could not slaughter them, and slaughter is the only term to describe that cruel and wanton destruction. But, in 1881, as strange as it seems to me now, it was the thing that I felt was the right thing to do.

Swift as the wind, those beautiful animals came on to be slaughtered. I stepped to one side and opened fire as those graceful creatures tried to leap the gap. They fell into the gap, sometimes two falling at a shot. Some made it across, only to flounder in the deep snow where they fell to my well-aimed shots.

Frank soon joined me and we crossed over on our snowshoes to finish off the cripples. Some we shot, and some we cut the throats of. We finished skinning when the afternoon sun was low; we had taken 56 hides. A good day's work by our standards then.

After taking the choicest pieces of meat, we left the rest for the coyotes and wolves. In the years that have gone by since, I have often longed for a piece of that tangy, gamey antelope meat we left as a feast for the wolves.

With our routine buffalo hunting underway once more, we had better and better luck in getting large stands. About a week after we had killed the antelope herd, I reached the pinnacle of my success in killing buffalo; the most buffalo in one stand with the fewest shells. That day, without changing position, I killed an entire herd of 54, using 79 shells. During the firing, the barrel became so hot that I could not hold it in my bare hands. I laid it carefully in the snow to cool, and then I hastily wiped out the barrel with a piece of flannel on the ramrod.

During the latter part of December it warmed up so much that the snow was melting rapidly from the ridges and tablelands. The skinners were occupied part of the time in turning over buffalo that had frozen before we could get them skinned. They would skin the top side before turning the animal over. The next day, we would return and skin the other side. In this way we added a great many hides to those we already had. We wanted to get them to the Yellowstone for shipping on the spring rise now while we could travel in warmer weather.

The big buffalo herd which was moving slowly and steadily to the south when we first came out on the range was now gone entirely. A month earlier we had seen numerous herds daily; during this holiday season at the close of 1881, we saw practically none. The warmer weather had doubtless enhanced their movement. Occassionally we saw a few cripples or calves, but the big herd was gone.

Grimmit had already taken another load of buffalo hides to Miles City, and this time when he returned, he brought our ponies with him. We led the ponies about the range picking up six to ten hides each load. We would take the load to camp where we made piles of hides, strapping them down with rawhide strips. We loaded these bales of hides into the wagon and freighted them to the Yellowstone about forty miles away. At the river they were counted and stacked to await the spring rise and the first river boat that would take them down. Nearly all these hides were shipped to Bismarck, Dakota, where they were reshipped to the tanneries in the east.

The hides were paid for according to their grade. Prices ranged from $2.75 for the poorer hides up to $3.75 for robe hides.

There was considerable trouble on the range from thieves. The Sioux had been carrying on a sort of guerilla warfare with the hunters, stealing hides and looting camp equipment and supplies while the hunters were out on the range. A few days after our arrival, while we were still in the teepee camp, a band of these marauding thieves invaded our camp and took some of our army blankets, food, and ammunition. They left behind a few filthy calico shirts and badly soiled old blankets. We took up the trail and followed them almost to their village, about 20 miles northwest of our camp. We decided it was too great a risk to attack since we were so outnumbered, so we did nothing about the loss.

While we were collecting our hides just before Christmas, we found nearly a hundred carcasses that had been left frozen and unmarked, so we skinned these and added them to our bunch. We missed few of our own marked hides that had been left out for collecting later, but we thought that the Indians had probably gotten them.

One evening a group of buffalo hunters met at Grimmit's camp. They were up in arms about the numerous and systematic thefts of hides which had been taking place. Early in the season, some of the old-timers had caught one of the thieves red-handed. He was an older man who made camp with his nephew, a boy of about eighteen. Their camp was further down stream than ours, and they appeared to be hunters like the rest of us.

They had been caught taking fresh hides with the camp-marks of others on them, under a hide of their own. The hunters who detected them warned them the first time this occurred. Upon a promise to desist, the thieves had been let go. Since the warm weather allowed the hunters to get out and gather their hides, it was discovered that many of them were missing hides again.

Grimmit, with a couple of other old timers came to see me to see if I would go with them on some important business. On the way they told me that the same old man and his nephew had been detected stealing hides again. A delegation comprising the foremen of several camps (twelve of us) was convened to enforce the unwritten law of the open range. Stories these old-timers told me of similar incidents left me feeling uneasy, but I had to go along with them.

Two of us were selected to go into their camp and bring the offenders out. We drew our revolvers and went into their teepee where we found them asleep. We ordered them to dress and come outside. We marched them down to the creek where the rest of the vigilance committee was waiting under a big old cottonwood tree. We soon had a big fire going. With the prisoners seated on a log, the vigilance committee had a sort of criminal proceeding. It was a gruesome sight, with the flickering firelight throwing dismal shadows about the cottonwood trees.

The men whose hides had been stolen asked question after question. The old man was examined first. He had ready answers to most questions. Accuser and accused faced each other angrily as cries of "liar" rang out. After a short time the old man broke down and admitted that he had been guilty of some breaches of range etiquette, such as trail hunting, but he vehemently denied stealing any hides after he was first warned.

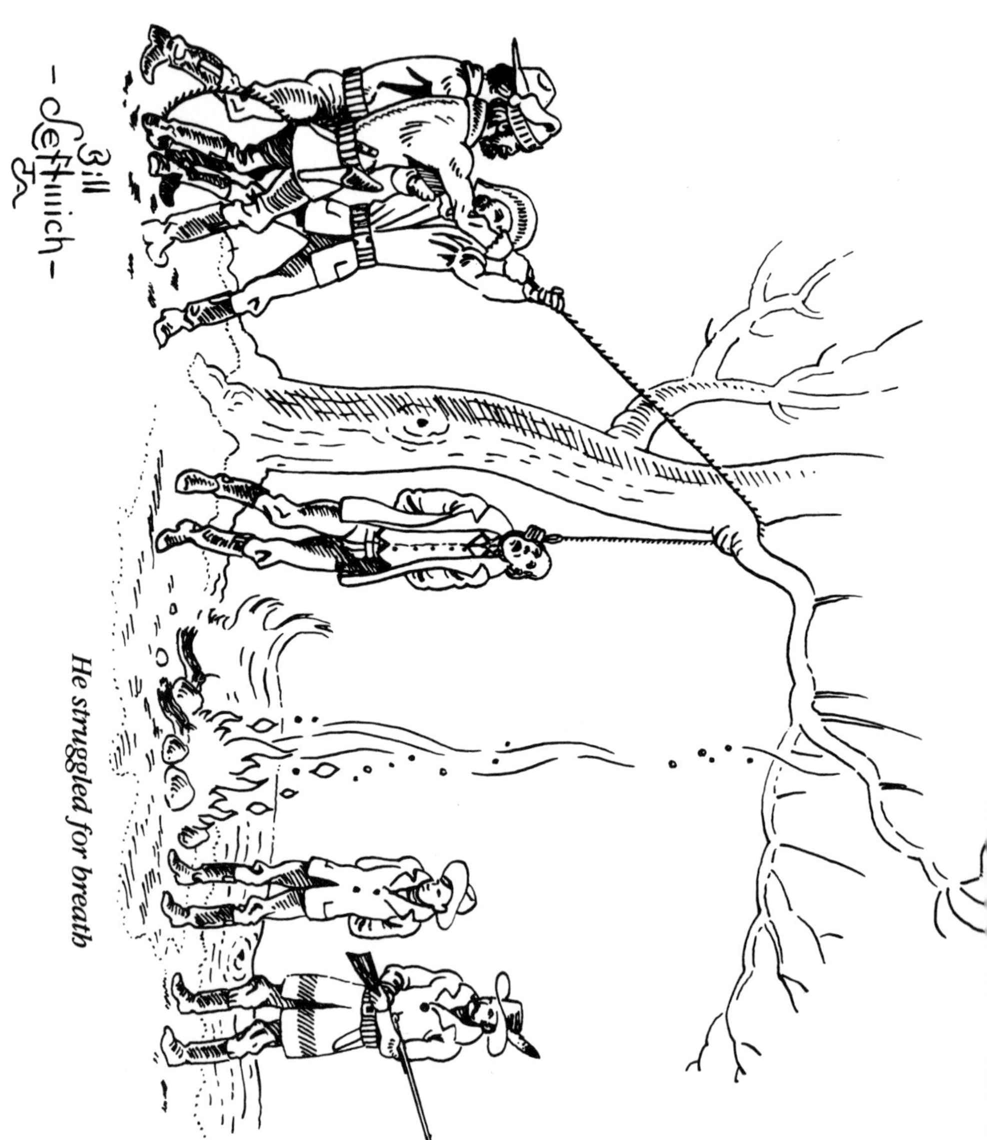

He struggled for breath

Suddenly a rawhide rope appeared in the hands of one of the vigilantes. One end was made into a noose and it was thrown over a limb of the cottonwood. The old man's head was forced through the noose, and he was hauled up onto tiptoe. It seemed to me like a nightmare. The firelight leaped and flared as I stood aghast at the proceedings. This couldn't really be a hanging.

One of the men startled me by saying, "Here, Bob. You take hold, too!"

With a feeling of horrible revulsion I placed my hand on the rope, protesting as I did that the punishment was far too drastic for the severity of the crime. My protests fell on deaf ears.

Very slowly the man was pulled up a bit higher. With a grunt and a sigh he struggled for breath, seeming to dance at the end of the rope. After a bit, he was let back down. As soon as he had his breath back enough to talk, he poured out a torrent of confessions. He admitted stealing the hides and begged to return them to their owners. He declared his nephew to be completely innocent. He pled with the men to let his nephew go; he alone was guilty and would take his punishment.

The hides had been stolen from almost every camp up and down the Porcupine, as we learned from the camp-marks on them. Feeling that all the thieving would be stopped, the vigilantes ordered the culprits to leave the range within 24 hours, warning them never to return. The stolen hides were turned over to their rightful owners and we all returned to our camps.

On the way back Grimmit commented to me that he did not like the feel of the weather. It felt like a bad snowstorm to him and he dreaded them. He told me about one of the men from his camp who had been out in the last blizzard we had endured. The man was quite some distance from camp when the storm broke. Blinded and confused by the swirling snow, he became lost. During the night there was a stampede of buffaloes. Some days later the lost man's campmates found his frozen body trampled in the snow.

The evening's "entertainment" by the vigilantes had not made me feel particularly jovial, and this story left me almost morose. By the time I reached our dugout camp, a light snow was falling. It snowed all the next day and night, and then the blizzard really hit with blinding snow and much colder temperatures.

Dutch Henry went out to see about his traps during a lull in the storm the next afternoon. When evening came with no sign of his return, I could not put from my mind the story of Grimmit's trampled hunter. I went out and called loudly, but my voice was smothered by the falling snow.

Close to dawn the storm abated and we began preparations to look for Dutch. Just as we started out, Dutch stumbled in. He was almost exhausted. His ears were frozen and two of his fingers were badly frosted. As soon as he realized that he was lost, he said, he knew that he must keep moving or he would freeze to death. So, he had forced himself to walk, walk, walk, until it stopped snowing and he could see where he was. We followed his tracks back to where he had spent the night: he had been walking in a circle all night long very close to the dugout.

We were all getting pretty homesick, but there was still several weeks of work to do before we finishesd gathering our hides. After the few days of idleness caused by the storm, I was eager to get back to hunting. I thought it might be possible that the storm would have driven some animals back near to camp.

Starting out at sunrise with the long swinging trot that we used to cover long distances over the snow, I went in a southeasterly direction, thinking that I might find some buffalo in the valleys. When I had gone nine or ten miles, I found myself in country that I had never been in before. I crossed several narrow ravines that led up from the Little Porcupine. Some of these gullies were difficult to cross because of their depth and steep banks.

Climbing down over a ridge, I saw several wild horses. I had frequently heard that there were some on the range, but these were the first I had seen. These wild ones were reputed to be descendents of horses that had gotten away from early hunters, explorers and travelers. The animals had made the open range their home and had survived and multiplied through the years.

I had heard many stories from the old timers about the ease with which one could catch a wild horse by "creasing" it. This meant shooting it just above the withers, or along and above the bones in the neck. This would stun it and knock it to the ground. Then all one had to do was run up and put a rope around it while it lay on the ground.

As the old timers told it, it sounded reasonable, so I decided to have a try for a wild horse.

Retracing my steps to a dead buffalo I had passed, I cut a 30 foot rawhide strip from it to use as a rope. I hurried back to the bottom where I had seen the horses, and cautiously worked into position to shoot. I took careful aim at a nice buckskin and fired. The horse fell as if poleaxed. The rest ran away out of sight before I could get up to the buckskin.

I put my lariat around his neck and waited for him to get up. The horse was alive, but it didn't make any effort to get up. In all the stories I had heard, the creased horse would jump up almost before you could get to it. I investigated and found that I had shot him too low, through the withers. He would never stand again. I wondered if all the stories I had heard were just campfire yarns and myths that gained credence by repetition. Sadly, I put my revolver to his head and put him out of his misery. I never attempted to crease anything again.

Traveling a few miles further I found a bunch of old, old buffaloes. They must have been a group of mavericks, or else they were just too old to keep up with the herd when it started north. I had a little difficulty in approaching them unseen, but finally I was able to get into a gully which would allow me to get up on them. By creeping up this little arroyo I was able to get within range in a few minutes. I crept up the side of the ravine and came within a few feet of the shaggy body of a large bull.

He was less than six feet from the muzzle of my gun when I fired point blank into his side. The big bull fell to the ground, fortunately in the direction opposite from me. I looked at the rest of the herd. They were all staring in amazement, apparently not knowing the direction from which the sound had come. Concealed behind the carcass of the big bull I had just killed, it was only a few minutes until I had shot the other eight. This was my last day's hunt on the buffalo range, and my last chance at getting a stand.

I decided that I would skin the buffalo myself before night and still have time to get back to camp. I didn't carry a watch and the sky had become overcast, so I didn't really know how much daylight I had left. Laying aside my rifle and revolver, I proceeded with the work of skinning the buffalo as rapidly as I could, hoping to finish before dark. While I was tugging at the forelegs of a cow in order to turn her over, I glanced up and saw another herd of buffalo congregating between me and camp. Working desperately at my self-appointed task, I didn't notice another snowstorm approaching until the first flurries of snow started to blow around me.

In only a few moments an absolute blanket of fluffy white snow fell and covered everything. The snow came down so fast that I could hardly see the carcasses of the buffalo that were only a few feet from me. I finished the hide I was working on when the snow started, skinning as fast as I could. I realized that if I did not hurry to camp, I might be lost in this blizzard like Dutch Henry and Grimmit's hunter had been. Knowing the awful danger I would be in out on the range, I decided to leave for camp immediately.

I had difficulty finding my guns because the snow had fallen so fast and so thick, and it continued to blur my vision. Because this was a strange part of the range to me, I took my direction from the position of the first dead buffalo. My course would probably have been all right if I could have kept to it, but I fell into some ditches and I couldn't be sure when I climbed out if I was still heading for Porcupine Creek.

I trudged through the blizzard for about two hours and every step seemed heavier than the previous one because the soft loose snow was up past my ankles. Suddenly I thought of the herd of buffalo I had seen, and I realized that if my direction was correct, I would now be upwind of the herd. Remembering the trampled hunter, and not being sure of my direction or distance from camp, I became panic-stricken. It would be like walking in front of a train to get in front of that stampeding herd, and being to windward greatly increased my danger of stampeding them.

From the blinding blanket of white I heard a noise, a rolling sound as if the herd were immediately in front of me. Then I saw them! They were coming right at me and would be upon me in a moment. I could not run. I could only stand paralyzed with fear. But nothing happened.

I put my hands out before my eyes and I couldn't even see them, so I knew that the image of a charging herd was just my over-wrought imagination at work. I trampled on and on, crossing a rough country that I could not remember crossing that morning. The hills seemed higher and the gullies seemed more numerous and deeper than any I remembered. Each time I fell into a ditch and climbed out, the snow seemed deeper and the wind colder and stronger. Suddenly I longed for my home in Illinois and I thought of a walk home from the spelling bee, walking safely through the snow with Abbie's hand in mine.

Here I was freezing to death, and seeing a fire in the snow

After what seemed like hours of travel, I found myself at the bottom of a gully almost exhausted. I sat there homesick, confused, frightened, and longing for the security of civilization, or the protection of our camp. I determined to make a continued effort to reach camp even though I was uncertain of its direction. I concluded that I had been traveling in northwesterly direction rather than a northeasterly as I should have been. This gave me cause for real alarm.

If, as I now believed, I was going northwest, I was in danger of blundering into the Indian camp. Some of the hunters who had scouted the neighborhood to determine how many warriors there were had reported that the Sioux camp was situated under a bluff just back of some very rough land. I decided that I was in just such a place, very near their village.

I tried to keep calm, although my hands and feet were freezing while the sweat of fear was running down my face. I changed course in an attempt to avoid the Indian camp.

After walking in the new direction for a few moments I stopped short. I heard the sound of brush and sticks being broken, as someone would in gathering firewood. I could not locate the source of the sound, but it seemed to be coming from below me! Listening in the dark, I realized that it was indeed not the sound of an animal crashing through brush, but rather the methodical action of a firewood gatherer. In spite of the danger that it might be Indians, I decided to investigate.

Shaking the snow off my cartridge belt and revolver holster and making sure that my rifle was in working order, I started forward to go down what I thought was a slope. Instead I plunged headlong over a bank almost fifty feet high. Fortunately, the snow cushioned my fall. Now I was frightened because I couldn't hear the brush breaker any more. I walked along the bank feeling my way until I came to a place where I could climb back up. Once more at the top, I went back to approximately where I had tumbled off and I listened intently.

Again I heard the crisp, clear snapping and cracking of a wood gatherer. Keeping within earshot of the sound, I circled carefully to the left. As I slowly made my way forward, I poked the ground with my rifle butt in order to avoid another fall. Glancing to my left. I saw a spark of a fire come up out of the ground! Facing the new danger, I stepped cautiously toward it, and saw a bright light shining up through the snow!

The fear of the buffalo stampede and of blundering into the Sioux village were as nothing compared to the terror I felt at this weird sight. I felt a chilll go through my entire body, and my scalp hair stood erect. I thought of all the witchcraft stories I'd ever heard, and of thirsty men seeing water - mirages in the desert. Here I was freezing to death, seeing a fire in the snow.

I turned my back on this fantastic sight and walked determinedly away. But, the mystery of it rankled my mind. It seemed cowardly to leave without a thorough investigation, so I went back and looked closer. As I approached, I expected the fire to recede and disappear, but it was still there brighter than ever. I cocked my rifle and edged closer and closer. With baited breath I leaned right over it and looked down into my own dugout! There were Frank and Wes sitting in front of our fireplace. With yells of delight, I brought them to their feet and in a few minutes I was inside, warming comfortably and telling them of my adventure.

During the last hour or more of wandering, I had been within hearing distance of camp. Wes had been out several times and shot into the air to attract my attention. They had given up finally and Frank went out to gather more firewood. That was the sound which I heard finally that saved me. There was not much left of night, but what there was of that New Year's Eve we spent in talking of our plans for the future.

For the next few days we were busy skinning and hauling hides before our return to Miles City. Ten or twelve hides were picked up with the ponies each trip. Occassionally we would come across a dead buffalo that hadn't been skinned, or marked for ownership in any way. Wes Morris skinned one of these that had already begun to rot. While he was working at it, he unconsciously ran his hand across his mouth. He had a cracked lip and some of the rotting matter must have gotten into it. The next morning when he got up, his lip was rolled out and swollen.

We went on about our skinning and hauling without his help, making him stay in camp, although we didn't have any medicine which would help him. Late in the afternoon when we got back, his upper lip was swollen as badly as the lower. The next morning his eyes were closed and his nose was swollen to almost three times normal size. His head resembled a battered pumpkin.

He could not eat. When he attempted to talk, his speech was just gibberish. We were all depressed, feeling that there was no hope for his recovery. We were afraid that we would have a funeral on our hands.

Wes called me to him. With great difficulty and much repetition he made me understand: "Bob, I'm going to die. When I'm gone, wrap me up and stick me in a snowbank until spring. When the ground thaws, please come back and bury me. And Bob, please write my mother for me."

That was a bad night for Wes, and for the rest of us. In the morning he didn't seem any worse. We wondered how long it would take the poison to kill him or leave him. He didn't attempt to talk again for the next four days. On the fifth day the swelling was down some and he managed to take a little soup. We had sat up with him all this time, and we were relieved to see him getting better.

After he had recuperated we teased him some about not suffering from the poison so much as from not being able to talk, for he was a great talker.

While Wes was still laid up, Dutch Henry volunteered to go out and help get the hides ready for shipment. He was bent over skinning a cow and I looked over just in time to see its calf headed for his rump with his head down. I hollered too late for Dutch to get out of the way, and over the cow he went sailing. He got up cussing, took his revolver and shot every calf in sight.

In hunting for just over forty days, I averaged about twenty buffalo a day from a herd that had seemed unending. The only animals that were about when I left were in almost inaccessible places. In that winter of 1881-1882 eighty-two thousand hides were taken from the range and shipped out of Miles City in the spring. The riverboats were often piled up to their smokestacks with hides. The next winter, with many more hunters out on the range, there were only eight thousand hides shipped out. The last of the great herds was gone.

When I left the range, I exchanged my share of the camp equipment (guns, powder, lead, bedding) for some Irish potatoes which were stored away in the woods about three miles from Miles City. There were supposedly ten thousand pounds of potatoes, and the price at which I traded was three cents a pound. I left Van Alstein to return to the range, and I took the stagecoach down the Yellowstone to Miles City.

Over the cow he went sailing

Upon my arrival, I was pleased to find that the whole town had been out of potatoes for about forty days, and the price was way up. The hotels, boarding houses and eating-places were bidding as high as ten cents a pound for potatoes.

I would realize a good profit on my trade if only I could find the potatoes. Trading for something sight unseen and finding the commodity in great demand elated me. I took a grocery store owner with me and we followed the directions I had been given. We found the cave where they were stored. The crop was there in good condition, and I sold the lot at ten cents a pound!

I sent this money to my brother in Illinois, who was holding my profits from buffalo hunting as well. I had wanted to make enough to go back to college, and I did.

I tried my hand at several things in and around Miles City, but I soon decided to return home. Throughout my career, first as a schoolmaster and later as an attorney, those months spent on the plains in Montana, peopled with Indians, Indian-fighters, buffalo hunters, and the buffalo themselves, have remained a vivid memory.

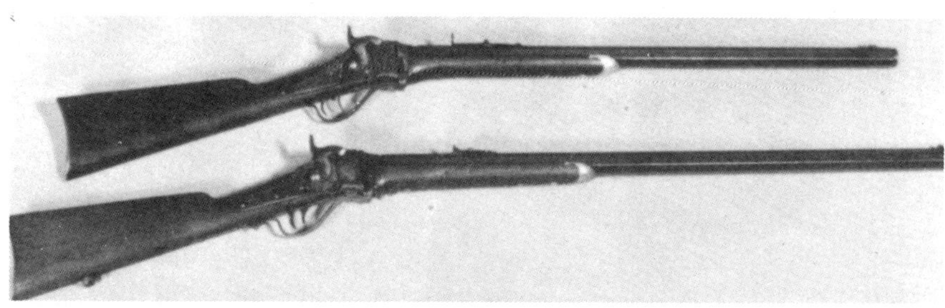

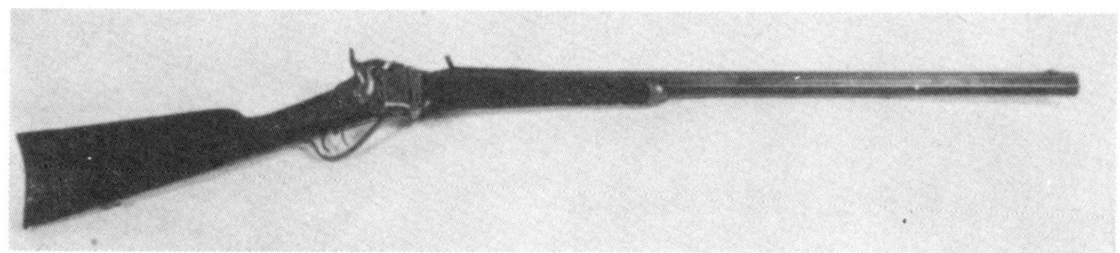

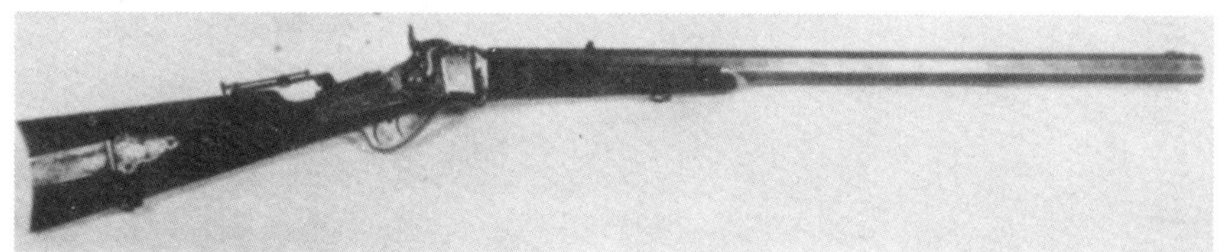

Tools of the trade

C54,336 a .40-90 BN shipped to Morgan Rood, Denver, Dec. 29, 1874.
C52,712 a .50-70 shipped to Schuyler, Hartley & Graham, New York, 1872. Author's collection.
C53,743 a .50-70 shipped to H. Folsom Co., St. Louis, March 27, 1873. Collection of Jerry Mayberry.
C53,637 a .44-77 BN shipped to Carlos Gove, Denver, Sept. 25, 1872. One of two 16 lb. guns shipped to Gove on that date. Author's collection. Photo courtesy of Tony Silveus, Silver Images Photography, Flagstaff.

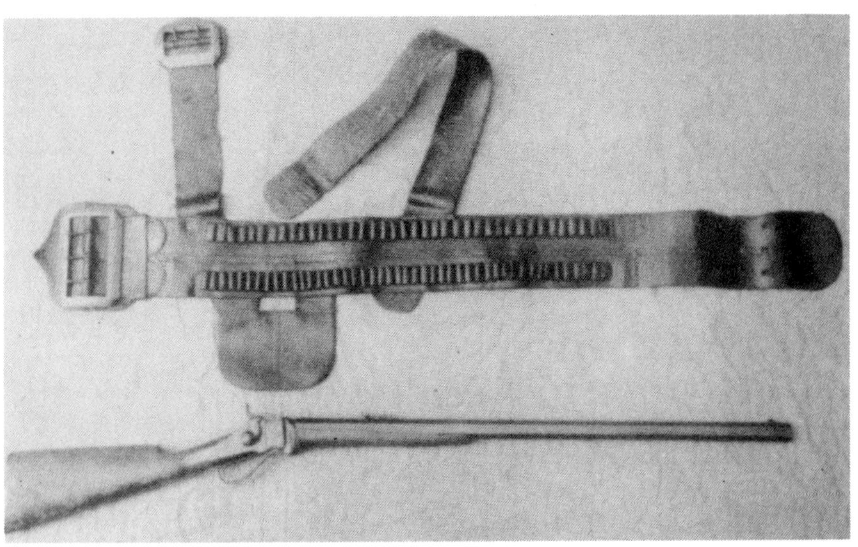

Tools of the Trade

Cartridge belt of the type issued to the NWMP, used by a buffalo hunter in Kansas. Collection of Jerry Mayberry.

158920 a .45 2 7/8, weighing 13 lb. 14 oz, shipped to lee & Reynolds, Dodge City, Dec. 27, 1876. The massive belt is 5 1/2 inches wide, accomodates .45 2 7/8 brass. Obtained from the Prairie Pottawatomie in northern Kansas. Collection of Stan Anderson. Photo courtesy of Tony Silveus, Siver Images Photography, Flagstaff.

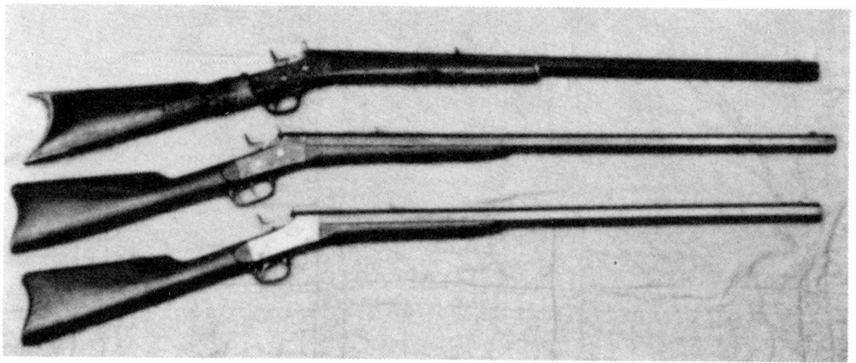

Tools of the Trade

Heavy barreled Remington Rolling Block rifles like these were also used by buffalo hunters such as the Cator brothers and Newt Moreland. Top: a .44-77 marked Carlos Gove, Denver; 13 1/2 lbs. Center: a .50-70, SN3807 12 lb. rifle with double set triggers. Bottom: a .44-77 13 lb. SN5478 rifle with single set trigger. Stan Anderson Collection. Photo courtesy of Tony Silveus, Silver Images Photography, Flagstaff.

George R.T. Gill (Right, front, holding reins) Raymond, Kansas 1913. Photo courtesy George W. Gill.

References Cited

Bicknell, P.C. letter Dec. 30, 1876 *In* Conger, Roger "A Buffalo Hunter's Letter" *Gun Report* Vol 27, No 3, 1981

Brown, George W. "Life and Adventures of George W. Brown" edited by Wm E. Connelley. *Collections of the Kansas State Historical Society* Vol XVII Topeka, 1928

Brown, Mark H. and W.R. Felton *The Frontier Years* Bramhall House New York, 1955

Chambers, Robert L. "Forty Days on the Montana Buffalo Range" MS Univ. Wyoming Library, Laramie

Cook, John R. *The Border and the Buffalo* Crane & Co. Topeka 1907

Dary, David *The Buffalo Book* Swallow Press Chicago, 1974

Dixon, William *Life and Adventures of Billy Dixon of Adobe Walls* Cooperative Publishing Co. Guthrie, Okla., 1914

Forrest, Earle R. "The Dodge City Buffalo Hunters" *Brand Book* XIII Los Angeles Corral, The Westerners n.d.

Garavaglia, Louis A. and Charles G. Worman *Firearms of the American West 1866-1894* Univ. New Mexico Press, Albuquerque 1985

Gard, Wayne *The Great Buffalo Hunt* Alfred A. Knopf New York, 1960

Glenn, W. Skelton "Buffalo Hunting in the Texas Plains 1876-1877" edited by Rex. W. Strickland. *Panhandle-Plains Historical Review* Vol 22, 1949

Grey, Zane *The Thundering Herd* Grosset & Dunlap, 1924

Hamner, Laura V. *Short Grass and Longhorns* Univ. Okla. Press, Norman, 1945

Hanna, Oliver Perry "The Old Wild West" MS Charles Hanna Carter

Hanson, Charles "The Greatest Years of Hide Hunting" *The Museum of the Fur Trade Quarterly* Vol 13, No 2, 1977

Hornaday, W.T. "The Extermination of the American Bison" *Report of the US National Museum 1887* (Washington 1889)

Jacobs, John letter to Joe S. McCombs July 13, 1924. Shackelford Co. Archives, Albany, Texas

Jacobs, John Cloud "The Last of the Buffalo" *The World's Work* Walter Page, ed. Doubleday & Page, New York. January, 1909

Lee, Ernest ed. "A Woman on the Buffalo Range: the journal of Ella Dumont (Bird)" *West Texas Historical Association Yearbook* October, 1964

Mayer, Frank and Charles Roth *The Buffalo Harvest* Alan Swallow, Denver, 1958

McCombs, Joe S. "First Buffalo Hunt Out of Ft. Griffin" MS Panhandle-Plains Museum, Canyon, Texas

McHugh, Tom *The Time of the Buffalo* Univ. Nebraska Press, Lincoln, 1972

Mooar, Josiah Wright "The First Buffalo Hunting in the Panhandle" *West Texas Historical Association Yearbook* Vol 6, 1930

letter to J. Evetts Haley Nov 25, 1927. Panhandle-Plains Museum, Canyon, Texas

Mooar, Josiah Wright as told to James Winford Hunt "Buffalo Days" *Holland's* March, May, 1933

Moore, R.L. "Fort Griffin and the Buffalo Sharps" *Arms Gazette* 1985

Raymond, Henry Hubert "Diary of a Dodge City Buffalo Hunter 1872-1873" edited by Joseph Snell *Kansas Historical Quarterly* Vol 31, No 4, Topeka, 1965

Reighard, George W. "Recollections of the Buffalo Hunt" *Kansas City Star* Nov 30, 1930

Roe, F.G. *The North American Buffalo* Univ. Toronto Press, 1970

Russell, Osborn *Journal of a Trapper* Boise, 1921

Sandoz, Mari *The Buffalo Hunters* Hastings House, New York, 1954

Sellers, Frank *Sharps Firearms* Beinfield, North Hollywood, 1978